BEST NEWSPAPER WRITING 2004

WINNERS: THE AMERICAN SOCIETY OF NEWSPAPER EDITORS COMPETITION

Featuring
Community Service Photojournalism Award
and Companion CD-ROM

EDITED BY KEITH WOODS

**The Poynter Institute
and
Bonus Books**

08 07 06 05 04   5 4 3 2 1

International Standard Book Number: 1-56625-234-2
International Standard Serial Number: 0195-895X

The Poynter Institute for Media Studies
801 Third Street South
St. Petersburg, Florida 33701

Bonus Books
875 North Michigan Avenue, Suite 1416
Chicago, Illinois 60611

Book design and production by Billie M. Keirstead,
Director of Publications, and Vicki Krueger, Publications
Assistant, The Poynter Institute

Cover illustration by Director of Publications Billie M. Keirstead
from a concept developed by Phillip Gary Design, St. Petersburg,
Fla. Photos for the cover illustration were provided by the Associated Press and are used with permission. Photo credits: Robert E.
Klein (nightclub fire), Dr. Scott Lieberman (space shuttle), pool
photographer Tony Nicoletti (Iraqis), and Brian Vander Brug
(grieving woman).

Photos in the Community Service Photojournalism section were
provided by the photographers. Photos of winners and finalists were
provided by their news organizations.

Printed in the United States of America

To the journalists who still believe
there is no excellence without truth.

An enduring icon of excellence

MAY 2004

Smiles come easily to Neal Shine, and he draws them from those around him. He glides through newsroom stories that begin with humor and end as salutes to journalists and their great work.

Shine's career spanned 45 years at the *Detroit Free Press*, beginning as a part-time copy boy in 1950 and ending with his retirement as publisher in 1995. His stories, like those you'll find in this book, capture the energy of newsroom successes.

He spun some of those yarns at a reception one day in the spring of 2004 as a guest at Michigan State University's Neal Shine Ethics Symposium. The setting created powerful contrasts, beginning with the sight of the 75-year-old Shine and his wife greeting student journalists just out of their teens.

Then there was the difference between the mood inside the conference center and a symbol outside. Inside, the crowd faced societal uncertainty about the job market, the economy, the war, and the news business. Outside, there was Michigan State University's most recognizable landmark: a statue of a soldier from antiquity, a Spartan grasping his helmet, sure of himself and his mission.

Shine and "Sparty" have so much in common. Both are tall with strong features. Neither has much hair. They have memorable expressions: Sparty has the vaguely stern look of his cousin, the Academy Award's Oscar. Shine has the constant look of one enjoying a private joke. The two share a sense of purpose. Sparty's bearing evokes determination. Shine's life reveals a commitment to excellence.

For most of 2003 and much of 2004, student journalists heard about highly publicized failings. They heard about journalists who deceived, fabricated, plagiarized, and manipulated facts and photos. At the Neal Shine lectures, by contrast, students reading the printed program learned about a man "dedicated to fairness, accuracy, and a humanitarian approach to reporting." They learned about "his commitment to ethical journalism."

Shine once wrote a column that told of his start at the *Free Press* and how, as a copy boy in the 1950s, he regularly talked with a staffer who was in his 70s. Shine called him Eddie Guest, but many people know him as the poet Edgar A. Guest. He started at the newspaper in 1895 and remained throughout his career, often writing verse for the editorial page.

Guest taught Shine this lesson: that the newspaper's purpose was to use its power to help those who had run out of choices.

During his first decade at the *Free Press*, Shine learned another lesson. City editor John Driver told him, "People have to believe in your paper or else it's all a lost cause."

Shine's stories are about journalists who believed in those values of integrity and purpose. They tell of a newsroom in which people made sacrifices to help those with nowhere else to turn; of staff members who worked long hours to nail an important story; of journalism that touched lives, revealed wrongs, and made things right.

At the top of that list of stories is one from 1967, when Shine's staff covered Detroit's riots. When the violence ended, the *Free Press* staff wondered, "Why did 43 people die?" A staff effort to answer that question took five weeks of 12-hour days. They found the answer: Most of the deaths could have—and should have—been prevented. The effort also led to the 1968 Pulitzer Prize for local reporting.

Quality journalism didn't end with Shine's stories, and it isn't confined to Detroit. Each year, this book makes that point. Once again, *Best Newspaper Writing* holds up examples of excellence from news organizations and individuals from across the country.

This year, led by Tim J. McGuire of Plymouth, Minn., the judges were:

Jim Amoss, *The Times-Picayune*, New Orleans
Caesar Andrews, Gannett News Service, McLean, Va.
Gilbert Bailon, *The Dallas Morning News*
Amanda Bennett, *The Philadelphia Inquirer*
Peter Bhatia, *The Oregonian*, Portland
Neil Brown, *St. Petersburg* (Fla.) *Times*
Jerry Ceppos, Knight Ridder, San Jose, Calif.
Milton Coleman, *The Washington Post*

Gregory Favre, The Poynter Institute, St. Petersburg, Fla.
Deborah Howell, Newhouse News Service,
    Washington, D.C.
David Laventhol, New York
Pam Luecke, Washington and Lee University,
    Lexington, Va.
Rich Oppel, *Austin* (Texas) *American-Statesman*
Chris Peck, *The Commercial Appeal*, Memphis, Tenn.
Skip Perez, *The Ledger*, Lakeland, Fla.
Maddy Ross, *Pittsburgh Post-Gazette*
Janet Weaver, The Poynter Institute, St. Petersburg, Fla.
Jim Willse, *The Star-Ledger*, Newark, N.J.

They were aided in selecting the community service photojournalism award by Carolyn Lee, formerly of *The New York Times,* and three other experts:

Vin Alabiso, Associated Press
Marcia Prouse, *The Orange County Register*,
    Santa Ana, Calif.
Kenny Irby, The Poynter Institute, St. Petersburg, Fla.

The Poynter Institute congratulates the winners and thanks writing committee members for their good work. These stories offer reporting that informs communities and helps those who have run out of choices. Their selections remind us that believable journalism is not a lost cause. Like Neal Shine and his inspirational stories, excellent journalism endures.

> Karen Brown Dunlap, President
> The Poynter Institute

Acknowledgments

The making of *Best Newspaper Writing* can sometimes seem like an orchestrated train wreck. In four short months, the crush of interviews, essays, and photographs collide constantly with the clock as a team of people report, write, and pore over every word and image. But when the smoke clears, journalists are left with a book that uplifts, illuminates, and instructs. Many people make that happen.

It begins with the winners and finalists who pushed their craft to a higher plane. They were chosen by judges from the American Society of Newspaper Editors, who give of their time each winter to make the selections. And our efforts are helped greatly by the work ASNE executive director Scott Bosley and assistant Suzanne Martin did in getting the materials to us quickly. But it's impossible to overstate the role publications director Billie M. Keirstead and assistant Vicki Krueger have played in herding writers, photographers, interviewers—and the editor. They got editing help from John Schlander, Kathleen Tobin, and Mark Wood.

Thanks, too, to Poynter faculty members who conducted interviews and wrote biographies and Writers' Workshops: Poynter vice president Roy Peter Clark, Aly Colón, Kenny Irby, Kelly McBride, Bill Mitchell, Christopher Scanlan, and dean Janet Weaver. Their efforts during one of the Institute's busiest times are deeply appreciated.

Poynter design editor and faculty member Anne Conneen designed the CD-ROM presentation with technical help from multimedia editor Larry Larsen. Others from Poynter put time and energy into producing this book, including library director David Shedden and Bobbi Alsina.

Each year, we all arrive at the nexus of journalistic excellence and academic inquiry, to sometimes-cacophonous effect. The result of that collision, though, is another volume of this series that celebrates the best of journalism.

Contents

Editorial Writing

Community Service Photojournalism

In praise of writing's unsung heroes

BY KEITH WOODS

Writing, for me, has not gotten easier with time. After more than 25 years at the professional keyboard, the words come no quicker. I still loiter interminably at the lead, slog tortuously through the body, stumble giddily upon a kicker.

Then I pray for good editing.

That's the part of the writing process that we speak least about, especially when celebrating the accomplishments of great writers. But talk to many—maybe most—of the journalists whose stories are honored in this book, and eventually they'll mention people who had a hand in the winning work, people whose names never appear in the byline.

In many ways, *Best Newspaper Writing 2004* is an ode to editors.

They coach, inspire, and provoke. For the winners included in the 26th edition of this book, editors played a critical role, from idea to rewrite.

Take *The Charlotte Observer*'s Tommy Tomlinson. He won the ASNE Distinguished Writing Award for Profile Writing, and you'll get some insight into how he did that by reading his interview with Poynter's Chip Scanlan.

You'll also learn how his editor, Mike Gordon, would sit him down and read the whole story out loud—an "excruciating and incredibly powerful" experience, Tomlinson calls it.

S. Lynne Walker's editor did the same thing as she worked on the series for Copley News Service that won the Freedom Forum/ASNE Award for Distinguished Writing on Diversity. In Walker's case, though, editor Susan White from *The San Diego Union-Tribune* read the entire four-part series over the telephone from 1,500 miles away while Walker sat on the other end in Mexico City.

"That's an enormous commitment of time on the part of an editor, but it's just absolutely crucial," Walker tells Poynter's Aly Colón.

Writers can come up with lots of words to describe

what they think of editors, but not everyone will stop in the middle of a sentence, as the *Arkansas Democrat-Gazette*'s Cathy Frye did, and say, "This is why I love my editor." She was talking about how Jay Grelen, who edited Frye's non-deadline prize winner "Caught in the Web," had freed her, with a simple sentence of support, to reveal the facts of a tragedy the way the people in the story had lived it.

"I had struggled and struggled with that first draft," Frye tells Poynter's Kelly McBride. "Once I had the all-clear from [Grelen] to do it the way that he and I intuitively thought it should be done, it was just so much easier."

Sometimes the editor's most important contribution happens at an even higher level of abstraction. Sometimes before the first word is written.

Before the bombs started falling on Baghdad, Anthony Shadid of *The Washington Post* needed to decide how he would tell the daily tales of war in a way that had coherence and meaning beyond the moment. In his interview with Poynter dean Janet Weaver, Shadid describes how editors helped form the coverage that led him to the Jesse Laventhol Prize for Deadline News Reporting and a Pulitzer Prize:

"One editor, Ed Cody, said, 'You're there; say what it's like. Bring an authority to your voice that you wouldn't maybe have otherwise.' And another editor, David Hoffman, said to understand the forces from below; understand social forces; understand what's happening to the city. And finally, Phil Bennett said to really focus on sentiment. 'Those sentiments you're exploring may be one of the defining qualities of this war.'"

For finalists in the ASNE contest, the sentiments toward editors were similar:

■ *The Wall Street Journal* team credits an editor for negotiating a truce with sources irate about the newspaper's dogged coverage of an unfolding scandal at the New York Stock Exchange.

■ Lane DeGregory says her editor at the *St. Petersburg Times* gave her some common-sense advice as she wrestled with how to turn a tale she thought would take days into a daily story. The advice: "This is a simple, lovely story. Just tell it like it happened."

■ *Seattle Post-Intelligencer* columnist Robert L.

Jamieson gives credit to his editors because they were willing to "loosen the leash" and give him license to tell good stories.

It could be that these are all kind, well-placed words by politically savvy writers trying to curry future favor with their bosses. Read on, though, and you'll get the sense that they mean it.

How else to explain that the *Observer*'s Tommy Tomlinson has named a technique he used for ending one of his stories after an editor.

He called the ending a "Schwab."

Want to know why? I won't tell you just yet. I hear it's good to make the reader wait for some things.

I don't remember who taught me that, but I think it was an editor.

ABOUT THIS BOOK

Through recorded conversations, follow-up calls, and e-mails, members of the Poynter faculty produced the interviews that follow the stories honored in this book. For the sake of clarity, flow, and brevity, some of the answers have been compressed and reordered, and some questions have been edited or added. The biographies of winners and finalists were written by Poynter faculty and include information provided by the journalists.

Electronic versions of the winners' and finalists' stories were provided to Poynter by ASNE for publication in this book. They may differ slightly from the stories that originally appeared in print.

Best Newspaper Writing editors made minor changes in stories for style and grammar. Where editors found errors of fact, those were corrected after consultation with the writers.

Best Newspaper Writing 2004

Cathy Frye
Non-Deadline Writing

Cathy Frye's vision for a narrative series began where the story opens, just outside the home of a murdered child.

In December 2002, Frye stood on the front porch asking for an interview with the family of Kacie Woody, who had been kidnapped and killed. The family said no. Frye walked away. She called back and sent letters. She went on maternity leave. She came back to work. And still she couldn't stop thinking about how much more there was to say about Kacie's death.

Before her arrival at the *Arkansas Democrat-Gazette* in 1999, Frye, 34, spent her entire journalism career in a series of Texas towns.

After graduating from the University of North Texas in Denton, she worked as a copy editor at the *Corpus Christi Caller-Times*, where she found herself desk-bound, addicted to caffeine, and gaining weight. "Copy editing was not for me," she says.

She moved on to a reporting job at the *Lubbock Avalanche-Journal* and then to the *Odessa American,* where she also spent a year as the night city editor.

Her favorite stories out of Odessa were about a stand-off in the remote Davis Mountains. A militant separatist group called the Republic of Texas held state troopers at bay for a week in 1997. Frye and her fellow reporters covered the story around the clock. She came home with the worst sunburn of her life and bruises from sleeping in the bed of her pickup. "I had a marvelous time," she says.

Shortly after the standoff, Frye took a job with *The Beaumont Enterprise*. When James Byrd Jr. was dragged to his death behind a pickup truck, Frye was the lead re-porter. A few days later, while the town was swarming with national media, Frye persuaded the sheriff to let her and a photographer take a look at the murder weapon—a primer-gray 1982 Ford pickup.

Small-town journalism has taught her the importance of accuracy, credibility, and staying in touch with readers. It's impossible to get away with sloppy work when you are constantly running into your sources at the grocery store, she says.

For the *Democrat-Gazette*, Frye has covered several national stories, including traveling to Oklahoma City for Timothy McVeigh's execution and to New York af-ter Sept. 11.

Frye is known in the newsroom for her compassion, humor, and persistence. It took months to get Rick Woody to talk about his daughter.

"Most reporters quit trying. And the story fades away," she says. "I don't forget."

It took three months to report the series, "Caught in the Web." On Oct. 1, 2003, Frye stood in the front yard of the Woody home as a photographer took pictures. It was dusk. They looked through the windows and saw what the killer saw. That became the introduction to her series.

Frye is married to photojournalist Rick McFarland. Their daughter, Amanda, sometimes shows her affec-tion for her parents' work by eating the Sunday paper.

—Kelly McBride

Caught in the Web:
Evil at the door

DECEMBER 14, 2003

He could see his 13-year-old prey framed in the living-room windows—cozy in her favorite nightclothes and typing speedily at the family computer on this rainy, 39-degree December night.

As usual, Kacie Woody had switched on all the lights as she walked from room to room, and the small house now glowed against a backdrop of towering trees.

He stepped closer. Kacie was there for the taking—typing, distracted, her silhouette melding with that of the computer monitor before her.

She was right there, only a stretch of dark and the front door between them, and she had no idea he had come for her.

* * *

Meanwhile, police officer Rick Woody—Kacie's dad—was on patrol in nearby Greenbrier, cruising the swath of U.S. 65 that cuts through this central Arkansas town. The traffic was mostly 18-wheelers, headed either north toward Missouri or south to Interstate 40.

Like most nights in Greenbrier, population 3,042, this one had been uneventful. Rick, suffering from a sinus infection, almost had called in sick. The night was cold and rainy, and his chief had told him to take it easy. Rick still felt poorly, but he figured he could make it through his shift, which would end at 2 a.m.

Rick liked policing the sleeping town. He made few arrests, but that was OK. His idea of good law enforcement was to prevent bad things, not to step in after the

---

This series of stories is based on interviews with investigators and Kacie Woody's family and friends, as well as police reports written at the time and a transcript recovered from the Woody family's computer. All direct quotes in the narration are based on the recollections of those interviewed. The parents of Scott, a 14-year-old Internet friend of Kacie's from Alpharetta, Ga., asked that his last name not be published.

crime. That's why he watched out for the young women making nightly bank deposits after Greenbrier's stores and restaurants closed. They often neglected to call for an escort, so Rick would just show up when they were due to leave work.

While on duty, Rick kept his cell phone close so he could check frequently on Kacie. He never really worried, though. Kacie had grown up motherless and had assumed much responsibility at home. She laundered her own clothes, cooked dinner for herself and did her homework without being told. If there were an emergency, Rick could get from Greenbrier to the house in 15 minutes.

Kacie didn't mind her dad's late hours. She had always lived in the little gray house on Griggers Lane, on the outskirts of Holland, population 597, a tiny community in the center of rural Faulkner County. The solitude didn't faze her. Nor was she disturbed by the seemingly impenetrable darkness outside.

Most nights, Kacie didn't even lock the front door.

One of her older brothers, Tim, 19, still lived at home and was usually there with Kacie at night. Tim's friend, Eric Betts, also 19, had taken up temporary residence at the Woody house. So he, too, was in and out. If the guys weren't around, there was always her Aunt Teresa, who also lived on Griggers Lane.

But on this bone-chilling evening of Dec. 3, 2002, a Tuesday, Tim had left for the University of Central Arkansas library at 6 p.m. Eric was at his electrician's class. And Aunt Teresa was in Conway, cheering at her daughter's basketball game.

Kacie was home alone.

EARLIER THAT DAY

For Kacie and her circle of seventh-grade friends at Greenbrier Middle School, the day had begun with an argument. At the heart of the tiff were Kacie and one of her closest friends, Samantha Mann, also 13.

The girls all normally agreed on pretty much everything—which guys were hot, which girls were popular and, of course, the belief that "school sucks." The group convened each morning before walking to class arm in arm. A sense of security pervaded these locker-lined hallways, where blue-and-white panthers prowled and pounced across cinder-block walls.

Kacie's social path at school was neatly paved. She had attended Greenbrier schools since kindergarten, and her sunny nature attracted new friends each year. She also was the younger sister of two former football stars.

Her days were plagued by little more than the usual teenage worries—weight gain, grades and guys.

Like her friends, Kacie was experimenting with eye shadow as well as boyfriends. But learning to put on makeup proved to be much easier than mastering the intricacies of teenage courtship.

In an e-mail sent to a male Greenbrier friend that autumn, she had confided: *My longest relantionship was… i think 3 months. I am usually the one that gets dumped…I have really bad luck with guys. Dude I am like sooo totally confused about guys right now!! ARGH! Sometimes guys really bad suck ya know? It's like… idk…weird…lol…well I am gunna jet bc i don't have nething to say…*

* * *

Samantha, a self-assured, outspoken blonde, could relate to Kacie's frustration. What Sam couldn't understand was her friend's fascination with the boys she met on the Internet. So far, Kacie had found love twice online. Both of these relationships bothered Sam. She worried about how freely Kacie was giving out her phone number to strangers. Several times, she had warned Kacie: "You can't be in love with someone from the Internet."

The girls' long-running disagreement peaked Dec. 3. It stemmed from a comment Sam had made the day before about a photo of Scott, Kacie's most recent online boyfriend. The picture, which hung in Kacie's locker, was of a young, dark-haired guy in a football uniform. Sam had said he was "hot." Kacie thought she said "fat." They had exchanged barbs, and by the following morning, the girls' mutual friends had taken sides.

Sam decided it was time to involve an adult.

For moral support, she took a friend with her to Room 214, where school counselor Dianna Kellar spends her days treading delicately through seventh grade's hormonal minefields.

With her maternal demeanor and lavish use of endearments, Mrs. Kellar, a middle-aged woman with salt-and-pepper hair, is a comforting presence in this small world of constant melodrama. She handled Sam and Kacie's fight as deftly as any other.

After hearing Sam out, the counselor summoned Kacie to the office and let the girls muddle through their grievances by themselves. By the time Mrs. Kellar reappeared, Sam and Kacie had patched up their friendship.

But Sam feared the truce would be short-lived. Kacie didn't know it, but Sam had told Mrs. Kellar that Kacie was giving out her phone number online. Mrs. Kellar had promised to talk to Kacie again, and Sam wasn't sure how her friend would react.

As the girls left that morning, Mrs. Kellar asked Kacie about the matter. Kacie assured the counselor she had shared her number only with people approved by her dad. But Sam knew this wasn't true.

During fifth period, Mrs. Kellar called Kacie back into her office and warned her about dangers online, but Kacie clearly had no fear of anyone she had met on the Internet.

In the months to come, Mrs. Kellar would wonder: *What else should I have asked?*

* * *

When Sam and Kacie met after school, Kacie was her usual bubbly self. But she made an unusual suggestion that later would cause her friends to wonder if she had sensed the horror to come.

As the girls prepared to leave, Kacie asked if she could spend the night at Sam's house. Sam, knowing her mom would frown on a school-night sleepover, said no.

Kacie also asked Jessica Tanner, a slender girl with large, earnest brown eyes. Jessica also said no.

Kacie persisted, asking a third friend, but received the same answer.

Kacie didn't explain why she wanted to sleep elsewhere that night. She just didn't want to go home.

The refusals didn't upset her. She laughed—that goofy, honking guffaw for which she was known—and headed to where her bus waited, its engine thrumming. Before boarding, she hugged all of her friends.

"Bye!" she called out. "See ya!"

A FINAL CHAT

Kacie spent the evening watching the weather, fervently hoping that the predicted sleet and snow might give her a day off from school.

She showered and put on what she always wore to bed—a favorite pair of blue sweat pants sporting the endearment "Baby Girl" and a gray sweatshirt. Then she returned to the computer, which sat in front of one of the two rectangular windows overlooking the Woodys' front yard.

Awaiting Kacie was an instant message from Scott, who was writing from his home in an affluent suburb of Atlanta.

Kacie loved instant messages, which, unlike e-mail, pop up on the screen as soon as they are written. Conversations are in real time.

Kacie had met Scott in a chat room in May 2002. He described himself as a 14-year-old boy living in Georgia. He liked football and wrestling.

Kacie and Scott had officially become boyfriend and girlfriend on Oct. 3, 2002.

Scott's online moniker was Tazz2999. Kacie's was modelbehavior63. Their rapid-fire conversation made abbreviations a necessity and misspellings inevitable:

Tazz2999: Hey Sweetie
modelbehavior63: hey
Tazz2999: how are you my angel?
modelbehavior63: ok…u
Tazz2999: better now that ur on sweetie

And they were off, fingers flying across keyboards as they bemoaned troublesome classes like math and Arkansas history, and analyzed Kacie and Sam's reconciliation. They also discussed Kacie's two favorite extracurricular activities:

modelbehavior63: GUESS WHAT…GUES WHAt… GUESS WHAT
Tazz2999: WHAT hehe
modelbehavior63: 23 kids outta 130 were picked to sing in frontof the school board and I AM ONE OF THEM…ooo adn wednesday i have band practice and

thursday i have choir practice

Tazz2999: Thats excenlant baby I told you You have the most beutiful voice I have ever hears

Tazz2999: *heard*

modelbehavior63: ☺

* * *

As she instant-messaged Scott, Kacie was on the phone with another Internet friend named Dave.

Dave was upset. His aunt, in a coma since a car wreck, was about to die. Kacie hurt for him. Her mother, Kristie, had died in an accident when Kacie was only 7. Kacie was certain her beloved mama was now a beautiful angel, looking out for her from above. Still, heaven was so far away.

Kacie had met Dave sometime during the summer of 2002 in a Yahoo Christian chat room for teens. From the start, their friendship was full of romantic overtones, and even after Scott became her new "official" boyfriend, Kacie had continued her online friendship with Dave.

Scott knew all about Dave. Kacie had introduced them online. The two had even talked on the phone a few times, mostly about cars.

In his Yahoo profile, Dave described himself as an 18-year-old living in San Diego. His picture showed a young man with wavy, sandy hair that fell below his shoulder blades. With his tousled mane, square jaw and pouting mouth, Dave looked like a cross between a surfer and the lead singer of a 1980s hair band.

* * *

As Kacie consoled Dave on the phone, she kept Scott abreast of the grim situation:

modelbehavior63: tonight…Dave's aunt is going to meet my mommy

Tazz2999: ☹ Im so so sorry baby…atleast we know that she will be happy there with your mommy…I am sure she will look out for her ...

modelbehavior63: yeah…i think they will be best friend…hehe

Tazz2999:…I hope Dave is alright

modelbehavior63: he is…i am on the phone… he has been laughing at me…bc he know it is the best...

Tazz2999: ☺ at least he is laughing

* * *

Kacie told Scott about her visit to the counselor's office:

modelbehavior63: so guess what i got…a lecture
Tazz2999: awww im sorry baby
modelbehavior63:…on how u could be a 80 year old rapest…lol
Tazz2999: lol
modelbehavior63: hehe…and that the picture was ur grandson
Tazz2999: how many times have u gotten that 1 hehe
modelbehavior63: um…i lost count…well…then… she is like…"do ur parents know u talk to ppl u dont know" i was like "yeah" and she was like…well careful…and dont agree to meet them less ur mom or dad is with you" i was like…okay…and she is like…well remember this lil talk…i was like…ok...
Tazz2999: uh oh. prolly means she is going to talk to u again…
modelbehavior63: i kno

* * *

The young couple moved on to more pleasant topics, like the fact that this day marked their two-month anniversary:

Tazz2999: I will always be your teddy graham and you will always be my angel and we will be together forever and always and longer
modelbehavior63: awww
Tazz2999: hehe what r u doing sweetie
modelbehavior63: eating and talking to dave and singing…Dave and i were crying together for a sec…i told him i loved him…and momma told me she did too…and that mommy talks to me…and that she said she would take care of his aunt

'R U OK?'

Kacie sent Scott a link to a weather Web site.

modelbehavior63: look at what it feels like outside!!
Tazz2999: awwww *holds her tight and rubs her arms to keep her warm*

Meanwhile, outside in the chilly darkness, someone crept across the Woodys' front yard—someone who had come for Kacie.

He had driven to the Holland community in a rented silver minivan, slowing down when he reached Griggers Lane, a narrow dirt and gravel road that dead-ends at the Woody home.

The house, illuminated by interior lamps and a single porch light, stood out in sharp relief against the blackness. Inside, Kacie still sat at the computer, reading Scott's fumbling attempts to wax poetic:

Tazz2999: hehe ill always be with u my angel becouse ur all I want to be with
Tazz2999: hehe i put my screen saver as the picture i have in my locker
Tazz2999: ur the most beutiful angel in the world Kacie
Tazz2999: r u ok sweetie?

When Kacie finally responded, her message was uncharacteristically brief:

modelbehavior63: yah

It was 9:41 p.m.

* * *

Maybe the intruder knocked. Or maybe he just walked in.

Either way, he caught Kacie completely off-guard, covering her face with a chloroform-soaked rag and knocking her glasses onto her dad's recliner. He dragged the thrashing girl through the living room and hauled her out into the cold darkness, across the damp ground and into the waiting minivan.

Throughout the violent struggle, Scott's loving entreaties continued to pop up on the Woodys' computer screen:

Tazz2999: r u busy baby?
Tazz2999: …hehe guess so...
Tazz2999: u there baby?
Tazz2999: sweetie r u ok...

Tazz2999: please talk to me baby...
Tazz2999: ☹
Tazz2999: when u r ready to talk sweetie ill be here...
Tazz2999: r u mad at me sweetie? ☹
Tazz2999: please talk to me baby...
Tazz2999: r u ok sweetie

No response.

* * *

For the next 35 minutes, Scott filled the Woodys' monitor with increasingly frantic pleas:

Tazz2999: please GOD let her be ok
Tazz2999: Kacie please tlak to me
Tazz2999: please…please...

Still, no answer. Scott kept trying.

Tazz2999: Kacie Im so so scared I dont know what to do.
Tazz2999: …please…Say something

At 10:15 p.m., Scott called the Woody house.

Tazz2999: why isnt anyone answering the PHONE!
Tazz2999: UGH
Tazz2999: Please
Tazz2999: PLEASE PICK UP KACIE
Tazz2999: PLEASE
Tazz2999: GOD PLEASE LET HER PICK UP
Tazz2999: please be ok Kacie…GOD let her bo ok

Scott e-mailed Kacie's friend Jessica: *Jessica please let this be u something is wrong with kacie her s/n is still on and she all the sudden left during our convo but didn't log off and i tried to call her and no one answered and we weren't fighting or anything so i e-mail the cops to make sure she is alright i hop they get it soon...I'm going crazy I don't know what I would do without her please God let her be ok.*

But it was 10:44 p.m. on a school night, and Jessica wouldn't find the e-mail until the next afternoon.

Frustrated, Scott went back to instant-messaging the Woodys' computer:

Tazz2999: ERIC TIM DADDY DANNY ANYONE PLEASE BE THERE TO HELP HER PLEASE I KNOW SOMETHING ISNT RIGHT PLEASE PLEASE PLEASE

AT THE WOODY HOME

When family friend Eric Betts returned home from his electrician's class at 10:17 p.m., he assumed Kacie was already in bed. For more than an hour, he watched television, getting up periodically to do his laundry.

At 11:30 p.m., during one of his trips to the utility room, Eric noticed that Kacie wasn't in her room. He assumed she was out with friends or family.

Minutes later, Kacie's brother Tim arrived home.

"Where's Kacie?" Eric asked.

"I thought she was here," Tim replied. Concerned, he called his dad. The time was 11:40 p.m.

"Where's Kacie?" Tim asked.

"At home," Rick replied.

"No, she isn't," Tim said.

Rick had last talked to Kacie at 7 p.m. She had been practicing her saxophone.

Rick told Tim to call Kacie's friends. He also told him to check with Aunt Teresa next door. Meanwhile, Rick drove to the Greenbrier Police Department. When he arrived, he called Tim again.

"Nobody knows anything," Tim told him.

Rick notified the Faulkner County sheriff's office. Then he headed home. His little girl wasn't where she was supposed to be, and he was certain someone had taken her.

When Rick arrived, he noticed that both of Kacie's coats—a brand-new yellow one and her band jacket— were draped over a chair in the kitchen. Her tennis shoes and boots lay by the computer, where she always kicked them off.

At the time Kacie disappeared, the temperature had been 39 degrees and dropping. Heavy rains were moving through the area.

At 12:24 a.m., Deputy Dalton Elliott arrived at the Woody home. After looking around, he asked sheriff's investigator Jim Wooley to join him at the scene. Elliott also notified area law enforcement agencies that a girl was missing.

Meanwhile, phones rang all over Greenbrier as Rick, Tim and Eric quizzed Kacie's friends.

"Is Kacie at your house?" Rick asked Sam when a family member brought the phone to her at 1:11 a.m.

"No," a still-groggy Sam said. "Why?"

By the time Sam hung up, she was fully awake. "Pray for Kacie," she told her mom. "She's missing." Sam sat up the rest of the night, telephone in hand, repeatedly calling Kacie's house.

By now, Rick and the boys had noticed a phone call from Georgia on their Caller ID. The call had been placed at 10:15 p.m.

They made another discovery as well—a long dialogue on the computer between modelbehavior63 and Tazz2999.

AT SCOTT'S HOUSE

Scott checked his computer frequently. Every so often, he fell into a troubled slumber. Finally, five hours after the last message from Kacie, Scott's computer monitor flickered to life:

modelbehavior63: hey scott ru there this is eric

modelbehavior63: as soon as u get this ANSWER back PLEASE i have GOT TO TALK TO YA

Tazz2999: im on...

modelbehavior63: what happened with u and kacie tonight...did she just quit talkin...

Tazz2999: yeah...just went silent

modelbehavior63: did any thing seem like something was wrong?

Tazz2999: nope not at all

modelbehavior63: what was the last time that u talked to her...i need as close as a time as possible

Tazz2999: 9:41 was her last message...

modelbehavior63: ok...did she say anything out of the ordinary

Tazz2999: no just quiet I can send you aour whole convo if u like

modelbehavior63: no i already got it i just need to know if she has seemed like something has been bothering her or if she needed to talk to someone

* * *

Eric confirmed Scott's phone number. He also asked him for his full name, age and address.

modelbehavior63: what was she saying bout the school consoler and this guy dave? anything wrong with her

Tazz2999: well umm her ans Sam have been having a fight and they talked abot it with the consoler then Sam told the consoler that she was dating me and she got lectured...dont worry about Dave he is just a good friend I would have said something if i didnt htink he was a good guy but he is cool

modelbehavior63: so has it just been tonight that she seemed quiet?...and did she talk about goin some where or with someone?

Tazz2999: Eric...can u tell me the [truth] now... where is Kacie

modelbehavior63: just tell me...i got to know it is VERY important

Tazz2999: ummm...i dont think so... not tonight...but she was on the phone...

modelbehavior63: do u know with who?

Tazz2999: Dave

Scott told Eric he didn't know when Dave and Kacie had ended their phone conversation. Nor did he know Dave's last name, only that he lived in San Diego. Scott promised to ask Dave for a phone number if he encountered him online.

modelbehavior63: i am going to get off of here but i will leave it connected just in case...thanks so much for the help

Tazz2999: anytime but can answer sumthing 4 me

modelbehavior63: whats that?

Tazz2999: what happen to Kacie...

Caught in the Web:
Entryway to danger

DECEMBER 15, 2003

Something bad had happened in this living room.

State police investigator Karl Byrd knew it as soon as he saw 13-year-old Kacie Woody's mangled eyeglasses, which lay beneath a pile of towels in a tan recliner. The frames were bent and one lens had popped out.

Kacie had been missing for six hours now.

It was 3:35 a.m. Dec. 4, 2002, a half-hour since the persistent ring of Byrd's telephone had jarred him from a deep slumber. The caller had been Jim Wooley, a Faulkner County sheriff's investigator.

"Karl, I've got a girl out here missing," Wooley had said in worried tones.

"I'm not sure what to make of it, but I don't like the way it looks."

Byrd had hastily donned his clothes and driven to the rural Holland community, snowflakes melting on his windshield. Byrd couldn't imagine a kid taking off on this cold, wet night.

The misshapen eyeglasses confirmed his suspicions: Kacie hadn't left this house willingly.

Kacie's dad, Greenbrier police officer Rick Woody, told investigators that nothing was missing except his daughter's nightclothes. Both of her coats were in the kitchen. Her shoes lay in a pile near the family's computer in the living room. Kacie's beloved Yorkshire terrier, George, was limping.

The last person to have seen Kacie was her brother Tim, who had left the house at 6 p.m. for the University of Central Arkansas library in Conway, 12 miles southwest of their home. At the time, Kacie had been on the Internet. She was wearing her glasses, as she always did when she was on the computer.

Dialogue still on the monitor revealed to the investigators that Kacie had been exchanging instant messages with someone named Scott, who appeared to be a 14-year-old living in a suburb of Atlanta. According to the dialogue, Kacie also had been talking on the phone with someone named Dave.

Kacie's messages ended abruptly at 9:41 p.m., in mid-conversation with Scott, further convincing Byrd and Wooley that she had been kidnapped.

As other lawmen throughout the county were roused from their beds, Byrd and Wooley went door to door on Griggers Lane, awakening neighbors and asking questions; volunteers searched the dark woods surrounding the Woodys' property.

At 5:14 a.m., investigators issued a Level II Morgan Nick Alert, which allows state police to notify the media of a missing child.

GREENBRIER MIDDLE SCHOOL, DEC. 4

For Samantha Mann, 13, the bus ride to school was unbearable. Her friend Kacie was missing, yet everyone was acting so...*normal.*

But most Greenbrier Middle School students hadn't yet heard that one of their schoolmates had vanished from her home the night before. So they chattered and bantered as usual, secure in their belief that bad things don't happen to 13-year-old girls living in the middle of nowheresville.

Sam, who knew better, sat numbly in her seat, unsure whether to say anything.

Jessica Tanner, 12, also part of Kacie's circle, heard the news when she walked into her first period-class, where two girls were discussing her friend.

"Kacie Woody's been kidnapped," one of the girls said.

"Y'all are lying," Jessica declared, and burst into tears.

Jessica's teacher sent her to the counselor's office. As soon as she walked in, Jessica encountered two other distraught friends, who clung to her and sobbed.

Moments later, Sam rounded the corner.

She made a beeline for Jessica, and the two girls locked in an embrace of grief and disbelief.

At 9:20 a.m., Sam sat in school counselor Dianna Kellar's office, trying to answer the questions of investigators Byrd and Wooley.

She had been here just the day before to tell Mrs. Kellar she was worried about how freely Kacie gave her phone number to people she met on the Internet.

Now Sam was here to talk about Kacie again, this time to policemen.

LOVE ONLINE

The Woodys live so far out in the country that phone calls to Greenbrier, 12 miles to the northwest, are long-distance. So Rick laid down strict rules about using the phone.

Kacie turned to the computer, discovering quickly that instant-messaging was almost as good as talking on the phone. Unlike e-mail, instant messages pop up immediately on the screen, allowing conversations to be held in real time.

Kacie's screen name was modelbehavior63, inspired by *Model Behavior*, one of her favorite Disney movies. The 63 came from older brother Austin's football jersey.

For a while, Kacie was content with her network of local friends. But like many teens, she couldn't resist the lure of chat rooms and ventured into these online social hubs. By autumn 2002, modelbehavior63 had become a regular presence in Yahoo's teen and Christian chat rooms.

Kacie's Yahoo profile, which included a photo of her, was there for anyone who wanted to learn more about her.

She last updated her profile in November 2002:

Real name: Kacie
Location: Arkansas
Age: blank
Marital Status: Long-term relationship
Gender: Female
Occupation: Messenger of God
More About Me: (Hobbies): I write love poems, play alto sax, am in the school choir and recently tried out for soccer. I'm 13 now.
Latest News: October 3rd I started going out with Scott. The sweetest, cutest, smartest, funniest, sexiest guy ever. I love him with all my heart.
Favorite quote: "They wear so many faces, show up in the strangest places. To guide us with their mercy, in our time of need. Oh I believe there are angels among us, sent down to us from somewhere up above. They come___"

* * *

Kacie first bumped into Dave in a Yahoo chat room for Christian teens during the summer of 2002. They struck up a friendship and began instant-messaging each other regularly. Kacie brought Dave into her group of online friends. She introduced him to her "real life" friends as well, setting up three-way phone calls and sending him photos of her schoolmates.

Kacie and Dave's shared love of music likely helped draw them together. Dave played guitar. Kacie loved to sing and play her sax. Both were Elvis fans.

Dave's profile was sparse:

Real name: Dave
Location: San Diego, Ca
Age: 18
Marital Status: Long-term relationship
Gender: Male

The accompanying photo showed a blondish, long-haired guy, sort of a younger version of the model Fabio. Kacie thought Dave was cute, but her friends didn't like his long hair.

Kacie briefly considered Dave her boyfriend but became interested in a local boy in early autumn. She later broke up with this boy for Scott, whom she had met online in May 2002.

Kacie and Scott became an official item on Oct. 3, 2002.

In Scott, Kacie found someone proficient in all the intrigue and drama of adolescent puppy love. Scott's profile identified him as a Georgia teen who loved football and wrestling. His photo, which Kacie hung in her locker, showed a dark-haired boy in a football uniform, No. 79. Unlike most young players posing for their team photos, Scott didn't wear the standard menacing scowl. Instead, a wide grin creased his face.

Sam disapproved. She had never liked Dave. And Scott didn't strike her as much of an improvement. His mushy prose struck her as excessive.

Sam warned Kacie several times about "dating" people she had never met in person. How, she asked, could Kacie be sure of someone's true identity?

Kacie was so trusting that it worried Sam.

Another Greenbrier friend expressed similar doubts after Kacie e-mailed him an excerpt of an instant message from Scott.

Hey Sweetie, Scott had written. *I miss you so much…I have barely talked to you all day. I Hope Your doing ok sweetie…I Love You so much…ur everything and so much more to me ur my moon and my sun u light up my world your my angel My love for you will never end…Sweeter Dramz…*

Kacie gushed: *Isn't he a sweetie?*

Her Greenbrier friend replied bluntly: *do u believe all that stuff that dude is saying? How long have u known him?*

Kacie responded: *i actually do believe him…i have known him for over 6 months…*

* * *

Even after Kacie fell for Scott, she maintained her friendship with Dave, who didn't seem to mind Kacie's new boyfriend. Twice, Dave even talked to Scott on the phone.

The first time, Scott's mom answered.

"Who's calling from California?" she asked. "Is this a salesman?"

Scott took the phone from her, explaining, "Oh, it's just a friend of a friend."

The second time Dave called, Scott's dad answered.

"You're not a kid," the irate father declared. He told Dave not to call back.

Rick Woody had a similar reaction when Kacie told him that her online friend Dave was celebrating his 18th birthday.

"Eighteen is too old," Rick said, ordering Kacie to cease her correspondence with Dave. Rick didn't catch a name at the time—he was more concerned about the unknown boy's age.

Kacie obeyed. "My dad said I can't talk to you anymore because you're too old for me," she wrote to Dave.

So Dave switched from the computer to the telephone, calling Kacie frequently and talking about his dying aunt. Kacie also phoned Dave, but would quickly hang up. Then Dave would call back.

The phone calls made Sam even more uncomfortable

with Dave. For one thing, Dave didn't *sound* 18. He used outdated words of a different generation—"groovy" and "righteous" and "wicked."

Kacie once told him: "You people out in California talk a little bit differently."

Sam would later put it this way: "I was like, okaaaaay. He needed to get a teen slang book or something because no one says wicked or groovy. It was like my dad trying to act cool but actually sounding really retarded."

But Kacie always expected the best of people.

On two occasions, Kacie set up three-way phone conversations so that she could talk to Dave and Sam at the same time.

Dave described trips to the beach and how he loved fourwheeling. Mostly, though, he listened to Sam and Kacie talk.

At one point, he interjected.

"How old are you?" he asked Sam.

"Thirteen," Sam said.

"Oh…cool," Dave replied.

* * *

Jessica had talked to Dave, too, one weekend night shortly before Kacie's abduction.

Jessica was at the Woody home, feeling ill after a Dr Pepper burping contest. Kacie was on the phone with Dave.

"Here," Kacie said, handing the receiver to Jessica. "Talk to him. He'll make you feel better."

During the conversation, the girls heard noises outside, maybe someone walking around the back of the house, his feet crunching the leaves and sticks. Hastily, they shoved a dresser in front of Kacie's bedroom door. Minutes later, they were certain they heard the kitchen floor squeak.

"I'm scared there's somebody in my house," Kacie told Dave.

"Oh, there's nobody in your house," he replied. "You're just imagining things."

And then the noises stopped.

SHY AND TRUSTING

Kacie was born Oct. 17, 1989. She almost died from lung complications.

Rick and Kristie Woody named their baby after K.C. Koloski, a character on the television series *China Beach*, and took her home to the house on Griggers Lane. The couple's sons, Austin and Tim, doted on their sister.

Kacie was quiet around people she didn't know. But at home or around friends, she loved to perform. Whenever she visited friends for sleepovers, she took her worn video of the musical *Grease* and would sing along with every song as she subjected her friends to repeated viewings.

Parents saw Kacie as a "model child," as one mother put it, a good friend for their own children. She possessed an empathy beyond her years, impressing her counselor, Mrs. Kellar, as the only student willing to befriend a lonely schoolmate.

In the years after Kacie's mom died, Kacie fretted over her dad, believing that he was lonely. Many times she climbed into his lap, asking anxiously, "Are you OK?"

Kacie was always in search of a mother figure. She latched on to one of Tim's girlfriends, Carlee Hensley, who frequently took Kacie shopping. Carlee once spent a whole day trying to find someone who would pierce Kacie's ears without a guardian present.

The kindness that Carlee and other women showed Kacie made her far more trusting than most kids. People had always been good to her. She couldn't imagine anyone wishing her harm.

* * *

The Woodys moved from the North Little Rock area to rural Faulkner County in 1984 for the Greenbrier schools. The sparsely populated area appealed to Kristie and Rick, who had always wanted to live somewhere quiet and safe.

Their new homeplace served another purpose. Kristie and her mother, Illa Smith, loved horses, and this place was perfect for keeping them.

The women each owned several horses, and they spent countless hours grooming, riding and showing their prized animals. One Christmas, Illa made Kristie and Kacie matching Western outfits and took a picture of the pair, with Kacie posed on a toy horse.

In a strange twist, though, horses led to tragedy.

* * *

On June 19, 1997, Rick, Kristie, Tim and Kacie were

on their way home from Tim's baseball game when two horses ran onto Arkansas 287 in front of the family's Lincoln Town Car.

Rick hit one of the horses, which slammed through the windshield on the passenger's side. After the car shuddered to a stop, Rick looked at his wife.

And he knew.

He couldn't let Kacie see her mother, not like this. But with his ribs broken, and shattered glass littering the car's interior, Rick couldn't reach his daughter. He turned to Tim, who sat in the back seat with his little sister.

"Get Kacie on the floorboard," he instructed his son.

"I can't," Tim answered helplessly. "There's glass."

At that moment, some family friends pulled up behind the Woodys' car. They ushered Tim and Kacie into their own vehicle, where the kids waited until help arrived. Kacie had been sleeping before the accident, so Rick was hopeful she hadn't seen her mother.

But she had. Kacie later told her Aunt Teresa about it, how her mom made an "uh" noise and that when she saw all the blood, she knew that her mother was dead.

From that night on, Kacie hated horses.

Even so, she kept her mother's collection of horse figurines. They filled an entire shelf in Kacie's bedroom.

* * *

On June 27, 2001, Rick went on part-time patrol for the Greenbrier Police Department. He was elated.

Rick had been working for the department as a dispatcher, a job that evolved from serving as a computer and security contractor for the agency. Rick liked dispatching, but he had longed to be on the streets.

The only drawback was the hours. Rick typically worked the night shifts, which could pose problems for a single dad. Normally, Tim was around. And on weekends, Kacie always went to her grandma's house, where she ate Chinese food and pizza, and chased yellow butterflies across the lawn.

Still, there were some evenings when Kacie was home alone for several hours. Rick believed she was safe though. He had lived on Griggers Lane for 18 years with no problems. Most of the time, the Woodys left the door unlocked. And as a cop, Rick believed most crimes were random.

Never had this policeman imagined that a kidnapper would pull right up to his doorstep.

DEC. 4, MIDMORNING

After Jessica's interview with the investigators in the school counselor's office, she and Sam compared notes. Both girls were certain Scott was behind Kacie's disappearance. He was all Kacie talked about lately, and after the previous day's fight, Scott was fresh in their minds.

Sam and Jessica sat in silence for a moment, lost in their thoughts. Something niggled at the edges of Jessica's consciousness, something she should have told the lawmen. She flipped through her memories of Kacie, mulling the events of recent months. Then the nebulous cloud of recollections crystallized.

She turned to her friend in a moment of horrifying clarity.

"Omigod, Sam—what about Dave?"

At this same moment, FBI agent Jerry Spurgers was in Kacie's bedroom, wondering the same thing.

Caught in the Web:
Running out of time

FBI agent Jerry Spurgers knelt on the floor of 13-year-old Kacie Woody's bedroom, holding two crumpled pieces of paper that might reveal the identity of Kacie's kidnapper.

Kacie had been missing for 12 hours now, snatched from her living room as she typed at the computer, and the lawmen investigating her disappearance desperately needed leads.

Surrounded by the stuffed animals lining the teen-ager's top bunk, the hundreds of Beanie Babies perched on shelves and the angels scattered here and there, Spurgers carefully smoothed the creases from the scraps of paper he had just pulled from Kacie's trash can.

One read:

Kacie Rene Woody
Loves
David Leslie Fagen

The other declared:

Kacie Rene Woody
Loves
Scott G —

The letters had all been numbered so that Kacie could compute the percentage of "true love" in each relationship.

But for Spurgers, the wadded-up papers held other significance.

When Kacie was abducted on Dec. 3, 2002, she had been exchanging instant messages with her online boyfriend Scott, 14, who lived in Alpharetta, an upscale suburb of Atlanta. At the same time, she had been talking on the phone with another Internet friend named Dave.

At 9:41 p.m., Kacie had abruptly quit responding to Scott's messages, and Scott had quickly become concerned. He had called the Woodys' home in rural Faulkner County and sent frantic instant messages to the family's computer, hoping that Kacie's dad, Rick, or her brother Tim would see them.

Dave, on the other hand, hadn't been heard from. Authorities had no idea who he was, only that he was supposedly an 18-year-old from San Diego.

As Spurgers examined the doodlings of a love-struck girl, he realized that Dave and David Fagen were quite possibly the same person.

The Woodys' computer soon yielded confirmation. Stored on the machine were a Yahoo profile and photo of someone named jazzman_df. FBI agents also found earlier correspondence between jazzman_df and Kacie.

Jazzman_df lived in San Diego. He had registered with Yahoo as Dave Fagen.

GREENBRIER MIDDLE SCHOOL

Meanwhile, Samantha Mann, 13, and Jessica Tanner, 12, sat in school counselor Dianna Kellar's office waiting to talk to investigators a second time.

Sam and Jessica had initially blamed Scott for Kacie's abduction. Now, however, they realized they had forgotten to tell the detectives about Dave.

The girls told Mrs. Kellar they needed to talk to the police again.

As they waited, Sam and Jessica hastily composed a note for the cops:

Dave has been tellin Kacie that his aunt is in a coma and he has been driving 4 dayz. Dave is Kacie's X boyfriend

For the past month, Dave had kept Kacie updated on his aunt's condition. Her coma, he said, was caused by a car wreck. She wasn't expected to live much longer.

The aunt lived in Arkansas. Dave didn't say where.

Kacie had told her friends about Dave's aunt. She felt really sorry for him. And then, one night in mid- to late November, when Jessica was sleeping over at Kacie's house, Dave had called to say he was on his way to Arkansas because his aunt's condition was worsening. It was the same night the girls had heard strange noises and barricaded themselves in Kacie's bedroom.

During the hour-long conversation, Dave had told Kacie and Jessica that he planned to remain in Arkansas until his aunt passed away. Doctors were giving her a few months at most.

Several times, Jessica and Kacie tried to end the conversation. But Dave told them he had been driving for 11 hours and needed the company.

Sam also had heard that Dave was heading to Arkansas.

A few weeks before her abduction, Kacie had turned to Sam one day and asked, "Remember Dave?"

"Yeah," Sam had said.

"Well, he said he was going to be in Arkansas seeing his aunt who's in a coma," Kacie had told her.

Dave never said anything about wanting to see Kacie during his visit. Even if he had, Sam and Jessica were certain Kacie never would have agreed to meet him in person.

But what if he had decided to show up unannounced at Kacie's house?

RACE AGAINST TIME

At 1 p.m., a fourth law enforcement agency joined the Faulkner County sheriff's office, Arkansas State Police and FBI in the search for Kacie when investigators asked Conway police to canvass their town's motels for suspicious guests.

Conway, just south of Greenbrier, is the biggest city in Faulkner County.

Investigators were looking for someone registered as David Fagen. Or anyone with the first name David. Or the initials D.F. Or anyone from California.

Conway police Sgt. Jim Barrett divided the town into two sections. He and one detective took the east side, and two other investigators headed to the northern part of the city.

About 30 minutes later, the detectives on the north side called to say there was a David Fuller from California registered at the Motel 6.

Fuller had arrived Dec. 2 and was scheduled to stay for seven days. He had requested that the maids skip his room.

Barrett headed to the motel.

The manager there vividly remembered Fuller, who had become angry when he couldn't connect to the Internet from his room and huffed off to the county library with his laptop.

The detective walked over to Room 115, where a

1993 Buick Regal with California plates was parked out front. When no one answered Barrett's repeated knocks, the manager opened the door with a passkey.

A cursory search revealed a suitcase, still neatly packed, on the luggage rack. A laptop was set up on the table, and two 3-1/2-inch floppy disks lay on the floor. The bed hadn't been slept in.

Barrett put a surveillance team in the room next door in case Fuller returned.

It was now 1:30 p.m.

Barrett asked another detective to check with car rental businesses. Had Fuller, perhaps, rented a car? Just 10 minutes later, the detective called back: On Dec. 2, Fuller had rented a silver Dodge Caravan for seven days from the Conway Enterprise Rent-A-Car.

At the rental agency, Barrett interviewed an employee named Steve Tate.

Fuller, Tate said, had behaved strangely while filling out his paperwork. The Californian had been fidgety, repeatedly interrupting the process to go outside and smoke.

So Tate had made a note of Fuller's California license plate number and motel room number. Also listed in the paperwork was Fuller's cell phone number.

At 2:45 p.m., state police investigator Karl Byrd and a few other detectives were eating a quick lunch at the Conway International House of Pancakes when Barrett called with David Fuller's phone number.

Byrd then phoned his supervisor, Sgt. Paul Curtis, who had subpoenaed the Woodys' phone records.

"Give me the number she's been calling," Byrd said.

Curtis read it aloud.

The number had been dialed repeatedly from the Woody home. And it matched the one Fuller had given the car rental agent.

Byrd called Barrett: "That's our boy."

A description of Fuller's rented minivan immediately went out to law enforcement agencies and the media.

Wherever it was, Kacie might be there, too.

DAVE VS. DAVID FULLER

As investigators delved into Fuller's background, they learned "Dave" wasn't the long-haired, handsome youth pictured on his Yahoo profile. David Leslie Fuller was

47, balding and scrawny. And his life was falling apart.

Fuller was born Jan. 18, 1955, into a devout Mormon family. His parents, Ned and June, were proud of the secure and stable life they had created for their four children. They brought up their brood in an upper-middle-class Salt Lake City neighborhood, in a home they had built in 1956.

The three oldest children, two boys and a girl, thrived—enthusiastically involved in school, church and family life. But young Davie was different—aloof, hanging back.

Davie was a lackadaisical student, and by the time he entered his teens, his friends were the rebellious, trouble-making, school-skipping kids. After high school graduation, he played bass guitar in various rock bands.

Davie's lack of interest in the church had long distressed the Fuller family. By the time he was a young adult, Dave had shunned Mormonism altogether.

At 19, he married a girl who was a year or two younger, and they made their home in Moab, southeast of Salt Lake City. The marriage quickly dissolved.

In the early 1980s, Dave was still living in Moab and playing bass guitar at a local bar. His band covered popular sing-along tunes, relying on crowd-pleasers such as Jimmy Buffett's "Margaritaville."

One night, a bandmate's girlfriend showed up at the bar with her sister, Sally.

Sally and the bass player really hit it off.

Dave and Sally's courtship ran smoothly. Dave didn't say much about himself, but he was a good listener.

Like Dave, Sally also had married and divorced young. Now she was in her mid-20s and wanted to settle down and have kids.

The couple wed on May 21, 1983, and moved to Salt Lake City. Sally worked as a commercial artist for an advertising agency. Dave drove a tow truck and then worked for a car dealership.

In 1989, Dave joined the Navy Seabees, and the couple moved to Gulfport, Miss. Over the next several years, they moved to Maryland and then San Diego. Son Dillon was born in Mississippi and daughter Stacie in Maryland.

Motherhood suited Sally, but she was increasingly

unhappy with her marriage. By their 18th anniversary in May 2001, Sally wanted out.

In the early days, Dave and Sally had done a lot of social drinking. Alcohol mellowed Dave out, made him more talkative and pleasant. But once Dave eased up on the drinking, Sally learned it was best to tiptoe around her husband. It was the only way to deal with his unpredictable temper.

Sally sensed a hatred—toward an unknown someone—simmering beneath Dave's moodiness. He would brood for days and then explode into an inexplicable rage. Sally was afraid to probe too deeply. Dave's past was off-limits.

"I don't want to go there," he would tell her. "Everything was fine. I had a good childhood."

Nor would he discuss the problems in the couple's relationship. Dave liked to deal in facts—bills or car repairs, day-to-day issues he could resolve and file neatly away.

There were troubling incidents, too, like the time Dave was arrested for exposing himself to two young girls. Sally was skeptical of Dave's explanation: that he had simply stopped to ask the girls a question, but they had run off screaming.

Dave never tried to defend himself. He skipped his court appearance and quietly paid a fine for indecent exposure, a misdemeanor.

* * *

By the summer of 2002, Dave and Sally's marriage was in its final months.

For the previous five years, the family had lived at 7216 Pearson St. in La Mesa, Calif., just outside of San Diego. By then, Dave had left the Navy and was working for a Saturn dealership.

Dave was more secretive than ever, spending long hours on the computer and walking alone through the neighborhood at night as he chatted on his cell phone.

Sally had stopped asking questions.

The turbulence in the Fullers' disintegrating marriage was affecting the couple's children, Dillon, now 11, and Stacie, 7. Concerned, Sally took Dillon for counseling.

In June 2002, Dave took the kids to visit his parents. Before he left, the couple argued, and Dave angrily threw out the word "divorce."

Great, Sally thought. *He's ready.*

While Dave and the kids were gone, she attended a nuts-and-bolts divorce workshop, and by the time they returned, Sally had done everything but file the papers. She thought Dave would be pleased. Instead, he was furious.

This time, however, his tantrums had no effect. Dave's formerly timid wife was resolute: The marriage was over.

* * *

During the next four months, Dave's once-orderly life crumbled.

In August, California's Child Protective Services division investigated a report that Dave was taking showers with 7-year-old Stacie.

The agency got involved after Sally started asking questions. Dave was livid. "I am not molesting my daughter!" he bellowed in front of the children. Investigators ultimately concluded nothing had happened. But Sally remained uneasy.

By September, Dave had moved into an apartment. One night, he showed up at his old home and demanded that Sally let him in. When she refused, he pushed her aside and barged into the kitchen.

After a screaming match, Sally locked herself in the bedroom with the kids. Dave used a screwdriver to open the door. Sally called 911, and the kids watched out the front window as police handcuffed their father and led him away. Authorities charged Dave with spousal abuse.

That same month, Dave lost his job at the Saturn dealership. The firing happened in front of his son, who had gone with Dave on his day off to pick up his paycheck. His bosses cited a lack of productivity but suspected Dave was visiting child pornography sites on company computers.

The couple's house sold Sept. 26. By this time, Sally had found a new home in Hemet, a town in Southern California's San Jacinto Valley. The move was a leap of faith, but Sally felt strong. She home-schooled the kids, practiced yoga and wrote in her journal of her new hopes.

She hoped to finalize the divorce by the end of 2002.

* * *

On Dec. 3, the day of Kacie's abduction, Dave called

his mother. He seemed fine. Sally was in Utah visiting her family, and Dave asked if she had brought the kids over to see their grandparents.

"No," June Fuller told him.

"That figures," Dave replied, his irritation obvious. He didn't mention that he was calling from Arkansas.

Dave became uncharacteristically emotional. "I love you, Mom," he said, a phrase he never uttered first.

And then he hung up.

DEC. 4, MIDAFTERNOON

Authorities now had a suspect in Kacie's kidnapping. But no one knew where he was or if he still had the girl.

After linking Fuller's phone number to Kacie's house, Barrett called the detectives who were staking out Fuller's motel room: "If Fuller shows up, arrest him."

Meanwhile, investigators subpoenaed the suspect's car rental paperwork, complete with Fuller's credit card number, the same one he had used to pay for his motel room.

His recent credit history revealed that earlier that day, Fuller's card had been charged by Guardsmart Storage in Conway. Fuller had traveled to Conway a month earlier to rent the unit.

Maybe, Barrett thought, Fuller was holding Kacie captive there.

He headed to Guardsmart.

En route, Barrett heard from state police that a caller who had heard news reports about the suspect's rented minivan claimed to be following it down University Avenue in Little Rock. Barrett was elated.

We've scared the crap out of this guy, and he's leaving, Barrett thought, assuming that Fuller was reacting to the publicity surrounding Kacie's kidnapping.

He's split. He left her tied up, and there'll be a happy ending.

Barrett and two FBI agents arrived at Guardsmart Storage a little after 5 p.m. The managers, a married couple, led the lawmen to unit No. 313.

The door wasn't padlocked. The latch was unfastened. Barrett was sure the suspect had fled in haste.

Unholstering his gun, the detective lifted the door and peered inside.

He saw a silver minivan. Its engine was running.

Barrett stepped inside, gun still drawn. Just as his foot hit the concrete floor, a shot rang out. Barrett and the FBI agents ran for cover. The detective made a breathless call for help:

Dispatcher: 911

Barrett: Sgt. Barrett. Shots fired, shots fired, Guardsmart Storage, Prince Street.

Dispatcher: Where at?

Barrett: Guardsmart Storage, shots fired. Got me and two FBI agents out here. Send backup now.

Dispatcher: At Smart Storage?

Silence.

Caught in the Web:
But not forgotten

DECEMBER 17, 2003

The kidnapper still clutched his 9 mm Luger in a lifeless hand.

A few feet from his body, in the rear of his rented silver minivan, his victim lay on her back, her wrists and ankles chained tightly to the four corners of the van's floor.

He had been hiding in storage unit No. 313 since the night before.

Throughout the day, he had cranked the engine and run the heater to warm himself.

As he had listened to the radio news reports about 13-year-old Kacie Woody's abduction of the night before, he learned that police knew his name and were looking for the minivan.

The engine was still running, the radio playing, when Conway police Sgt. Jim Barrett had approached the unit and raised the door.

That's when David Fuller shot himself in the head.

When Barrett and other investigators entered the unit more than three hours later, they found Fuller at the back of the unit, a few feet from the rear of the minivan, dozens of cigarette butts, a lighter and a bottle of Mountain Valley Spring water littering the concrete floor near his feet.

Fuller, 47, had backed the silver Dodge Caravan into the unit at Guardsmart Storage after snatching Kacie from her home in rural Holland. At some point, Fuller had removed the vehicle's two back seats to make room for his victim.

The seats now rested on the floor. One was folded. The other, on which Fuller had been sitting when he pulled the trigger, remained upright.

Fuller had been looking directly into the back of the minivan, where Kacie lay. He had raped her. And he had shot her in the head.

The final hours of the drama had begun a little after 5 p.m., Dec. 4, 2002, 19 hours after the abduction, when

Barrett had heard the gunshot and summoned the SWAT team.

The lawmen had spent more than three hours in the sleet and snow waiting, unsure whether Kacie and her kidnapper were dead or alive.

Just before 8:30 p.m., the SWAT team entered the unit with Barrett close behind.

The detective identified Fuller, using the dead man's California driver's license. Then he looked in the mini-van, and the image of Kacie there would haunt him for months each night when he put his own daughter to bed.

As investigators searched the unit, they found a half-empty bottle of chloroform and a purple rag next to Kacie's head.

Later, after police had studied the medical examiner's report, they would conclude that Kacie likely had been unconscious from the time she was kidnapped until she was killed, a small comfort amid the ruin.

According to a security box at the storage facility, Fuller had punched in his access code at 10:15 p.m., Dec. 3, which meant he had driven straight there from the Woodys' home in rural Faulkner County after abducting Kacie from her living room.

No one who worked on the case would ever agree on the time of Kacie's death. With the chloroform, she could have remained alive but unconscious for hours. Detectives don't know if she was dead or alive when Fuller left the unit on foot at 7:24 the following morning to buy water and cigarettes at a nearby convenience store.

The security box showed Fuller was gone 21 minutes.

He spent the rest of the day chain-smoking and, police speculated, waiting to flee the unit on foot after dark.

As investigators examined the crime scene, several lawmen gathered for a somber discussion: Who was going to notify Greenbrier police officer Rick Woody of his daughter's death?

Faulkner County sheriff's investigator Jim Wooley and state police investigator Karl Byrd volunteered. They had worked this case from the outset, and they would see it through.

DEC. 4, LATE EVENING

Jessica Tanner, 12, and several of Kacie's other clos-est friends were keeping vigil at 13-year-old Samantha Mann's house. By now, the local TV news broadcasts were reporting that police had cornered a man named David Fuller. Reporters described his rented minivan, and Fuller's face appeared on the screen.

Sam and Jessica looked at each other and spoke in unison:

"It's Dave."

Dave, whom Kacie had befriended on the Internet, had claimed to be 18. The picture on his Yahoo profile was of a good-looking young man with long, wavy hair.

Sam stared, disbelieving, at this new version of Dave. He was balding and had a mustache. "He's ugly," Sam said. "And old."

And then there was an update: Authorities had stormed the storage unit. A news conference was sched-uled for 10 p.m. The briefing opened with the first re-port of Kacie's death. Sam and her friends huddled on the staircase and wept.

At 12-year-old Haley Allen's house, the phone rang. The caller was her father, checking on her. Haley and Kacie had been friends since kindergarten.

"Are you doing OK?" he asked.

"Hopefully, they'll find her," Haley replied.

"You don't know?"

There was an uncomfortable silence. Then Haley's dad said, "Let me talk to your mom."

Before she took the receiver, Leah Compton sent Haley to bed.

Haley obeyed reluctantly. For the next hour, she lay there, staring at the ceiling, wondering.

Finally, Leah and Haley's stepdad entered her bed-room.

Haley asked, "Is she going to be at school tomor-row?"

"No," Leah said softly. "She's gone."

Haley cried and cried. And then, as many other kids in Greenbrier did that night, she crawled into bed with her parents.

Over on Griggers Lane, a handful of people had gath-ered at the home of Teresa Paul, Kacie's aunt.

Teresa, the older sister of Kacie's late mother, had moved next door to the Woodys in 1990, a few years after her husband, a native Alaskan, had drowned in the Yukon.

Teresa didn't say so, but she knew Kacie was never coming back. When she had returned from Rick's house at 6 a.m., she had seen an owl perched on the deck. In her husband's clan, the owl was the symbol of death.

She was prepared when a family friend arrived at her front door.

Teresa spoke first. "She's gone, isn't she?"

Like Rick, Teresa had lost her spouse. And she, too, had lost a daughter. Her oldest girl, Jonna, died in a car accident in 1994. She was only 17. Heartbreak was an old, familiar acquaintance.

Teresa turned to her elderly parents, Chuck and Illa Smith.

"Mother," Teresa said gently, "it's over."

"Oh, they got Kacie?" Illa asked, hope lighting her face.

"He killed her," Teresa said flatly.

There was a stunned pause. And then the Smiths sobbed. First their granddaughter Jonna. Then their daughter Kristie.

Now Kacie.

Chuck turned to Teresa: "Why can't we keep our girls?" he asked. "We keep losing our girls."

Down the road from Teresa's house, dozens of people filled Rick Woody's home. Rick slumped in his recliner, watching the TV for updates on the standoff between the SWAT team and the man who had kidnapped his daughter. Rick also listened to the chatter on his police radio.

But as a TV news crew announced that there would be a news conference at 10 p.m., Rick's radio went silent.

And he knew.

ALPHARETTA, GA.

In this affluent suburb of Atlanta, 14-year-old Scott was telling his parents that something horrible had happened to a girl he had met on the Internet. It was some time after 9 p.m., EST, and Scott, known online as Tazz2999, had just learned from Internet news reports that Kacie was dead.

His parents, Steve and Pamela, were baffled. Who, they asked, is Kacie? And all of this is going on where? In Arkansas?

So Scott explained everything, starting with how he had met Kacie in a chat room in May 2002 and how she had disappeared the night before while chatting with him on the computer.

"This is not small stuff," Pamela told her son. "This is either a really sick joke, or it's something so terribly sad."

She looked at Scott's pictures of Kacie. There was a school portrait, a formal photo of Kacie in all her finery as Fall Festival Queen and a few candid shots from Kacie's webcam.

It would be several days before Pamela grasped the magnitude of what her son had gotten himself into—a murder case involving a girl from Arkansas, a killer from California and, eventually, a coast-to-coast FBI investigation.

Pamela hadn't even known that Tazz2999 had a girlfriend.

DEC. 5, 2002

School counselor Dianna Kellar's office at Greenbrier Middle School was filled with crying students.

Flowers, stuffed animals and other teen paraphernalia soon covered locker No. 427, where Kacie had once gossiped with friends as she stashed her books.

Throughout the afternoon, teachers comforted sobbing girls and tried to soothe fears. By the end of the day, an oppressive grief had sucked the laughter and chatter from the halls.

THE GIRLS SAY GOODBYE

On Dec. 8, the night before Kacie's funeral, her friends arrived at the visitation with yellow roses and a group picture of themselves making goofy faces.

Sam tucked the photo under Kacie's pillow.

Then the girls took their roses, which had handwritten notes attached to each stem, and placed them one by one in the coffin. Except for Haley. She couldn't look at her friend. She gave her rose to Rick.

Kacie was wearing a yellow dress her grandma had

made. It was a little tight on her, but it had been her favorite. Her Aunt Teresa had made sure two matching jackets went into the casket. She knew Kacie would want to show them to her mama in heaven.

During visitation, Rick said to Sam and Jessica: "Don't quit coming around. You're my girls too now."

OVER THE NEXT FEW WEEKS

In La Mesa, Calif., FBI agents searched Fuller's orderly apartment. They found a framed montage of photos of Kacie near his computer.

Dave had two computers: one in his apartment and the laptop he had taken to Arkansas. Authorities examined both, looking for other victims.

Soon, the FBI arrived at Sam's house with printouts: a picture of Sam, pointing to a photo of singer Justin Timberlake; a webcam picture of another of Kacie's friends; and Dave's Yahoo buddy list, which included the names of lots of Greenbrier kids.

Sam was alarmed. So was Jessica, who remembered clearly the night she and Kacie had sent Dave a picture of themselves posing with Kacie's dog, George.

Dave had wanted to see what Jessica looked like.

* * *

The FBI was quickly finding out that Dave Fagen, as Fuller was known online, had been a regular presence in teen chat rooms for at least two years. He also had been targeting three other girls about the same age as Kacie.

The first lived in Michigan. She met Fuller in the winter of 2000 in Yahoo's teen chat room. They had talked for several hours and the girl put Fuller, known then by the screen name daves_in, on her buddy list. He claimed to be a 17-year-old living in San Diego. The girl chatted with him every day. She told the FBI that Fuller was always a gentleman, sticking to innocent topics like school, friends and family.

Fuller had asked for her phone number, saying, "I want to hear your voice," but the girl said no. She also refused his offers to fly her to California. The girl corresponded with Fuller for nearly two years, primarily on a public-library computer. Fuller never learned her real name.

Another of Dave's interests lived in Dallas. This girl met Fuller online in March 2001.

She had never given Fuller her address, she told detectives, but in March 2002, flowers from a Dave Fagen had arrived at her home. The girl's father was furious. And that was the end of her correspondence with Dave.

In Pennsylvania, FBI agents discovered a third girl who knew Dave, but after making certain that she was safe, agents didn't press for details.

Investigators ran Fuller's DNA through a national databank, but that produced no matches linking him to other crimes. Authorities were surprised. Fuller's planning had been so meticulous, they thought he must have struck before.

A KILLER'S PLOT REVEALED

Fuller, police learned, made his first trip to Arkansas on Oct. 11, 2002, nearly two months before he executed his plan. He flew into Little Rock National Airport, Adams Field, where he rented a car, drove to Conway and checked into a Motel 6. No one is sure what Fuller did during this first trip to Arkansas, although police believe he spied on Kacie and the Woody home.

The weekend he was in town, Kacie was crowned seventh-grade queen at the annual Fall Festival's Night of Coronation. On Oct. 12, a Saturday night, Kacie wore her first grown-up dress, a long, shimmering black confection, and a self-conscious smile.

She had 52 days to live.

On Oct. 15, 2002, Fuller sent this e-mail to Alltel Communications: *I am planning an extended trip to Arkansas and the ISP I am currently using doesn't have a local dial-up number there. Are you an actual ISP and if so, how do I get software and set up an account to use your service?*

Two days later, Kacie turned 13.

On Nov. 2, when he had his kids for visitation, Fuller bought a gun. He told them he needed it for target practice.

Kacie also had been shopping. She excitedly described her purchases in an e-mail to a school friend: *I got a new sweat shirt today...its really cute...and it is YELLOW! Yellow is the best color in da world!*

On Nov. 4, Fuller flew back to Little Rock, once again renting a car, driving to Conway and renting a room at the Motel 6. Two days later, he showed up at the Guardsmart Storage facility in Conway looking for the largest unit available. Fuller told one of the on-site managers that he traveled the country buying cars and needed a place to temporarily store vehicles.

On Nov. 8, he extended his stay at the motel. Authorities later speculated that Fuller had planned to abduct Kacie during this trip, but something thwarted him.

When he returned to California, Fuller went shopping again. He bought chain, duct tape and zip ties from his local Home Depot. He also obtained a bottle of chloroform from a chemical supply company. Soon he would pack his supplies in his Buick Regal for a final trip to Arkansas.

* * *

In Kacie, Fuller had found the perfect victim.

She was gullible, freely giving him her real name, address, phone number and pictures of herself. Also stored on Fuller's computer was a poem Kacie had sent him:

It was about nine p.m.
When everything got so dim,
In the road was a horse,
How could things get any worse?
We hit it hard and fast,
And in it came through the shattered glass,
There was blood everywhere,
The moon shone a big glare,
I wondered if she was alright,
This was one horrid night,
We all were rushed in the room,
Where my daddy lay full of gloom,
I was only seven,
I heard the prayer that said she was in heaven,
Oh that was such a horrid night,
And as I stared at the sky with fright,
I wondered why she had to go away,
Even though I knew now she'd be happy everyday,
I hated horses from that day on,
Because now my mommy was gone.

Such outpourings from Kacie were Fuller's inspiration. His fictitious aunt, who he said had been in a car wreck and was dying—like Kacie's mother—was key to gaining Kacie's trust and sympathy.

Byrd, the state police investigator, would later surmise:

"On the night Kacie died, she was telling the Georgia kid the story [Dave] told her—how he was going to see his dying aunt and how [the aunt] was going to go meet Kacie's mother. As it played out, he was playing a mind game with her. He was talking about her.

"Kacie was the one who was going to meet her mother."

A YEAR LATER

When Fuller's parents learned of their son's crime and death from reporters, they were skeptical.

"My son Dave would not be involved in anything like that," Ned Fuller declared indignantly. "Don't bother me anymore."

But then the police came, and they had to believe. In the months that followed, Ned wanted to call Rick Woody, but the officers discouraged him.

"I just wanted to tell him how sorry I was and that I still—I can't understand—that Dave must have been out of his normal mind-set when this happened because he was never violent," he says now.

"I'm just sorry his was the daughter he got involved with. I'd have probably come charging out here with a shotgun if it had been me."

* * *

The Santa Ana winds will sweep across Southern California in the coming days, carrying the stinging smoke of wildfires. It is late October, a week before Halloween, and in the dusty, palm-dotted San Jacinto Valley, Sally Fuller has found serenity.

Sally is tall, lean and lightly tanned, her patrician features emphasized by the short, stylish cut of her salt-and-pepper hair. She lives in San Jacinto, just north of Hemet.

She now recognizes the red flags she missed: the late nights Dave wandered the neighborhood to talk on his cell phone; the tantrum when Sally proposed moving the computer out of his bedroom; his insistence that the couple have separate Internet passwords and e-mail accounts; the framed photos of a smiling young girl in Dave's new apartment.

At the time of Kacie's murder, Sally and Dave's divorce was not yet final.

Sally heard what her husband had done from the reporters who called as the SWAT team surrounded the storage unit. "I was not as surprised as I could have been because of how I saw him deteriorate," she says. "I guess I had this feeling—he is going to crash. He is just going to crash.

"My feeling is that this was the only time," she says, referring to Kacie's murder. "Of course, he was gone for months at a time, so I really don't know."

Sally has been cautious in what she has told her children. Dillon, now 12, knows that his father killed a girl and then himself. Stacie, 8, knows only about the suicide.

Dave's ashes are still in Sally's closet. Someday, when the kids are ready, she will take Dillon and Stacie to Mount Olympus to scatter their father's remains.

* * *

Rick Woody, now 46, sits in his dimly lit, paneled living room, staring at the row of photos that line his mantel.

There is his wife, Kristie, her striking features framed by a mass of dark, tumbling curls. And there is Kacie, who possessed the same soulful eyes and enigmatic, close-lipped smile.

"I've gone through all kinds of emotions," Rick says, his face unreadable. "I've gone through the bitter stage, the questioning-God stage, where I've asked, 'How can you take my wife and then turn around and take my little girl?'"

He recognizes the irony in this tragedy—that the man who became a cop to help others wasn't here when his own daughter needed him most.

Last spring, Rick agreed to allow federal and state authorities to share Kacie's story in a nationwide effort called "Innocent Images" to train law enforcement officers and educate parents—even though he isn't ready to hear the story in its entirety.

"I can't let this be meaningless," he says. "I've got to make it do somebody some good."

In June, the FBI presented Rick with one of 100 commemorative patches bearing Kacie's name. The blue-and-gold patch depicts a teddy bear sitting next to a computer. "Kacie Woody, 1989-2002" is printed on the computer screen. FBI agents and local law enforcement officers who are part of the Innocent Images task force will wear the patches.

Guilt and what-ifs haunt Rick. What if he had called in

sick that night, like he had been tempted to do? What if he had kept a closer eye on Kacie's computer activities?

"It can't lead you anywhere but in a circle," he says. "You want to know everything that's going on in your kid's life and you think you've got a good idea...." His voice trails off. "You want to protect them...." Again, a pause before Rick concludes: "She didn't have any fears."

OCT. 28, 2003

White tombstones glitter against the late-afternoon shadows on this gray, overcast day. Crickets chirp, and a breeze rustles trees on the cusp of autumnal glory.

Rick pulls up on his motorcycle, parking directly in front of Kacie's grave. He takes off his helmet, walks to the grave and kneels. Eleven days have passed since what would have been Kacie's 14th birthday. Tenderly, Rick scoops up the cards and notes that Sam, Jessica and other friends have left.

In years past, Rick came here each Sept. 4, his wedding anniversary, to leave red roses for Kristie—one for each year they would have been married. This year, he left 22.

But now there is a second grave in need of flowers, yellow ones, Kacie's favorite. Rick comes here three times a week, usually on his motorcycle. Kacie loved to ride with Rick. So it seems fitting to thunder into this peaceful spot on his bike.

Kacie was excited when Rick bought a motorcycle. During their first excursion, she leaned this way and that, glorying in this new sense of freedom. Rick finally pulled over and lectured her about holding on to him. He needed to know she was still back there. But Kacie wasn't afraid of falling off. She was with her daddy.

Rick leans against his Kawasaki Vulcan and gazes at Kacie's gravestone. He is clad entirely in leather. On his jacket, just over his heart, is the FBI patch that bears Kacie's name.

Briefly, a burst of sunlight pierces the clouds, warming the shoulders, but not the stone, on which a white ceramic angel slumbers. For much of her short life, Kacie wanted to be an angel, just like her mother. In second grade, for a school assignment, she listed two goals: to become a gold-medal gymnast, and then, someday, to go to heaven to see her mama.

Kacie now lies next to her mother. The epitaph on her gravestone is a single line, an allusion to the heart-rending fulfillment of a second-grader's goal: *I Am an Angel.*

The declaration comes from a poem Kacie wrote in sixth grade:

I'm an Angel

I'm an angel,
Sent from above,
To spread the world,
With lots of Love…

"It was like someone put that in her head," Rick says, still leaning against his bike, eyes focused on the past. "So I thought it just belonged there."

Rick glances once more at his daughter's grave.

And then he roars off, the seat behind him empty without the joyful girl who once rode there, the one who dreamed of angels.

A conversation with
Cathy Frye

KELLY McBRIDE: You originally covered this as a news story. What was your role in that?

CATHY FRYE: They wanted me to go out to the family's house to see if they wanted to talk. I was the lead writer for that story, but my role was mainly to go out and get the human side. I was hugely pregnant at the time.

Why did you stick with it?

I had worked on a story, or actually a series, on child porn and online predators. You know, you have these kids who have taken off to meet someone they've met online. It happens frequently and there's almost a jaded attitude toward it now. People forget that not only are these predators extremely savvy, but that children, and particularly teenagers, are first starting to think of themselves as individuals. They don't necessarily do what you think they're doing when they're online, and I wanted people to understand that. Kacie Woody's father was so incredibly stunned to find out that all of this had been going on. It's just one of those stories that lingered.

The news story about Kacie ran in December, and I went on maternity leave in February. Before I went on maternity leave and again when I came back in April, I was trying to convince the family to let me come out to talk to them. At that time I did not envision a series. I was just planning to do more of an in-depth story. There were a lot of things that we never had reported. And we kept hearing things over the next few months—that there had been this dialogue on the screen with this kid in Georgia. It wasn't until I started researching it and I actually had the father's agreement to participate in the story that I found out that, just that very day, Kacie had been to the counselor's office.

So there was a lot more.

Oh, there was a whole lot more, which was my argument, you know. You have editors who say, "Well, everyone knows she dies." I said, "Yeah, but, my God, we didn't know this, we didn't know this, and we didn't know that there were all these opportunities where either someone could have intervened or someone did try to intervene." I wanted to really drive that point home. The more I kept hearing, the more details that trickled out here and there, the more I thought you couldn't read or hear this stuff and not wonder what your own child might be doing online.

So you went on maternity leave and you came back, and you still had the drive and desire to do the story.

Yeah. At one point, I even sent a letter to Rick Woody. And I also sent several other stories I had done, all of which dealt with parents who had lost children and that sort of thing. I finally got hold of him at the end of July. At that point he seemed ready to talk. You know, I was close to thinking I should just give it up.

You have a four-paragraph introduction that reads like the intro to a novel. When did you type those four paragraphs for the first time?

Initially, what you read at the end, the part about the angels, is what I had as my intro. And then it was more of your standard opening with Rick Woody in the present and so on. I didn't start writing until November. I mainly did all the reporting up until then. The first time I wrote this beginning, we had just had an editors' meeting and I came out of there not really knowing what they wanted. Jay Grelen—he is my immediate editor, and he's wonderful—said, "Ignore all the other editors. Do what you were going to do."

And so you had taken several stabs at drafting this?

Once Jay said, "I'll back you on it," it was really easy. You know, I had struggled and struggled with that first draft, and once I had the all-clear from him to do it the way that he and I intuitively thought it should be done, it was just so much easier.

When you wrote these four paragraphs, did you intend them to be the lead-in to the whole series?

Once I started the second draft, yes. At that point, the photographer and I had been out there. We went out one night to shoot. Rick Woody was getting ready for work but he would periodically come outside and chitchat, go back in, work on dinner, and then come out again. We were asking him very specific questions about the house and how it looked that night, because at one point he had joked about how Kacie always left the lights on. And just standing out there that night, just looking at that house, in that window—I can't even really describe it—it was just the eeriest thing to think of this child sitting in there, the computer is still right there at the same place it was and you can see it in that window, and we could see Rick in there moving around. It just seemed fitting to open with that. You know, she's there. She's right there. She's in the window. He's out there. He can see her.

Let me read you a bit of your story. "His idea of good law enforcement was to prevent bad things, not to step in after the crime. That's why he watched out for the young women making nightly bank deposits after Greenbrier's stores and restaurants closed."

You start with a bad guy standing in the dark watching a girl who doesn't know she's being watched, and pretty soon you've got a good guy watching women in the dark who also don't know how vulnerable they are. Is that intentional?

I was trying to drive home the point that this is a child whose father is a police officer. He's very safety conscious. As a result, so is she. And here she is at home alone. There's this guy watching her, making his approach. And meanwhile, here's her father, who is a cop, on patrol and out there looking after someone else's daughters even as his own is most vulnerable. That really ate at him. You could see just how tormented he was by the fact that he was not there when she needed him. I guess I was trying to put it all into context for people. Not only was this man a cop, but this is why he got into this. And yet here, right now, this is about to happen.

Here's another piece a little bit later. "But on this bone-chilling evening of Dec. 3, 2002, a Tuesday, Tim had left for the University of Central Arkansas library at 6 p.m. Eric was at his electrician's class. And Aunt Teresa was in Conway, cheering at her daughter's basketball game.

"Kacie was home alone."

Okay, I'm totally creeped out, and I've only read 12 inches of the story. Did you realize when you wrote this that it would have that effect?

I hoped it would, but you know how it is when you're so close to something, and you've heard all the details, and you've pored over all these police reports, and you start to wonder if you're being as effective as you can be. I passed around copies—I'm a big believer in subjecting my friends to reading things before they get to the editor —so that I can get a feel for how they're reading it and how they're taking it in. And I also want to know where it gets slow or boring or starts to drag and that sort of thing. I was fairly optimistic because, when I did have people read some of the early drafts, I felt like I was accomplishing what I was trying to do—I wanted people on edge from the very beginning.

The other thing you do successfully is embody the voice of a 13-year-old girl in the story, and you even got "school sucks" in the paper. Was that difficult?

Actually, no, not with my editor. We had one meeting and some of the editors said, "Do we have too much of this? Do we have too much of what it's like to be a 13-year-old girl?" I really wanted people to remember what it's like to be that age and to understand what it's like to be that age, because you have to get where she's coming from to understand why she's doing these things and how this happens.

If you hadn't succeeded in doing that, as a reader I would have thought, "Oh, well, what a silly girl."

Right. And that's exactly what I worried about. A lot of parents were kind of reluctant initially to let me come talk to the girls. I had to assure them that I was not out to belittle or to lay blame. I don't think that parents understand the appeal of chat rooms and they don't understand why this is so fascinating and they don't understand what it is teens are getting from chatting. You really do have to put people back in junior high. The counselor's office was another thing we debated. Is there too much about this whole theme with the girls and how she mediates? Again, that's such a part of that age group, all these little fights. Back in our day we wrote notes. Now you hop online and instant message.

You gained the trust of a lot of people who were probably in the throes of some serious guilt. Why do you think Kacie's dad, Rick, eventually let you in?

When the FBI started talking about how they could use this as an educational tool, I think that was also about the time the attorney general's office here started making its push. I told Rick I wanted to intrude on his life and make him relive all of these painful memories because I thought it would serve a purpose. And he was very agreeable once he could see how it would do that. I don't know if he realized at the time how much I was going to be around, but he never said no.

He never got sick of you?

No, he didn't seem to, and I pestered him quite a bit and we went out there many times. Then I tagged along when he was on patrol. We went out to the cemetery one time as well.

The excerpts of online conversations are amazing. How did you get them?

The state police officer, Karl Byrd, had printed it out, and when I went to interview him, he had it there. The original version has different colors. Modelbehavior and Tazz are two different colors. When I brought it back to the newsroom, everyone just pounced on it and made copies. Everyone wanted to read it. I had sat in Byrd's office and read it already, and as soon as I did, I thought, "My God, how can we get all of this in? There's no way I could write anything that's stronger than this."

What does it convey?

You get a sense, first of all, of what Kacie was like. You get a feel not just for how she was, but also of how these exchanges occur. I don't think parents really understand—there's the use of acronyms and all of that. You walk by a kid's computer screen and you just see all this stuff.

It's like a foreign language.

Yeah, and a lot of parents are intimidated by that. I wanted people to hear her voice, and that was one way of accomplishing that. There were so many parts of it that were just so chilling. You know when Kacie is talking about her visit to the counselor's office and she said that Tazz might be an 80-year-old rapist and that was probably his grandson's picture. And there's the hee-hees and the LOLs [laugh out loud].

And so here she is, right before she's going to be abducted by someone she's met online and she's joking about this visit to the counselor's office, and there's no way I could have rewritten or paraphrased. You just have to let the kids tell it. To me, that was the most effective way to do it.

Now that whole conversation with Scott makes me uncomfortable. He's not the bad guy. But he comes off seeming manipulative and imposing and almost inappropriate in that relationship. Why did you include that in the story?

I wanted parents to see how their kids talk online. Secondly, her friend Sam had misgivings about Scott. Initially Scott is the one everyone is suspicious of, with good reason. You read this and you're thinking it's just a tad on the excessive side. And it's funny, too. When you read the dialogue in its entirety, every time he starts getting too mushy, I guess you could say she switches topics altogether.

Really?

Yeah. She heads him off at the pass—pardon the pun—
every time. We did have a little bit more in there. It was
another chunk of dialogue, kind of the same stuff, and at
that point, one of the male editors was like, "Okay, please,
enough already. You've already subjected us to Romeo.
Got the point. No more."

**You dribble out the fact that several of Kacie's friends
had actually talked to Dave on the phone. It would
have been tempting to just hit the reader over the
head with that right off the bat. How did you resist?**

Well, it just seemed like it would have more oomph.
When you think about how this evolved, there's so much
randomness to it. You've got a kid who frequents chat
rooms. She happens to be in there at the right time of day
and he is, too, and they meet and strike up a conversation
and it continues. I don't think parents understand that
these aren't people who just get online. They know how
to win your child's trust. And if I'd hit them over the head
with, "Here's this guy mingling with all your teenagers,"
they're not really going to understand how he got there.
He got there because he befriended one girl in one small
community, and he used her dead mother and her vulnerability and her desire to be liked by boys to manipulate
her. And then it starts branching out. He starts talking to
her friends. He starts getting pictures of them. And then
when you find out at the end that he had these online relationships with other girls, then you get a sense of just how
this expands and expands, and how frightening it is. He
has a victim pool. And it's all due to one friendship he
struck up with one child. I wanted that to be very clear. I
felt that if I just went ahead and threw that out there—
yeah, it has a nice startling effect—but I thought people
needed to understand how it grows.

**You knew a lot of things that Kacie's dad did not know.
Did he learn the truth by reading the story in the
paper?**

I tried very hard not to surprise him in any way. At one

point, I asked him what he knew, because that was one of the difficulties with this story. He had never wanted any details. He knew she was raped. He knew she was shot. And he had heard things here and there. He was very adamant about not wanting to know. And I had difficulty with other police officers at first because they were extraordinarily protective of Rick. It took a lot of phone calling and dropping in and so on before they felt comfortable. And I had told them from the beginning that we would be extremely judicious. I wasn't out to be gratuitous. They finally got comfortable enough that it ceased to be an issue. But it was very much a problem in the beginning weeks.

And I did tell Rick before the series started that on Day Four I would be discussing the crime scene. "It's right up front, and it's up to you whether you want to read that or not." It's often different hearing it and reading it. It sometimes hits home a little bit harder when you're sitting there reading it in black and white, so I did give him forewarning as far as that went.

How much time did you spend tracking down information about David Fuller?

Oh, Lord. I talked to his parents early on and I was really surprised they talked to me. But that one was kind of difficult. I didn't want to lose track of what we were doing, and it was tempting to just go on and on about David Fuller. I had a lot more than we printed.

You only devoted a small part of the copy to him. It must have been hard to leave out something.

Oh, it was incredibly hard. I cut and then I'd go back and say, "Okay, do you think it's still too much?" I didn't want it to be about David Fuller. We weren't out to solve this case. We weren't out to explain why he did what he did. I'm not trying to explain the mentality of a pedophile. I wanted people to understand enough so that they could see how he operated, and I wanted people to understand how he was successful in what he did. But at the same time I didn't want to lose sight of what I was trying to do, and so I tried to rein myself in when it came to him.

On Day Four your description of Kacie's dead body is minimal: half a sentence in the second paragraph. Yet the image is haunting. In fact, you used that word to describe the effect that it had on one of the investigators. What were you aiming for as you crafted that image?

I wanted people to see it, but I didn't want to go overboard with it. I felt like it wouldn't have been as strong if I had gone into as much detail as I could have. At that point I had read the autopsy report, I'd seen the crime scene diagrams, I'd seen the crime scene photos. I wanted people to see it, but I felt that if I had gone on and on and on about it, it would lose that effectiveness. So I reworked and reworked and reworked that sentence before I finally felt it was right, that it would do what I wanted it to do.

Another great passage in the last installment—in fact, probably one of my favorite passages—is, "Haley cried and cried. And then, as many other kids in Greenbrier did that night, she crawled into bed with her parents." How confident were you writing that?

Oh, extremely. By that point I had interviewed a lot of her friends. Every parent I talked to, as well as the school counselor, described children in their beds for months afterward. So I felt extremely confident.

The bulk of your narrative takes readers from the day of Kacie's disappearance to the visitation the night before her funeral. How did you arrive at that as a structure?

I wanted it to be chronological. I wanted people to be in the position of Rick Woody. You know, he comes home, his daughter's missing, there's this dialogue on his computer monitor with some guy, and then there's this phone call that's described in this dialogue, and then suddenly he's having to absorb all of this in 24 hours. And I wanted people to get that effect. He is finding this out and then there's *this*, and then there's *this*, and then there's this stand-off, and now his daughter is dead. And, oh, by the way, here are all these other pictures of these kids floating around. And, oh, there were these other girls Fuller was talking to in other states. And that's a lot, that's a hell of a lot. Aside from the fact that his daughter has been kidnapped and is dead, there's so much Rick is finding out. I wanted readers to have to take it all in the way that he did.

Tell me a little more about how you constructed these chronologies.

I'm a big believer in chronologies because they come in so handy when you start writing. It was a long period of time to keep intruding on people's lives. I don't think I've ever had to be quite this persistent and patient in trying to get a story. And for me, that was tough—just having to wait and then try again, and to wait and to try again. And then once I got their agreement, I worried, "Are they going to change their minds and are they sick of me?" So there was a lot of stress and worry.

This one was the chronology from hell. It was huge. I like timelines; they make it easier. It's kind of the backbone. And I'm a person who, when I write anything, even if it's a short little daily, I will do the lead and then I have a very rough outline. Otherwise I can go off on numerous tangents. But I have to have that timeline to follow. First I used the police timelines and then, as I went through interviews, I would keep adding: "At this point at 1:11 a.m., Sam gets the phone call." "At this hour they're out doing a search," and every little thing. By the time I finished it, it was very long. I think it was several hundred inches.

So you do this just in a word processing document?

On our software. Printed out, it looks a little intimidating. How did I amass this much information? And how can I possibly get it all in without editors having a coronary when they see the length?

Where did you learn to do this?

I'd done them periodically when I was writing a detailed story. I also sat next to the courts reporter, who loves chronologies. And I just got hooked on them shortly after I came here, and I started using them regularly as opposed to just when it was a big project. You know, you miss so many details or little ironies or things that you might not necessarily put together when you don't look at it that way.

There were four law enforcement agencies involved, and I had all of their case files and all these interviews and everything and I might not have necessarily connected things or thought about them a certain way. The e-mails, they were such innocent topics. But those e-mails really helped me piece together her final weeks. Along with her friends' recollections and descriptions, it gave me such a clear picture of what was going on. You know, she's crowned Fall Festival queen, and I didn't realize that Fuller was in town that weekend until I did the chronology. And I was thinking, good God, here's her great shining moment. She's wearing her little crown, her first formal, and she's all dressed up, and meanwhile here is this guy in town staking out her house and planning on how he's going to kidnap her. If I hadn't done the chronology, I would never have realized that he was lurking around town that same weekend.

This story lends itself to cliché, yet I don't think I read "every parent's nightmare" once in the whole thing. Was that hard?

No, not really. I had journalism classes in college. One professor's favorite tactic was to stand up and bellow out a cliché when he read your story out loud to the class. So I've had many years of fear instilled in me where clichés are concerned, and that's hard to get over.

What was his name?

Roy Moses. It was at the University of North Texas, and he taught what they call desk work and feature writing. He was very dramatic. But it was effective. I left that class thinking, "Jeez, never, ever, ever will I allow that to happen."

At the end of each installment is an editor's note explaining that the stories were mostly reconstructed

from interviews. How comfortable were you doing that?

I wanted it to be clear how we got this. I wanted people to understand the depth of research that went into it. You have to be so careful when you try to reconstruct things, and it always bothers me when I read narratives and I don't understand how the reporter did something. You can tell a lot of the time when you read it, "I bet the reporter did this or I bet that's how they got that." But you still want that extra reassurance that this is where this came from. I was lucky in that I had so many people I could crosscheck things with—the friends, the family, the investigators, and I had umpteen documents.

Well, tell me how you reported this: "Chuck turned to Teresa: 'Why can't we keep our girls?' he asked. 'We keep losing our girls.'"

I talked to Teresa first. I also went out and talked to her mom, Illa Smith. It was such a powerful moment given what has happened in this family and hearing it—you know, I heard it from Teresa and then I talked to Illa, and each time I heard it, I knew I had to use that somehow. So I clung to that. I think at one point there was talk of cutting it, but I said no.

Do you write much narrative?

No. Well, I probably write in a narrative style when I do any type of story. I tend to do that. But, no, not really. This was the first huge series.

What was the response like from readers?

It was great. I was really nervous about it, and at our paper we don't normally put e-mail addresses on the bottom of our stories. When I came in on the last day, there were at least a dozen messages already there, and then they just kept on and kept on. Most of them were from teachers or grandparents or parents. And all of them seemed to have gotten it, which I thought was fantastic. A lot of the teachers wanted to use the series, and they were writing in to ask if there was a way they could get it in its entirety. They were asking permission to make copies and use it, and that was exactly what I had hoped to see happen. So that just made my day. Then the e-mails just kept coming in the rest of the week. You want to think you spend all this time on something hoping it's going to achieve a certain purpose, but you don't know. It's just a gamble, and sometimes it pays off and sometimes it doesn't.

What effect did this series have on you personally?

It's all I thought about for the months I worked on it. The crime scene photos were tough, and I've seen a lot of crime scene photos. I've been doing this for 11 years this summer, but those were just horrible. I worried a lot, too. When you have that many people trusting you, especially the girls and their parents, the family. We're not writing for them necessarily, but at the same time, you feel this sense of responsibility because they have put so much faith in you. And these aren't people on your beat. They are not public figures. They're people who just had something horribly tragic occur in their lives. So that weighed very heavily on me. And I was relieved to hear from them afterward and find out what they thought. In fact, two girls, Sam and Jessica, came and job-shadowed me last month, so I took that as a vote of confidence.

How has reporting and writing this story changed you as a journalist or a writer?

In numerous ways really. It was my first attempt to do something of this magnitude. I reported the way I normally would and I came in, I dumped my notes, I did everything I normally would, including a chronology. We discussed so many issues, dealing with these types of sources and how we handle this and at what point we are overstepping the line. So there were numerous issues that would come up throughout and we would sit down and have these in-depth discussions, and that was great. You don't often get to do that, especially with a bunch of editors who are on deadline. It was probably the most thought-provoking project I've ever done.

Writers' Workshop

Talking Points

1) There is a debate in American journalism related to story length. Consider the length of this series and the time it would take to read the whole thing. Discuss the following issues: Is the number of chapters ideal? Could it run on one day, two days, or eight days? Does the content of the series, and the issues associated with it, justify its length? Could it be shorter? If you think so, where would you cut? Are important questions left unanswered? What strategies does Cathy Frye use to keep you engaged in spite of the length?

2) Louise Kiernan of the *Chicago Tribune* says that enterprising reporters should take full advantage, not just of public records, but of "private records," some of which become public as a result of trials or criminal investigations. How often does Frye make use of documents that usually are private? What important insights can be gained by the readers' eavesdropping into these personal communications? Is there a personal revelation you would have left out? Why?

Assignment Desk

1) Re-read the final paragraphs of each of the first three parts of the series. You will see that each one ends with a small cliffhanger, a revelation or foreshadowing that forces you to turn the page. Roy Peter Clark of The Poynter Institute encourages writers to place a mini-cliffhanger at the end of any part of a story of any significant length. The next time you write a story with parts, look for an opportunity to use the mini-cliffhanger.

2) See if you can get a young teenager—with the permission of a parent or guardian—to show you several examples of instant message exchanges. Write a story describing what you learn about this form of communication and the insight it gives you into the lives of young people.

Los Angeles Times

Robert Lee Hotz

Finalist, Non-Deadline Writing

Robert Lee Hotz is a science writer, a specialty he has maintained for nearly all of his journalism career. That career began in 1976 at *The News Virginian* in Waynesboro, Va., where Hotz was a general assignment reporter.

He moved to the *Pittsburgh Press* in 1979, did general assignment work for another two years, then became a science writer. He held that title when he moved in 1984 to *The Atlanta Journal-Constitution,* where he also had brief stints as an assistant metro editor and science editor before moving on to the *Los Angeles Times.*

Hotz has been rewarded for his writing since the earliest years of his career, beginning with awards for news reporting in Virginia. He twice received national reporting awards from the Society of Professional Journalists and three times won the science writing award given by the American Association for the Advancement of Science. He was a Pulitzer Prize finalist in 1986 for coverage of genetic engineering issues and again in 2004 for coverage of the *Columbia* accident. He shared in a staff Pulitzer in 1995 for the *Los Angeles Times*'s coverage of the Northridge earthquake.

He has written on matters of science and how the media handle it for books and the *Times*'s Sunday magazine. He and his wife, Jennifer Arlen, have two boys: Michael, 12, and Robert, 8.

"Decoding Columbia: A Detective Story," the story of a space shuttle's disintegration, is a study in the power of narrative storytelling that employs the tools of that genre to lyrical effect. The *Los Angeles Times* published this story in a six-part series called "Butterfly on a Bullet."

Decoding *Columbia*:
A detective story

DECEMBER 21, 2003

James Hallock discovered just how little it takes to bring down a space shuttle.

He did it by playing with pencils.

As a member of the *Columbia* Accident Investigation Board, the pear-shaped, bewhiskered expert on flight safety had a New Englander's flinty skepticism and a physicist's distaste for untested accident theories.

On this day, Hallock, 62, scowled at specifications for the reinforced carbon panels that shielded the leading edge of *Columbia*'s wings from the heat of re-entry.

If one of the $800,000 panels had cracked, it might have been the flaw that on Feb. 1 caused the $1.8-billion spacecraft and its crew of seven astronauts to plummet in a shower of molten debris across six states.

Hallock brooded over a simple question: What would it take to break one?

Engineers gave him the original 25-year-old NASA specifications, which said the panels must withstand an impact equal to the kinetic energy of 0.006 foot-pounds.

What did that mean? Hallock twiddled a yellow No. 2 pencil between his fingers. How far, for instance, would he have to drop the pencil to generate that kind of impact?

In the mailroom at the board's makeshift headquarters in Shirlington, Va., he found a box of pencils and a postal scale.

He weighed the pencils, then calculated the mass of the average pencil. With that number, he worked out how much punch each pencil would pack.

"The answer," he would say later, "is that a No. 2 pencil dropped from about 6 inches equals the kinetic energy number they had."

The panels, in actual manufacture, were much stronger. But that remarkably low standard, Hallock believed, was a tangible measure of how confident NASA engineers were that nothing would hit the leading edge of the wing.

"The number didn't matter to them," Hallock said, "because they assumed nothing would ever hit the shuttle."

* * *

Call it forensic engineering or, more plainly, detective work.

The *Columbia* accident investigation was the most exhaustive scientific inquest ever undertaken.

Suspicion led down a hundred blind alleys. Investigators quarreled. Mission insiders tried to control the probe. Outsiders railed about secrecy.

The investigators mustered the most sophisticated techniques that science could devise—X-ray scanners, neutron beam machines, hypersonic wind tunnels.

They also used red food coloring, a bicycle pump, a hobby-shop hacksaw and a steam iron.

They conducted some tests in classified military laboratories, others in the nearest kitchen sink.

In arcane debates about trapped-gas analysis, radar cross sections and spatter metallurgy, they stalked answers to wrenching questions of guilt, shame and responsibility.

Every imperfection they found revealed a human face.

All that they discovered reinforced what Hallock learned by dropping his No. 2 pencil.

The space shuttles are by design unsafe.

As the most complex flying machines ever assembled, each shuttle contained more than 2.5 million parts, 230 miles of wiring, 1,060 valves and 1,440 circuit breakers. All of it had to function properly at extremes of speed, heat, cold, gravity and vacuum—the interaction of its parts just at the edge of human understanding and control.

From liftoff to landing, the shuttles flew in peril.

In orbit, they maneuvered through a hailstorm of 10,000 man-made objects larger than a softball and millions of smaller pieces of debris. At orbital velocities, an object no larger than a pea carried the force of a falling 400-pound safe.

During NASA's first 75 shuttle flights, technicians had to replace 60 cockpit windshields—at $40,000 each—because of pitting from debris.

But launch was even more dangerous. Orbiting junk at least could be tracked by radar and avoided.

For all their efforts, shuttle engineers could not stop

ice and chunks of insulating foam from falling off the shuttle's 15-story external fuel tank and striking the spacecraft during its eight-minute ascent into orbit.

Agency engineers could not fix this fundamental flaw, nor could they craft a safer vehicle. They dared not abandon the only vehicle the country had to carry people into space.

So NASA continued to launch the shuttles, gaining confidence each time the crew returned safely.

"The program had been put in this box they could not get out of," said Scott Hubbard, director of NASA's Ames Research Center in Mountain View, Calif., and a member of the investigating board.

Blind to the consequences, they had constructed a trap and baited it with ambition.

* * *

In the winter darkness, Caltech astronomer Tony Beasley, 38, shivered in his front yard.

According to the announced flight path, *Columbia* would soon swoop over moonlit mountain slopes draped with snow and above the white, upturned antenna dishes of the university's Owens Valley Radio Observatory.

His wife and mother-in-law, wrapped in a rug to ward off the February chill, stood beside him. Stifling yawns, cupping hot mugs of tea, they scanned the star fields over Bishop for the returning shuttle.

Beasley rarely paid attention to anything so close to Earth. He managed Caltech's millimeter astronomy array and, in his spare time, studied the motion of galaxies through the deep cosmos.

Two local photographers, however, had convinced him that the sight of the shuttle's predawn re-entry over Northern California would be especially memorable.

Just before 6 a.m., *Columbia* slashed the dark from horizon to horizon. Staccato flashes punctuated its passage.

The fiery pink streak left the afterglow of a holiday sparkler. It burned in Beasley's eyes long after the shuttle itself, traveling at 4 miles per second 40 miles overhead, vanished in the eastern haze.

The burly Australian astronomer could not make sense of the bright pulses of light that trailed in *Columbia*'s wake.

His mother-in-law was puzzled, too.

They might be tiles, Beasley told her. I think the shuttle normally sheds some tiles on re-entry, he said. He didn't give it a second thought.

The stargazer ducked into the warm kitchen, ate a piece of toast with peanut butter, then drove to the observatory.

He had no inkling how obsessed he would become with the streak of light he had just witnessed.

* * *

One *Columbia* crew member didn't wear a space helmet, so smooth was the descent.

Too elated to bother, or perhaps too confident, three of them did not put on their orange pressure-suit gloves.

On the flight deck, shuttle commander Rick Husband, 45, chugged down three plastic flagons of saline solution to keep from getting lightheaded, a common side effect of re-entry. It tasted slightly like seawater.

Pilot William McCool, 41, pored over a pre-landing checklist. Crew members Kalpana Chawla, 41, and Laurel Clark, 41, sitting behind him, watched raptly as superheated gases licked across the cabin windows.

Seated back in the mid-deck area, Michael Anderson, 43, David Brown, 46, and Ilan Ramon, 48, could not see what lay ahead.

The seven men and women were plunging out of orbit into the atmosphere over the South Pacific on the last leg of a journey that 22 years of repetition had turned into a NASA routine.

For 16 days, they had circled Earth. Now they could return.

The shock of *Columbia*'s passage was ripping apart molecules of the thickening air. Atoms blazed furiously. Faster than a bullet, the shuttle hurtled down a tunnel of excited particles, glowing within a glow, like a firefly trapped inside a fiery neon tube.

"It looks like a blast furnace," Husband told his crew in cabin talk captured on Clark's video camera.

Gravity gently took hold inside the spacecraft. A notecard floated to the floor. At 24 times the speed of sound and 250,000 feet over Hawaii, the shuttle encountered temperatures of 3,000 degrees Fahrenheit, and the light danced even harder outside.

"It's really getting bright," McCool exclaimed.

Seething plumes of ionized gas—orange and yellow, reddish purple and pink—swirled around the capsule.

"You definitely do not want to be outside now," Husband replied.

They chuckled. *Columbia* automatically began banking to the right. The Earth below swung into view. Home.

* * *

In Houston, lead flight director Leroy Cain watched a glowing line track *Columbia*'s re-entry across a world map covering one wall in the windowless auditorium of Mission Control. This was his 12th mission.

Abruptly, instrument readings from four temperature sensors aboard *Columbia* flickered off.

No one in the five rows of systems engineers in front of Cain could tell him why.

To all appearances, the spacecraft was flying normally northeast of Yosemite, heading toward a routine landing in Florida.

Cain double-checked. "Everything look good to you?" he asked the engineer monitoring guidance and control.

"I don't see anything out of the ordinary," came the reply. The Johnson Space Center tape recorders and video cameras preserved every word.

Five minutes later, pressure readings from two of *Columbia*'s tires ceased. The shuttle flew on, approaching Dallas and Fort Worth, slowing to 21 times the speed of sound.

Cain's thoughts raced down a dozen avenues of contingency and response, as he had practiced in so many mission simulations. Each was a dead end.

Ninety seconds passed.

"*Columbia*, [this is] Houston," radioed Marine Lt. Col. Charles Hobaugh, 42, the astronaut in charge of Mission Control's communications with the shuttle crew. "We see your tire pressure messages, and we did not copy your last call."

Aboard *Columbia*, shuttle commander Husband keyed the microphone switch. "Roger," he replied. "Uh, buh…"

His transmission ended mid-word.

With all its electronic senses, NASA strained for a telling signal. Frantically, engineers paged deeper into thick manuals of procedures. They sought to restore communication.

"*Columbia?* Houston. UHF comm check," Hobaugh radioed, trying to raise the crew.

No response.

"*Columbia?* Houston. UHF comm check," he repeated.

Silence.

"*Columbia?* Houston. UHF comm check."

The minutes dragged. Mission Control, cut off from any sensation of the world beyond its unresponsive computer monitors, was paralyzed as if by a stroke.

Sixteen minutes after the first sensors faltered, a cell-phone rang. Someone watching television at home had called a NASA official in the control room, who in turn murmured the news to the flight director.

Columbia had burst into a confetti of debris.

Torn into thousands of pieces, it was falling with a rolling rumble of sonic booms across Texas and Louisiana. From the ground, the disintegrating spacecraft was a winter thunderstorm of wreckage.

Quietly, Cain worked his jaw. He wiped a hand across his face. He couldn't help it: A single tear slid down his cheek.

The shuttle team was no longer running a mission.

They were witnesses now.

Their statements would be taken. Their notes, logs and computer data would be impounded. There would be questions and a fever for answers.

All their decisions would be suspect.

"Lock the doors," Cain ordered.

Lessons Learned

BY ROBERT LEE HOTZ

This was a mystery story that began in the most public way imaginable.

America's space shuttle shattered in the sky. Wreckage streaked across seven states. As a matter of forensic engineering, the subsequent investigation into the accident that killed the seven crew members aboard the space shuttle *Columbia* was the most extensive scientific inquest in history.

At stake was the bureaucratic survival of the nation's space agency and a nation's commitment to manned space exploration. At direct issue was the personal guilt of the shuttle managers responsible and the potential corporate liability. There was no shortage of shame and indignation, of secrecy and misleading claims.

What I found was a story of the terrible human consequences of engineering ambition. I have covered complex science issues for a quarter century; yet every hour of the six months I spent reporting the *Columbia* accident, I relied most on the simple lessons I learned by trial and error during my first assignments as a raw reporter on a small Virginia country daily.

There is no mystery in these, but perhaps they bear repeating:

■ **Shed your preconceptions.** By necessity, we approach most stories with an expectation of what we hope to find. That can blind a reporter to what sources are trying to show him, make a reporter deaf to what they are trying so hard to tell him. At the same time, both NASA and the independent commission investigating the accident worked aggressively to mold the story into a narrative of their choosing.

■ **Look people in the eye.** Hang up the phone and get out of the office. Talk to people directly. I knocked on doors in nine cities, from Huntsville to Boston. It was time-consuming, lonely, expensive, and yet always revealing. The further I went away from managed news events, the more I learned.

■ **Good writing takes good reporting.** No one can honestly write what he hasn't first reported. At every stage, pay meticulous attention to sensory detail. Gather the facts of the senses that can later make the story come alive: colors, sounds, smells, textures. Pay the same attention to personal detail: what people wear, their hobbies, the family photos on their desks. They all are revealing pieces of the mosaic of human character. I remember one source who wore his Naval Academy class ring on the same finger as his wedding band. It seemed the apt symbol of his passion for public service.

■ **Organize as you go.** The series encompassed 130 interviews with accident investigators, scientists, and NASA employees across the United States. I also reviewed dozens of government reports and public hearing transcripts spanning the quarter-century of the space shuttle program. I met at length with members of the *Columbia* Accident Investigation Board. To digest it all, I built a searchable computer database, updating it every day. I relied most on the 10 yellow legal pads of handwritten interview notes I had indexed by topic. I typed up summaries of impressions, thoughts, and possible follow-ups after every interview session. And I made a detailed story outline.

■ **Give your curiosity free rein.** Under deadline pressure, we anxiously sprint for the money quote and the hard lead. Trust your instincts. Wander up blind alleys. One of them will lead to the heart of a story. It took me a month to identify and locate the firefighter who found *Columbia*'s OEX flight recorder.

■ **History matters.** The *Columbia* accident was two decades in the making. The conditions for the fatal flight were set by the political and economic decisions that shaped the original design of the shuttle spacecraft.

■ **Persist.** Many senior shuttle officials never talked directly to me or anyone else in the press. The head of the investigating commission never spoke to me despite repeated requests for an interview over three months. Yet many people inside the space agency and the investigation did talk to me at length. All of them had to be courted.

St. Petersburg Times

Lane DeGregory

Finalist, Non-Deadline Writing

Lane DeGregory began writing as an elementary school student and eventually edited the school paper in middle and high school. She started writing for *The Cavalier Daily* in her freshman year at the University of Virginia and was elected editor of the daily student paper in her senior year.

DeGregory interned at *The Charlotte Observer* and *The Virginian-Pilot* and eventually got a job with *The Daily Progress* in Charlottesville, Va. In 1992, she moved to the Outer Banks of North Carolina to work in a bureau of *The Virginian-Pilot*. When the newspaper formed a narrative writing team, DeGregory was one of four staffers picked to write off-the-news stories. She wrote about old nurses, young sailors, and a terrible flood.

She was hired by the *St. Petersburg Times* in 2000 and has since written about people in the shadows: young anarchists and old tap dancers, commune dwellers and white witches, fugitives and carnies and middle-aged yodelers.

DeGregory was a member of the team named as a finalist for the 2002 ASNE/Jesse Laventhol Prize for Deadline News Reporting. She won an Outstanding Media Award in 2001 from the National Alliance for the Mentally Ill. In 2000, her writing earned a second-place award from the American Association of Sunday and Feature Editors. In 1999, she won a Salute to Excellence Award from the National Association of Black Journalists.

She and her husband, musician and teacher Dan DeGregory, have two children: Ryland, 7, and Tucker, 6.

"A Message from Roger" solves the mystery of a letter in a bottle that was discovered nearly 19 years after a 7-year-old tossed it off a pier on Florida's west coast. DeGregory uses scenes and dialogue to tell a story sure to send a tingle up the spines of readers.

A message from Roger

JULY 10, 2003

At first, he thought it was trash.

The bottle was bobbing in a canal behind Don Smith's house in Venetian Isles, drifting toward his dock. He saw it on the Fourth of July, while he was playing with his grandchildren. He grabbed a fishing net and scooped the bottle out of the murky water.

One side was fuzzy with algae. The other was clear. Black electrical tape was wound tightly around the top. The rusty cap said "Pepsi" in an obsolete logo.

Inside, there was a note.

The paper was folded, scorched sepia by the sun. It had been ripped from a school writing tablet, the kind with dotted blue lines. Smith pulled it out and smoothed it on a table.

"To whoever finds this letter please write me a letter and let me know," the note said in shaky pencil. "Roger J. Clay, 890 Linwood Ave., Fairfield Ohio, 45014."

Don and his wife, Carol, know the place. They are from Cincinnati, about 25 miles from Fairfield. Their son Sean works in Fairfield. "What are the odds?" Don asked.

Then he saw the date. On the bottom right corner, the paper said: 12/27/84.

That bottle had been in the water for almost 19 years.

Don's daughter-in-law is a teacher. By the handwriting, she said, whoever wrote the note was probably 7 or 8 years old. Roger J. Clay would be 26 or 27 now.

"Wouldn't it be great if we could find him and let him know we found his bottle?" Carol said.

"I'll try," said Don. "But 19 years is a long, long time."

* * *

That night, after the fireworks, Don got on the Internet. He didn't find Roger J. Clay. He found this:

"Roger K. Clay, 890 Linwood Ave., Fairfield, Ohio."

A few more clicks and Don found public records showing Roger K. was 49. "Must be the kid's father,"

Don told his wife. "And it looks like he still lives at the same house. What are the odds?"

Don tried to find a phone number, but had no luck.

So he wrote a letter: "I found your son's message in a bottle behind my house in St. Petersburg, Florida," he wrote. "I just thought you would want to know."

He mailed the letter the next morning, Saturday.

On Monday, he called the *St. Petersburg Times*.

* * *

Don and Carol Smith are 56 and retired. Don owned a Cincinnati business that manufactured trailers to haul mobile television studios. Carol was a Realtor.

"I couldn't believe it. Could a bottle really last that long out there? In Tampa Bay?" Don asked. "Geez, 19 years!"

Back at work, we tried to find out more about the boy who wrote the message. Caryn Baird, a *Times* researcher, tapped into electronic databases, tracked all sorts of records. But she couldn't come up with a Roger J. Clay.

Then she scanned Social Security files. There he was.

"He's dead," she said.

* * *

There had been an article in the paper.

Nine days after his 21st birthday, Roger J. Clay was driving home on his new Suzuki. "His motorcycle went left of center and collided head-on with a pickup," *The Columbus Dispatch* reported. "Police are still trying to determine why Clay's motorcycle went left of center."

It happened on July 10, 1998. Five years ago today.

I called Don Smith and read him the news.

He coughed. Or choked. Or something. "Oh, my God. Oh, my God. I knew it," he said. "That's terrible. I can't explain it. Oh, my God. I just had this feeling something had happened to that kid."

Now Don was even more determined to find Roger's parents. "Imagine what that message would mean to them," he said.

So Caryn found a new address and a phone number for Roger's dad. Then she found a number for someone she thought might be his mom, at a different address. I gave the numbers to Don.

A half-hour later, he called me back.

"You're not going to believe this," he said.

Roger's dad wasn't home. So Don had called the other number, the one for Lisa M. Ferguson, who used to be married to Roger K. Clay. A woman had answered. No, Lisa wasn't home. "I'm Lisa's sister," the woman said. "Can I help?"

Don explained why he was calling.

"Oh, my God!" the woman gasped. "Lisa is away," she said. Every year this time, she goes away. "She can't stand to be in Ohio around the anniversary of the accident."

She gave Don a cell phone number.

"Lisa is down in Florida," her sister said. "In Seminole."

* * *

Lisa had just come back from the pool when her cell phone rang. She and her husband, Al, were cooling off in their hotel room.

When Don told Lisa he had found a bottle, she started screaming. She knew the rest. She remembers that note. She remembers the day her son wrote it.

They were in Clearwater, celebrating Christmas with her sister. Roger was 7. His dad took him fishing on Pier 60. Roger wrote the note and took tape from the tackle box and sealed the note in the bottle and tossed it off the pier. Lisa remembers telling him he was littering.

Roger was a happy, active kid. He liked to pretend to climb the walls like Spider-Man. He liked shooting squirrels with his dad. He raced dirt bikes. He fished. And he dropped a Pepsi bottle in the water even though his mother disapproved.

Now, 19 years later, a stranger had called and given her back her son.

"Here I am, trying to escape Roger's death, and he reaches out and gives me this message, this gift," she said.

Lisa told Don she wanted to see him. She wanted to hold that bottle. She wanted to touch that note, trace Roger's childish letters with her finger.

Don wanted to see Lisa, too. He wanted to learn about Roger.

They agreed to meet for dinner at 7:30 Tuesday night.

* * *

How does it happen? Can a message really float around in a bottle for 19 years and surface so close to where it started?

"I'm not at all surprised," said Robert Weisberg. He is a professor in the College of Marine Science at the University of South Florida, St. Petersburg. He makes models of currents, tracks tides and studies how objects travel in water.

"There would be no problem at all getting a bottle from Clearwater's Pier 60 to Tampa Bay. Water does move," he said. "There are currents out there that are driven by wind. There are tides. It certainly is reasonable for something like that to stay in circulation around this area."

The bottle could have gotten hung up in a mangrove somewhere and stayed there for 15 years, Weisberg said. It could have moved around a bit, floated down to Sanibel Island and come back up into the bay again. It could have circulated up the gulf toward the Panhandle, then gone to Texas and come back under the Sunshine Skyway bridge. "Once something drifts offshore, there's no telling," he said.

Vembu Subramanian, who works in USF's office of Coastal Ocean Monitoring and Prediction Systems, said the bottle could have traveled thousands of paths from Clearwater to Venetian Isles. "There could have been boats moving it. It could have bounced through all those little islands. Who knows what kinds of influences could have impacted its path all those years?"

* * *

All day Tuesday, Roger J. Clay's mother couldn't stop smiling. And crying. And smiling.

She called her daughter in Ohio. She called her brothers and sisters. She called Roger's dad, who cried so hard he had to hang up.

"I had forgotten all about that bottle. It's kind of hard to put into words, all the emotions that brings back," Roger K. Clay told me from Ohio. "I told Lisa, it was like he was trying to remind us he was still with us."

Lisa told Roger's dad she would get to see the bottle that night. She and Al got to the restaurant early. At 7:40 p.m., a man with blue eyes and salt-and-pepper hair walked up, holding a bubble-wrapped bottle. Lisa smothered him, weeping, without even introducing herself. Don hugged her back. Hard. Then they stood there, in the lobby of the restaurant, holding on and sobbing into each other's shoulders. Their spouses stood by, dabbing at their eyes.

"Isn't this unreal?" Carol Smith asked.

"He's still touching lives," Al Ferguson said. "He was an amazing kid."

Over Diet Cokes and iced teas, salads and flaky rolls, the two couples talked about Roger. How he loved to play practical jokes, rig buckets of water above his sister's bedroom door, string fishing line across the hallway. How he lettered in football three years in high school. How he played varsity baseball. How the girls all loved him. He loved country music, they said, and fishing and deer hunting.

"He was buried in his blue jeans."

Ever since he was a kid, Roger had wanted a motorcycle. He begged his mom, then—after his parents got divorced—he started in on his stepdad. They kept saying no. Too dangerous.

So the day he turned 21, Roger bought a brand new Suzuki GSX-R750W. He drove it to his mom's house, where he still lived. She turned white. He grinned.

But his bike kept breaking down. The fuel hose kept popping off, killing the engine. Roger took the bike back to the dealership four times the first week. Five years ago today, he picked it up after it was supposed to be fixed again. He and two friends headed down the highway. Roger's fuel hose dropped off a few miles from home. The engine cut out and he crossed the center line.

"It's not natural," Lisa said. Under the table, she cradled Roger's Pepsi bottle in her lap. "You're not supposed to have to bury your baby."

Lisa slipped her wallet from her purse and pulled out a photo. Roger's high school graduation portrait. He was wearing a blue oxford and jeans.

"What a nice-looking kid," Don said. "What a shame."

"He was studying to be an FBI agent," Lisa said. "He was going to school during the day and working third shift. Everyone loved him. More than 400 people came to his funeral."

A few weeks after the funeral, she said, a notice came in the mail. Suzuki was recalling its GSX-R750W line because of a fault in the fuel system. Lisa called a lawyer. She spent five years suing Suzuki. Finally, in February, she settled out of court for an undisclosed amount.

"The money will never bring back Roger," she told her dinner companions. "But you all have."

"I dread this time of year every year. It's the worst. But now I have something wonderful to think about," Lisa said. She reached across the table, grabbed Don and Carol's hands. "You all have given me so much to be happy about. You have given me this message from Roger. He's still playing tricks on me."

When dinner was over, the two couples walked out into the dark.

"Why don't you all come visit us in Ohio?" Lisa asked the Smiths. She plans to put the bottle on her mantel, and wants them to see it.

Lessons Learned

BY LANE DeGREGORY

When the phone rang, I answered it. I hardly ever do that.

I try not to be at my desk much. I'd rather be out reporting, or scouting subjects, or something. But over the July Fourth holiday, when this story started to unfold, I broke my foot. There I was, the Monday after the long weekend, with crutches propped beside me and my right foot in a cast, stuck at the office because I couldn't drive. So when the phone rang, I answered it.

"I found something. I'm not sure if you'd be interested," said a man's voice. "But I understand you like strange stories."

It's true. The slices of life I love most usually are ones no one else sees. I comb the back streets and bars, chat up bus drivers and eat at all-night diners. Co-workers kid me about seeing stories everywhere. That's my biggest asset. And my biggest downfall: I believe everyone has a story. And I believe almost everyone.

Sometimes, as a journalist, you have to be a cynic.

Or at least sit near one.

When I got off the phone, I was so excited, I shouted over my cubicle, "Some man just found a Pepsi bottle floating in a canal. And there's a note in it! He said it was written 19 years ago."

The reporter whose desk is across from mine has been writing for newspapers since before I was born. "No way," he said. "Not possible.

"Somebody's pulling your leg."

What? Who? Why would anyone do that? How could my colleague say such a thing?

Burst my bubble, would he? Well, I'd show him...

I called four oceanographers. Two called back. By making me want to prove him wrong, that reporter had forced me to show how something that seemed entirely implausible was, at least, possible. Scientists said so. That made the story so much stronger.

The man who found the note wanted help finding the boy who wrote it. That's why he called the newspaper.

When *Times* researcher Caryn Baird finally tracked down the boy and told me what had happened, I didn't know what to do. Should I call the boy's mother? After all these years? Would she want to know? "Let the man who found the bottle make that call," said my editor, Mike Wilson.

The hardest part of this story was trying to stay out of the way.

So I called Don Smith and he called the boy's mother and, of course, she sobbed and, of course, she wanted to see the note. And since she happened to be in Florida, a short drive from where Smith found the bottle, of course, they agreed to meet.

I needed to see the mother's face when she cradled the bottle. I had to be there when she opened the crumbling paper and traced her young son's words. Of course, I asked to come along.

But I had to be careful. I had to shut up and not ask questions and stay in the background and just observe and let the scene unfold on its own. So I could write it.

Roger's mom saw his message the night of Tuesday, July 8. I wrote the story the next day.

I hadn't planned to do this piece as a daily. A story this great deserves to be really well-written. I wanted to take my time, craft something special, draft and re-draft.

"This is a simple, lovely story," said my editor. "Just tell it like it happened."

Most of the time, I try to be invisible in my articles. But sometimes, as a reporter, you can't help but influence events. If the *Times* hadn't tracked down the boy and found his mother, Smith wouldn't have been able to pass on Roger's note. So how could I tell that segment of the story without being in it?

"Acknowledge your role when you need to, then step aside," said my editor. "Readers want to know how you know."

Sometimes the best narratives spin out naturally: Start at the beginning, when the phone rings. Drop clues about what's going to happen. Don't give away the ending.

And always edit out your last three sentences. Most writers tend to dribble on. See?

Anthony Shadid

Deadline News Reporting

Just read Anthony Shadid's travel itinerary since Sept. 11, 2001: Egypt, Lebanon, Iraq, Afghanistan, Pakistan, Israel, the Palestinian territories.

While so many of us on the homefront have stood bewildered, trying to understand our changed world, Shadid has been traveling the Middle East and South Asia providing us with some glimpses at the answers.

Posted to Baghdad by his still-new employer, *The Washington Post*, he arrived just a few weeks before the war began in 2003. He had been to Iraq in 1998 and 2002; already, he had used his extensive contacts among Iraqis in America and throughout the Middle East to start building sources for war coverage.

Between making contacts and laying in provisions for the coming war, Shadid was on the phone to his editors back home, trying to persuade them to let him stay once

the bombing started. They were worried about his safety. He was worried about being able to bear witness for his readers and the world to what soon would happen in Baghdad. He won the debate. He stayed, and his coverage provides readers with a vivid picture of what life was like for ordinary people caught in a war zone.

At age 35, Shadid already has a lifetime's experience as a foreign correspondent. He worked for the Associated Press for 10 years, serving as AP correspondent in Cairo from 1995 to 1999, reporting and writing from most countries in the region during that time. His work during that posting included interviews with young fighters of the Taliban on the Afghanistan front. He then worked for *The Boston Globe* in Washington for two years, covering diplomacy and the State Department.

As a unilateral reporter, unattached to a military unit and unencumbered by the rules of "embedding," Shadid was able to write stories about what was going on in the streets and households of the Iraqi capital before and during the fighting.

His stories weave a narrative, a picture of the human suffering and the human emotions of civilians caught in wartime. Shadid says he felt an obligation to be there, to document what was happening. He did more than document it; he captured it, whole and unblinking.

Shadid is an American of Lebanese descent. His grandfather immigrated to the United States, settling in Oklahoma City, where Shadid grew up. He studied Arabic at the University of Wisconsin and at the American University in Cairo from 1991 to 1992. He also did graduate work at Columbia University in New York from 1993 to 1994.

Shadid received the George Polk Award for foreign reporting in 2003 for stories he wrote from the Middle East. He won the 2004 Pulitzer Prize for international reporting. He is the author of *Legacy of the Prophet: Despots, Democrats, and the New Politics of Islam.*

He is married and the father of a young daughter, Laila.

—Janet Weaver

[*The Jesse Laventhol Prize for Deadline News Reporting is funded by a gift from David Laventhol, a former Times-Mirror executive, in honor of his father.*]

'We're in a dark, dark tunnel'

MARCH 24, 2003

BAGHDAD, Iraq, March 23—The melancholy wail sailed across the city and pierced the walls of the middle-class Baghdad home. The sleepless family listened in silence until the mother, her face lined with fear and pain, shook her head.

"Siren," she whispered.

At that, her daughter jumped up and threw open the door. She ran to open the windows next, fearful the blast would shatter them. The son sprinted outside, hoping to spot a low-flying cruise missile that would send the family huddling, yet again, in a hallway.

And they waited for the bombs.

"It's terrible," the mother said, as the minutes passed. "We really suffer, and I don't know why we should live like this."

Her daughter nodded. "I get so scared, I shake," she said. "I'm afraid the house is going to collapse on my head."

While the outside world has grown accustomed to detached images of fire and fury over Baghdad, and the government here boasts of victory over the invaders, this rattled family of five in the middle-class neighborhood of Jihad has watched war turn life upside down. Their world now is isolation, dread and a bitter sense that they do not deserve their fate.

"We're in a dark, dark tunnel, and we don't see the light at the end of it," the daughter-in-law said.

The family met privately with a journalist today, without the presence of a requisite government escort and with a promise that their identities would not be published. Over a lunch of Iraqi dishes—pickled mango, kibbe, *kufta* and chicken cooked with rice, peanuts and raisins—they spoke with unusual candor about politics and war. At times brashly, they discussed subjects that are usually hinted at, as if Baghdad were already in limbo between its past and its future.

"Iraq is ready for change," the father said. "The people

want it; they want more freedom."

But family members expressed anger at the U.S. government, which has promised to liberate them. They criticized President Saddam Hussein and his dictatorial rule, but insisted that pride and patriotism prevent them from putting their destiny in the hands of a foreign power.

They spoke most fervently of a longing for routine—the most mundane rituals of going to work, sharing dinner on a quiet night and sleeping at a set hour. They predicted little of that stability ahead. From a bloody battle for the capital, to lawlessness, to the humiliation of an occupation, they braced for a future that hardly anyone in Baghdad dares predict.

"Everything is turned around," the daughter-in-law said.

For weeks, the daughter-in-law helped prepare the house for war. She and her husband hauled a mattress downstairs, setting up their bedroom in the dining room. The family rearranged furniture so that they could sprint to open the windows. Sofas and tables were cloaked in dust cloths to protect them from flying glass and debris. Two rifles and bags of ammunition were propped against the wall.

Scattered around the two-story house were supplies to help them withstand a siege. Two tanks were filled with kerosene for cooking in case the electricity went out. The mother filled every pan, kettle and thermos with water, in case the pumps stopped working. Flour, sugar, rice, beans, powdered milk, biscuits, jam, cheese, macaroni, wheat, and cereal filled bag after bag.

"These will last three months," the son said, surveying the stockpile.

His wife interrupted to disagree. One month, no more. "The men in our family have very big appetites," she said.

It was a rare moment of levity in a city with little joy. The family members gazed out the window at a sky shrouded in black smoke from fires lit by Iraqi forces to conceal targets from U.S. strikes. The oil pits burned for a second day, turning a sunny, cloudless Baghdad sky into an eerie gauze. In vain, the family hoped the smoke would limit the air assault.

They had already had enough, they said. The worst so

far was Friday, when U.S. and British forces fired 320 Tomahawk cruise missiles at Baghdad, wrecking the symbols of Hussein's rule. Ten of the missiles landed near their home, shattering the window in the front of the house. The shock waves threw open the refrigerator, tossing its drawers on the kitchen floor.

"They were powerful, really powerful," the mother said. "They came one after another."

Baghdad is a city that takes pride in its toughness. Residents are fond of listing the challenges history has thrown before them. The men in the family sounded a similar theme.

"We have 11,000 years of history. I know it sounds facetious, but it gives you resilience," the father said.

Of the bombs, his son added, "The bark is worse than the bite." But in private moments today, the suffering was close to the surface. Friends, they said, had fled to Syria in January, only to run out of money before the war started. Others had headed north to the city of Mosul, hoping to endure the war with relatives.

Those who stayed have struggled to negotiate the uncertainty. A pregnant friend of the daughter-in-law was supposed to have a Caesarean section within 10 days. But her doctor has vanished. Hospital after hospital has refused to admit her, overwhelmed with the task of preparing for the wounded. Another friend who is seven months pregnant has begun taking Valium.

A neighbor said she stuffed cotton in the ears of her two young children every night. She fretted about finding diapers and milk.

"She's in a complete panic," the daughter-in-law said.

When it came to the cause of Iraq's predicament, family members pointed to Hussein, describing him as rash. He invaded Iran, trapping them in an eight-year war. He seized Kuwait, bringing on the Persian Gulf War and the devastation of sanctions that largely wiped out Iraq's middle class. After that war, they were ready to overthrow him themselves.

But they bitterly denounced the war the United States has launched. Iraq, perhaps more than any other Arab country, dwells on traditions—of pride, honor and dignity. To this family, the assault is an insult. It is not Hussein under attack, but Iraq, they said. It is hard to gauge if this is a common sentiment, although it is one heard more often as the war progresses.

"We complain about things, but complaining doesn't mean cooperating with foreign governments," the father said. "When somebody comes to attack Iraq, we stand up for Iraq. That doesn't mean we love Saddam Hussein, but there are priorities."

A friend of the family interrupted. "Bombing for peace?" he asked, shaking his head.

"I don't even care about the leadership," the daughter-in-law said. "But someone wants to take away what is yours. What gives them the right to change something that's not theirs in the first place? I don't like your house, so I'm going to bomb it and you can rebuild it again the way I want it, with your money? I feel like it's an insult, really."

Gathered around the table, the family members nodded their heads.

"There are rumblings of dissent," the father said. "But these rumblings don't mean: Come America, we'll throw flowers at you."

The family is Sunni Muslim, a minority from which the government draws its strength. Sunnis appear to have the most to lose in a postwar Iraq that would undoubtedly devolve authority to Kurds in the north and the Shiite Muslim majority in the south. The son acknowledged that some Shiite friends had a different opinion of the U.S. attack. But Iraqi nationalism—and a history replete with sometimes violent opposition to foreign intervention—could influence the course of the war and its aftermath.

On this day, though, survival was the more pressing issue. By late afternoon, the thunder of bombing broke across the horizon. The son said he heard a rumor that B-52s were on their way, and the family members guessed at the time it would take them to arrive.

They were jittery, flinching at the slightest sounds. "That's wind, that's wind," the father said when the door slammed shut. When the son got up, his chair banged the wall and the mother jumped. A few minutes later, he did it again.

"Quit doing that," his mother said. "I'm so scared. Every little noise."

Outside, the sounds of ordinary life came from the

street. A cart passed the house, its horn blowing. It had come to collect trash and refill kerosene tanks for cooking. As the cart passed, the routine it evoked seemed to anger the son.

"I should be able to live like other people are living," he said glumly. "I shouldn't fear bombs falling on my head. I shouldn't be hearing sirens. Why should I have to like this? Why should this be normal?"

Everyone looked to the floor, no one saying a word.

In a moment,
lives get blown apart

MARCH 27, 2003

BAGHDAD, Iraq, March 26—Shards of corrugated tin dangled from roofs like chimes, colliding on the winds of a savage sandstorm. Shattered pipes poured sewage into the streets. The charred carcasses of cars sat smoldering, hurled onto the sidewalk.

Ali Abdel-Jabbar watched helplessly as his friend, Mohammed Abdel-Sattar, lay on the ground, his legs torn off. He lived. Across the street was the severed hand of Samad Rabai, tossed gracelessly in a pool of blood and mud. He died.

In a moment, two explosions transformed a busy stretch of life today into a junkyard of mangled wires, uprooted trees, toppled lights, anguish and grief.

Iraqi officials said at least 14 people were killed and 30 injured in the blasts—a count that matched hospital estimates—in the biggest loss of civilian life in Baghdad since U.S. and British air attacks began last week. The explosions devastated a 100-yard swath of shops, homes and a restaurant in the working-class neighborhood of Shaab, on Baghdad's northern outskirts.

Pentagon officials denied responsibility for the bombing, saying there were no U.S. targets near the neighborhood. But U.S. military officials in Qatar said that U.S. aircraft targeting Iraqi surface-to-air missile launchers in a residential area in Baghdad had fired precision-guided weapons at about the same time as the bombing, possibly causing civilian damage.

In the Shaab neighborhood, the carnage spoke of the helplessness and dread that has enveloped the capital.

"Who accepts this?" shouted George Said, a mechanic whose store was littered with spilled oil, a door torn from its hinges onto the floor. "Does America like this, does Bush like this, do the American people like this? How can they accept the destruction?"

Crowds poured into the muddy, congested streets, shouting, "We will sacrifice our blood and souls for you, Saddam."

But in private, some residents complained bitterly that the Iraqi military had trucked missiles and other weapons to a grass-and-mud clearing at the neighborhood's edge. One neighbor said the trucks moved in from 11 p.m. to dawn, their movements shrouded to a degree by a two-day sandstorm that Iraqis said was the fiercest in years. Four tents and military equipment remained there today, concealed in part by trenches and dozens of industrial-size spools for cable. Down the road were at least four antiaircraft guns.

The neighbor said he blamed "both sides" for the destruction that sent shattered glass cascading through his apartment. His refrigerator and television rested against the pockmarked wall, tossed across the room by the force of the blast. Flying debris injured his mother, father, brother and sister, all of whom lived together in a cramped, two-room apartment.

"We are the simple people who get hurt. The government doesn't get hurt, but we end up getting hurt," the 35-year-old resident said. The government "is responsible for the people. They should take care of the people."

It was a day of menace in Baghdad, a capital forced to contend with around-the-clock bombing, smoke billowing from burning oil trenches that has compelled some to flee, and a sandstorm that has convinced many that divine intervention rules their fate.

On the storm's second day, the city of more than 5 million was coated in a film of dust, blown in from Iraq's deserts. The sky turned from a blinding yellow at dawn to blood-red in the afternoon. A dusk-like brown was followed by an eerie orange at nightfall. An occasional vegetable stand provided the city's few glimpses of color in its onions, tomatoes, eggplant and oranges. Rain fell throughout the day, bathing Baghdad in mud.

Cars drove with their headlights on at noon, and street lights cast a faint glow over the city streets. Residents complained of sleeplessness, some saying they had started taking Valium to ease the anxiety brought by the storms and the bombing. Few in the capital predicted that the worst was over; even fewer were willing to predict what the next few weeks would bring.

Shaab today was their worst fears made plain.

U.S. forces have, on the whole, waged their air assault

on Baghdad with precision, targeting presidential palaces, government offices and intelligence headquarters since last week. At dawn, blasts shook the area that houses the Information Ministry, knocking Iraqi television off the air for several hours. But there have been errant strikes too, demolishing a student union building at Mustansiriya University, a laundry in a village outside Baghdad and clusters of homes in the neighborhoods of Adhimiya and Qadisiya.

In Shaab, the bombs struck at 11:30 a.m., a time that the streets, even in war, were crowded with mechanics, vendors of auto spare parts, customers at electric appliance stores and families sitting down to a late breakfast after a jarring night of bombing.

Residents said they heard the murmur of a bomber in a cloaked sky. Seconds later, the first explosion struck.

Abdel-Jabbar was in his workshop, putting together cardboard boxes. The blast collapsed the shop's entrance, showering the store with bricks and cinderblocks. He said the shock waves tossed cars and people several feet. One of them was Sattar, a 22-year-old friend repairing his car in the street. Sattar survived, Abdel-Jabbar said, but his legs were severed.

"Does he carry weapons of mass destruction?" Abdel-Jabbar shouted, as the sirens of ambulances, police cars and civil defense vehicles tried, in vain, to navigate traffic that had come to a standstill in the wrecked street. "Do his wife and children carry weapons of mass destruction?"

Next door, two workers had been scurrying around the Dulaimi Restaurant, preparing for lunchtime. Both were killed in an instant. The restaurant's red and blue tiles lay splintered on the sidewalk, plastic white tables and chairs were turned upside down, wires hung from the ceiling like a spider's web and its sign dangled overhead, giving perch to a bird.

Within moments, the second blast struck the other side of the street. Qais Sabah and his family of eight were sitting down to a breakfast of falafel, boiled eggs and bread. They jumped at the first explosion, then were thrown to the ground by the second.

Hours later, the 35-year-old day laborer looked out over the detritus of his house. A cracked porcelain plate that read "God" hung askew on the wall. On the sidewalk outside was the severed hand of Samad Rabai, 17, the owner of an appliance store.

"It's a crime against us," Sabah said. "There's nothing here to bomb."

Tareq Abdullah was making a halfhearted attempt to wash the dust off his white Lada sedan when the bombs struck. He was thrown several feet, then crawled to his car. He said he was desperate. His 4-year-old son, Ali, was still inside, screaming.

In the hospital, Abdullah lay in a bed with bandages covering wounds to his head, chest and both legs from flying debris. He had trouble hearing, his ears still ringing from the bomb's percussion. "I feel pain," he said, over and over.

Next to him, his brother Ahmed, wearing a soccer jersey smeared with dried blood, looked at the bed and started crying.

"Look at my brother," he said, shaking his head. "Look at my friends."

In another room, Alawi, the nickname given to young Ali by his relatives, lay in a bed with a bandage over his head. With deep brown eyes and the look of a young child struggling to make sense of disaster, he said the Americans were trying to kill his father. He pulled nervously on the threads of the blue-and-white blanket covering the cut on his shoulder, recounting his fear.

"But I'm not afraid anymore. I'm brave," he said meekly.

Hours after the attack, residents piled trucks with their belongings. One patriarch threw mattresses, red and pink blankets and pillows off a ledge to his children below, careful to keep their few belongings out of the mud and sewage. Another man carted a refrigerator, chairs, shelves and blue bedding in a pile along the street. Workers emptied a workshop of battered machinery, then slapped mortar on cinderblocks to build a wall across its door.

"We'll clean up," Sabah said. "We'll find our relatives. We have to go somewhere else. We have no place left."

A boy who was 'like a flower'

MARCH 31, 2003

BAGHDAD, Iraq, March 30—On a cold, concrete slab, a mosque caretaker washed the body of 14-year-old Arkan Daif for the last time.

With a cotton swab dipped in water, he ran his hand across Daif's olive corpse, dead for three hours but still glowing with life. He blotted the rose-red shrapnel wounds on the soft skin of Daif's right arm and right ankle with the poise of practice. Then he scrubbed his face scabbed with blood, left by a cavity torn in the back of Daif's skull.

The men in the Imam Ali mosque stood somberly waiting to bury a boy who, in the words of his father, was "like a flower." Haider Kathim, the caretaker, asked: "What's the sin of the children? What have they done?"

In the rituals of burial, the men and their families tried, futilely, to escape the questions that have enveloped so many lives here in fear and uncertainty. Beyond some neighbors, family, and a visitor, there were no witnesses; the funeral went unnoticed by a government that has eagerly escorted journalists to other wartime tragedies. Instead, Daif and two cousins were buried in the solitude of a dirt-poor, Shiite Muslim neighborhood near the city limits.

The boys were killed at 11 a.m. today when, as another relative recalled, "the sky exploded." Daif had been digging a trench in front of the family's concrete shack that could serve as a shelter during the bombing campaign that continues day and night. He had been working with Sabah Hassan, 16, and Jalal Talib, 14. The white-hot shrapnel cut down all three. Seven other boys were wounded.

The explosion left no crater, and residents of the Rahmaniya neighborhood struggled to pinpoint the source of the destruction. Many insisted they saw an airplane. Some suggested Iraqi antiaircraft fire had detonated a cruise missile in the air. Others suggested rounds from antiaircraft guns had fallen back to earth and onto their homes.

Whoever caused the explosion, the residents assigned

blame to the United States, insisting that without a war, they would be safe. "Who else could be responsible except the Americans?" asked Mohsin Hattab, a 32-year-old uncle of Daif.

"This war is evil. It's an unjust war," said Imad Hussein, a driver and uncle of Hassan. "They have no right to make war against us. Until now, we were sitting in our homes, comfortable and safe."

As he spoke, the wails of mourners pouring forth from homes drowned out his words. He winced, turning his head to the side. Then he continued. "God will save us," he said softly.

At the mosque, hours after the blast, Kadhim and another caretaker prepared Daif's body for burial—before sundown, as is Islamic custom.

Bathed in the soft colors of turquoise tiles, the room was hushed, as the caretakers finished the washing. They wrapped his head, his gaze fixed, with red and yellow plastic. They rolled the corpse in plastic sheeting, fastening it with four pieces of white gauze—one at each end, one around his knees and one around his chest.

Kadhim worked delicately, his gestures an attempt to bring dignity to the corpse. He turned Daif's body to the side and wrapped it in a white sheet, secured with four more pieces of gauze. Under their breaths, men muttered prayers, breaking the suffocating silence that had descended. They then moved toward the concrete slab and hoisted the limp body into a wood coffin.

"It's very difficult," said Kadhim, as the men closed the coffin.

On Friday, he had gone to another mosque, Imam Moussa Kadhim, to help bury dozens killed when a blast ripped through a teeming market in the nearby neighborhood of Shuala. The memories haunted him. He remembered the severed hands and heads that arrived at the Shiite mosque. He recalled bodies, even that of an infant, with gaping holes.

"It was awful and ugly," he said. "This is the first time I've ever seen anything like this."

In an open-air courtyard, the men set the coffin down on the stone floor of a mosque still under construction. In two rows, they lined up behind it, their shoes removed before them. Their lips moved in prayers practiced thousands of times.

"God is greatest," they repeated, their palms facing upward in supplication.

In the background, men discussed the war. In the repression and isolation that reigns in Iraq, rumors often serve as news, and the talk today was of carnage unleashed on a convoy taking the body of an 80-year-old woman to be buried in the southern city of Najaf, where U.S. forces are confronting Iraqi irregulars and soldiers.

For Shiite Muslims, Najaf is among their most sacred cities, housing the tomb of Ali, the son-in-law of the prophet Muhammad, whom Shiites regard as his rightful heir. Tradition has it that the dying Ali asked his followers to place his body on a camel and bury him wherever it first knelt; Najaf was the site. Millions of pilgrims visit each year, and devout Shiites will spend their life's savings for the blessings of being buried in the vast cemeteries that gird the city.

The woman from Rahmaniya never made it. Residents said U.S. forces attacked three cars, one carrying her body. It was another ignominy visited on the city, the men agreed. They insisted that infidels would never enter the city by force of arms. The U.S. siege of the city—its severity accentuated as rumors circulated—was an act of humiliation.

"It's a disgrace," said Hattab, one of Daif's uncles.

Hussein, another relative, echoed the words of others. "They didn't come to liberate Iraq," he said, "they came to occupy it."

In his words was a fear that strikes deep into the Iraqi psyche. Many worry that the U.S. invasion is a threat to their culture and traditions. They wonder if an occupation would obliterate what they hold dear, imposing an alien culture by force on a society that, in large part, remains deeply conservative and insulated.

"We don't want the Americans or British here. Our food is better than their food, our water is better than their water," he said.

With the prayers over, the men hoisted Daif's coffin over their heads. They left through the mosque's gray, steel gates and ventured into the desolate, dirt streets awash in trash. Some were barefoot and others wore sandals.

"There is no god but God," one man chanted. "There is no god but God," the pallbearers answered. Bombing on the horizon provided a refrain. The men crossed the street, past concrete and brick hovels, the Shiite flags of solid black, green, red and white flying overhead.

As they approached Daif's house, its door emblazoned with the names Muhammad and Ali, they were greeted with wails of women covered by black chadors. They screamed, waving their hands and shaking their heads. The cries drowned out the chants, as the coffin disappeared indoors. The despair poured out of the home, its windows shattered by the blast that killed Daif.

"My son! My son!" his mother, Zeineb Hussein, cried out. "Where are you now? I want to see your face!"

The men in Daif's family embraced each other, sobbing uncontrollably on their shoulders. Others cried into their hands. From within the house came the sounds of women methodically beating their chests in grief.

In the houses along the street, neighbors and relatives spoke of injustice—a resonant theme in the lives of Shiite Muslims, whose saints and centuries of theology are infused with examples of suffering and martyrdom.

"We're poor. We can't go anywhere else. What is the fault of the families here? Where's the humanity?" asked Abu Ahmed, a 53-year-old neighbor sitting in a home with three pictures of Ali and a painting of his son, Hussein. "I swear to God, we're scared."

Their talk was angry, and they were baffled.

If the Americans are intent on liberation, why are innocent people dying? If they want to attack the government, why do bombs fall on civilians? How can they have such formidable technology and make such tragic mistakes?

In Hussein's Iraq, with a 30-year political culture built on brutality, some were convinced the Americans were intent on vengeance for the setbacks they believed their forces were delivered in Basra and other southern Iraqi cities. Others, in moments of striking candor, pleaded for the United States and Britain to wage war against their government, but spare the people.

"If they want to liberate people, they can kick out the government, not kill innocent civilians," one relative said. "The innocent civilians are not in business with the government. We're living in our houses."

Before dusk, Daif's coffin was carried from his house. It was set on the back of a white pickup truck headed for the cemetery. As it drove away, kicking up clouds of dirt, some of the neighbors and relatives shouted, "God be with you." Other men waved, a gesture so casual that it suggested the strength of their faith, that they would eventually be reunited with Daif.

Hattab, the uncle, looked on at the departing coffin. His eyes were red, and his face was drawn.

"He has returned to God," he said. "It's God's wish."

A conversation with
Anthony Shadid

JANET WEAVER: I want to start with your thinking as you went into Iraq. Now you'd been to Iraq twice before, is that correct?

ANTHONY SHADID: That's right. Once with the Associated Press in 1998 and again with *The Boston Globe* in 2002.

So you went in this time just as the war was starting?

I think I got there about 10 days to two weeks before the war, and I went in with the intention of just covering the war. That was my goal. There was a lot of concern at the time whether the *Post* would pull us out like a lot of other news organizations were, and that definitely was my most pressing concern at that time, maybe even more pressing than just trying to get a sense of the story. I felt strongly that it's part of the responsibility of journalists to have eyes and ears everywhere, not only with the troops, but in Baghdad and anywhere it's possible.

At what point did the *Post* say it was not going to pull people out?

It was definitely a last-minute thing. Most people pulled out maybe the day before the bombing started, and I had a conversation with my editor early that morning just pleading my case to stay in Baghdad. Obviously they were concerned—rightfully so—and I think at that point we put it on a 12-hour basis. Every 12 hours we'd re-assess where things were at, and within 24 hours the war started and there wasn't any way to get out.

What other things were going on as you were getting ready for the eventuality that the bombing was going to start?

I think what definitely dominated those few days before

the war was logistics, in every sense of the word. Is the security threat too great that we do need to pull out? I felt it wasn't, but there was a lot of analyzing and thinking about that, trying to figure out what you could do in a worst-case scenario. Then another part of logistics was just preparation. We expected electricity to go out. Do we have fallback plans for that? We expected food to be hard to get. Do we have supplies? Water? We were pretty much preparing for a siege in a lot of ways.

To be honest, the week before, I think journalism was secondary. It was just trying to figure out how we would get by. You're not just dealing with the war situation, but you're also talking about the government that was pretty nasty and didn't want us to have our cell phones, one that wanted to stay around us as we worked at our computers. We were really trying to find two, three, four fallback plans that would enable us to file every day.

The last thing was what kind of approach we wanted to take toward the war, and obviously that evolved as time went on.

This may be the next question, but I'll just go ahead and mention it. I think it was the first day of the war, and I heard advice from my editors that I thought was just seminal. One editor, Ed Cody, said, "You're there; say what it's like. Bring an authority to your voice that you wouldn't maybe have otherwise." And another editor, David Hoffman, said to understand the forces from below; understand social forces; understand what's happening to the city. And, finally, Phil Bennett said to really focus on sentiment—and this was after I'd actually written a couple of stories—but Phil said, "Those sentiments you're exploring may be one of the defining qualities of this war and don't let go of that."

Taken together, it did start to shape the approach I wanted to take. You could look at covering the war as a war, or you could look at covering the war as a backdrop. In other words, the war's a backdrop to a capital that's under siege. [I'm] trying to understand the city and people's lives with the war as the backdrop.

So it wasn't that you went in with this approach in mind. It evolved as things were starting and as you were having conversations with Washington?

As I said, I felt very strongly that it was my responsibility as a journalist to be in Baghdad as this unfolded. I felt that it was even worth taking some risks to make sure that happened. Part of that was a determination to humanize the conflict. I think often, as war correspondents, we struggle with readers who are just inundated with the violence and strife and chaos, and I think they get deadened to a certain degree to what we're reporting. To me, the way around that is to humanize the people you cover, to make their lives understandable, to make their lives resonate somehow. And that was my intention going into Baghdad, to do that. How I would do that was something that definitely evolved. Do we try to understand the city? Do we try to understand its people? Do we cover the war as a war? The tactic is something that evolved over the first few days of the conflict.

Talk a little bit about that tactic. I know you did some work beforehand trying to make contact with people through expatriates and through other sources you have, but how did you get to some of the people you spent time with?

That was definitely the toughest thing, and again, because it wasn't just covering a war, it was also dealing with a government that could be exceedingly difficult. I had a couple of lucky breaks. One, the minder, the escort who was assigned to me, became an ally, to put it bluntly. There was a certain bond we created as the war unfolded, and just as you would cultivate a source when you're reporting in Washington, I had the same approach toward this minder during the war. I knew that he was going to enable me to get to things that I wouldn't be able to get to otherwise. That gave me a certain freedom of movement that I think was so crucial in trying to get to those stories. To get the subjects themselves was also difficult. I was able to do a little bit of work ahead of time on that, relying on people who I knew in the States who had relatives in Baghdad, NGOs [non-governmental organizations] in Baghdad that knew people, and then people I had met or befriended before the war with whom there was a certain element of trust.

I think trust might have been the biggest challenge

because no one trusted anybody, and even to this day in Baghdad, you really deal with this lack of trust in almost every relationship. So how do you create even just a certain element of trust, even just a degree of trust, that you can maybe break through the rhetoric and the kind of clichés that you heard so often before the war?

I think these stories proved to be the most interesting and the most compelling in a lot of ways. There are three that come to mind. One was entered in the contest, and that was of the family. And there's another one in which I profiled a woman, a mother, who'd sent her son off to war. Then there's a third about a doctor whose son I knew in the States. All three gave very, very different perspectives, but perspectives that struck me. I actually revisited them a year later for an anniversary story that I just finished, and it struck me how much those perspectives on what they had told me at that time held true a year later. What they had said to me they still believed at this point, and I thought that was in some way—I don't want to say vindicating, because it wasn't about me—but it was refreshing, I guess, or reassuring to hear that it turned out that there was a certain element of trust that we created.

The family story is such a wonderful piece. It's interesting to me to read that story as an American and get a sense of what one family is doing to prepare for catastrophe. It resonates in a different way since Sept. 11, after we've all been told to get plastic sheeting and water but then nobody here really follows through with those instructions.

And I'll tell you, it was a tough story because I had been invited to lunch at their house, and it wasn't made clear that I was going as a reporter. I don't think I pulled out my notebook for the first hour or two. I was rigorously trying to commit to memory everything I was seeing, because in the words they were saying to me there was a certain elegance, I think, that people have in times of conflict, in times of strife. Almost everything they said to me was just incredibly elegant.

Finally after an hour or two, I did broach the subject. I said I'd like to write about it, and we reached an agreement that I couldn't mention their names but that I was free to write whatever they said. Over that day I think most of the conversation was political at a certain level and surprisingly so. I mean, I was hearing things that I probably hadn't heard that much in Baghdad. I wanted this story to be about a family, not about politics, not about Saddam, not about the war, but instead, how a family fares in this conflict. So it was funny, when the family read the story, they were so surprised that it wasn't about the politics they had been discussing. But to me it wasn't politics. It was life. And that was the thing I wanted to understand and then report on.

I think some of the elements are just so human. I love the part when the son says they have a stockpile of food for three months and his wife says no, the men eat too much; they would never make it three months. It's the humor in that moment while also knowing that there's a tension behind that humor, because it's probably true that the food wouldn't hold out that long.

It's true. In fact, going back to visit that family, that son and his wife actually left the country. They went into exile this summer. It was kind of bittersweet. They survived the war, but they didn't stay in Iraq to survive the aftermath.

It's wonderful that you've been able to keep track of them and get to go back a year later.
The nominating letter for the entry talks about your daily routine as a drive-around approach of getting out and looking for the story of the day. I think all general assignment reporters can relate to that approach, just not under wartime conditions. Was that the best method for finding out what was going on?

Well, again, it was that idea that you could stick close to the war as a story, and there were plenty of news conferences to keep you busy, plenty of these tours that would take you out to places, or you could try to break away from that. You're taking a great risk as a daily journalist in breaking away from that because you may miss something. I was rooming with the Associated Press reporter and that was a great crutch in the sense that he would share stuff and he would keep me informed and keep me posted, and he did it as a friend rather than as a colleague.

But in driving around, the idea was to just keep looking, looking, looking. In a story in which information is such a commodity, almost everything you see becomes a detail for the story. It becomes a paragraph of color. It becomes a way to describe the atmosphere. I remember before the bombing at Shaab ["In a Moment, Lives Get Blown Apart"], we were just driving around and the sky was changing from blinding yellow to blood red in the afternoon, and then at other times it was kind of a brown, almost like at dusk. And then I noticed a vegetable stand. It just struck me that the vegetable stand was the only color in the city being overwhelmed by dusk. It ended up being only a few sentences in a story and just the very little idea that something so inconsequential as a vegetable stand somehow helped you describe what the city looked like at that point.

Driving around was when we stumbled onto one of the more dramatic stories that was entered into the contest, and that was the funeral of the young boy. We were asking about where one bombing had happened, and we were asking some guy on the corner of the street and he said, "Which bombing? The one that just happened about 30 minutes ago?" I'm like, "Oh, my God." So we went to where the bombing had happened. And then when I found it, it wasn't like the other bombings I had covered where you had 20, 30 dead, just this scale of carnage. It was three boys, and so I knew you could write it several ways. You could write it as a spot story. You could write it as what happened in this neighborhood. Or you could try to understand death in a different way. What I wanted to do through that story was to understand the ritual of death, and pretty soon, I think probably within a half hour of getting there, I wanted to follow it from the moment the boy died until the moment he was buried and just describe what happened, without being too dramatic, without letting people yell so much that it kind of overwhelms the ritual itself. I wanted to describe that ritual and try to humanize it at a certain level, and so that's what I ended up doing, just following in almost the mundane way from step one to step two to step three until his burial.

How did the people you were reporting on react to your presence for this intensely personal thing?

In these types of stories, there's a little more tension in the relationship, because I had to be very aggressive in the reporting. It was AP training in a lot of ways—I worked for the AP for 10 years—I had to get names and ages and I was insistent on that. To me, it's the very basic element of turning this person into a real person in that story. And ages are not something the people necessarily know in Iraq. When you ask them their age, they'll sit there and think for a few seconds and then they'll say the year they were born, and you'll ask the day and they don't know. So even that becomes a little bit of a hassle. I would always ask people what they ate. When a certain thing happened, I want to know what they were eating or what they were doing at the moment that something happened.

A lot of times I'd say the color's more important than the quote, and so questions would seem bizarre to them a lot of times, but these were details I thought would be the only way to bring them to life to a reader, and I had to be very insistent on getting them. I also was traveling without a photographer, so a lot of times in the reporting I would try to almost be like a photographer trying to capture the scenes. So in the situation with the funeral, for instance, when I would fade into the background, there was usually no problem. They're so overwhelmed by the grief of the moment that I think they ignored me. When I had to bring myself into the reporting, when I actually had to ask them questions, I think they found it difficult to be honest because the questions were in some ways very bizarre. Why would somebody want this kind of detail? Why would somebody want to know such facts that seem so inconsequential at a moment of such tragedy? It was difficult.

You feel awkward but you do understand that if you don't ask these questions, then you'll never be able to convey the humanity of that moment.

As you're talking about asking these kinds of questions that people might consider strange or weird, it

makes me think about the fact that you were able to speak Arabic. How big of an advantage do you think that was?

It's hard to say—I have been in situations in Afghanistan or Iran in which I had to use a translator, and I've never found it impossible. I found that you can get what you want even with a translator. But I think in a situation like Iraq, where trust does matter, because I was speaking Arabic and I am Arab-American, there was a certain shared culture or—this is going to sound strange—but a shared kind of historical memory. They knew that I knew something and that they could start from a different departure point. I guess the best way to describe it is that it does introduce me to a very small degree of trust, but even a small degree of trust at that time was incredibly important for reporting.

So you can get the job done with a translator, but there may be some issues of trust and maybe some subtleties in what people tell you and even what you think to ask.

Right. And even something almost as superficial as religious invocations. I'm always struck by how Arabic is a language at once formal and personal. Sayings that to most people seem almost clichéd, and they're said very often, almost in any situation. You use this phrase, but at the same time that phrase becomes so personal and it becomes so reassuring and comforting in a way. And the fact that you're even understanding those phrases and translating almost directly, I thought, was a way to introduce humanity into the situation.

You wrote 24 front-page stories in 21 days. You were telling me before we began the interview about how tired you were, how you were writing from a point of exhaustion. As a reader of your stories, I found that they wove together. It's almost like chapters of a book when you read them. Did you have a sense that that was what was happening as you were doing it?

I wish I were smart enough to deal with it and do it that

way, but I'm not. I did have an approach that I wanted to develop throughout the war, and I didn't want to do certain things with the reporting and writing. But often it was luck. It was luck that I was able to find these people or situations that could bring something to the story that might not have been there otherwise. But exhaustion was always a factor. I was sitting with the *Los Angeles Times* reporter one night, I think it was 3 or 4 in the morning, and we'd both finished filing, and we said if this war goes on for two months, we can't make it. I mean, it was grueling.

On a typical day, you try to get up by 9 or 10 if you could and then you just go all day. You come back to your room at maybe 6, 7, or 8 and try to formulate what you want to do with the story. I always outline stories, and I would go through my notes pretty relentlessly because I didn't want to miss anything. I often spend as much time outlining stories as I do writing them, and sometimes I wouldn't have my lead done until 11 at night and then probably not have the story finished until 2 or 3 in the morning. Then you talk to your editor, do the editing, and then start another day. It was like that day after day. We lived on canned tuna and canned cheese, which I'd never seen before and I don't think I'll ever eat again. I was sick probably a third of the time, dealing with the exhaustion. If it wasn't for adrenaline, I probably wouldn't have been able to make it through the whole time.

What was your relationship like with the desk in Washington? What kind of conversations were you having with the people back home and how able were they to give you direction from that distance?

I had just been with the *Post* for a month, so I had very little institutional knowledge of the newsroom, and that was intimidating at a certain level. But the assistant managing editor, Phil Bennett, pretty much took charge on the stories I was writing out of Baghdad. And I say this without any flattery: He's a brilliant editor. He was able to take the stories, and even with the exhaustion, he was able to see what should come out. He was often very good at taking out the nut graph, for instance, seeing that the narrative itself stood and it didn't need to have a nut graph, and that, I thought, was a brilliant move.

An editor who'll take out a nut graph?

Exactly. It was brilliant.

He is brilliant.

Phil was always incredibly reassuring. It was probably the best experience I've ever had with the desk on any one story because there was a lot of trust they gave me and I had a lot of trust in what they were doing with the stories, and it worked out well in the end.

You've been covering the Middle East for a long time and this was not the first time you'd been in a situation that was dangerous.

The year before I had been in the West Bank, in Ramallah, as a reporter for *The Boston Globe,* and I was shot in my right shoulder there. To be honest, the fear I felt in the West Bank was greater than the fear I felt in Baghdad.

Really?

Yeah. I'm not sure exactly how to describe it, but to me journalists are a target in the West Bank, and I never felt that we were ever targeted specifically in Baghdad. At the end of the war, a U.S. tank had fired a shell at the Palestine Hotel and killed two journalists. But before that, I never felt that we were in any great danger as journalists. It was always in the wrong place at the wrong time kind of thing. I mean, not that that didn't create fear—I was anxious throughout the conflict—but I didn't feel like I would avoid doing things because of the fear of danger.

How do you manage the fear? Do you ever think, "Boy, I'm really scared right now?" Are those conscious, front-of-the-mind thoughts, or is it something you try to put in the back of your head?

Most of the time I did try to keep it in the back of my head, especially because the reporting was so grueling. It was a new type of reporting in a way, because you had so little time and you had to produce so much that you really tried to find an economy of reporting. I remember it struck me a few times as I was going about work during the day that I was trying to write the stories as I reported them. It was like I was almost casting two or three paragraphs at a time as I was going through the reporting, because I knew I didn't have the time to do more.

In some situations, you couldn't stay longer than 15 or 20 minutes. You had to know exactly what you wanted for your story and then move on. So as I was reporting, I would try to create as much as possible, within the space concerns that we have as daily reporters, small narratives within that story. I would try to develop characters, even if it's in two or three paragraphs, at least develop them a little bit. But you also have 15 or 20 minutes with those people and so you have to be so specific, often very aggressive and more blunt than you'd want to be, just to be able to capture that detail. And I think that was the toughest thing, more so than the danger maybe, was trying to balance everything at once and know that you were going to have to write this story in six or eight hours and you have a lot to get done in that time.

So I imagine that's something you're always thinking about: "What am I missing?"

Right, exactly. In fact, since then I've felt myself almost relaxing because I can go back to these people. At the time, you couldn't. Because of that, and because of the exhaustion, you had to write very directly and very simply just because you're too tired to develop anything more complicated. I think that in the end it worked well for the stories, but I think it did kind of give the stories a tone that they might not have had otherwise.

Do you know what happened to your minder?

Oh, yeah, definitely. He's one of my best friends.

So you're still in contact?

Oh, yeah. It's actually a sad story in a way. He stayed with me afterward and worked as my fixer, and we had a great year, got stories that I don't think we would have ever been able to do if we weren't together, and he did become one of my dearest friends. His house was bombed last month by people who accused him of working with the Americans. He had to relocate his family.

I'm going to write a book later this year, and I'm thinking about how that relationship was probably the most complicated relationship I've ever had. He started off as a minder, he became sort of a fixer and an assistant, and he ends up a dear friend. In the oddest of ways, he was probably one of the best experiences that came out of the war.

What's your book going to be about?

It's going to be about Baghdad, basically understanding Baghdad before the war, the war, and then after the war, and part of the story is following some of the families I met before the war, during the war, and how their lives evolved over the conflict, or in its aftermath. A person remarked to me, and I'm not going to get his quote exactly right, but he said to me something like, "Baghdad is more of an idea than a reality." And it struck me so much because I know it's true, especially in the Arab world. When you say the word "Baghdad," it evokes something that today's city doesn't even come close to. I was trying to describe it to some person, and I said it's kind of given majesty by its memory. And so, just understanding Baghdad and what Baghdad has become or what it was, I think that's going to drive the book in a lot of ways.

You've had a lot of experiences in the Middle East. What's changed for you going through the experience in the war and then the aftermath in Baghdad? Has that informed your thinking about the region at all or has it changed any of the impressions or ideas you had formed from previous years of reporting?

One of the ironies of the aftermath is that, during the war and what followed, we were often told that Iraq would be an engine for change in the rest of the region. As a reporter over there for the last year, as time goes by, Iraq becomes much more familiar to me. Having spent time elsewhere in the Arab world, I see that Iraq is more apt to become much more like the rest of the Arab world than the Arab world is being changed by Iraq. And I think maybe there are two elements to that. One is that what I saw after the war were these arcs of change that took maybe years or even decades to play out in other parts of the Arab world. They played out within weeks and months in Iraq. I think the other thing was how powerful the sentiment of religion became in Iraq, especially when—you know people there refer to the war as the collapse, they use the word *suqut* in Arabic, which means "collapse" or "fall," and I've always been struck with the use of that word because I think it signals an end but not necessarily a beginning.

How did your family feel about your work?

It hasn't been easy. I think it's created a lot of stress for them, and I think the worst part of the job is that you know you can take care of yourself, but you can't really take care of how other people are worrying about you. My conversation daily with my father is, "When are you leaving?" That's all he can talk about. To the point that during the war, I had to say, "I'm going to quit calling if you don't quit asking about when I'm leaving." That's been definitely the most difficult part of the experience.

Anything that I haven't asked you that I should have asked you?

There was one thing I was going to mention: the idea of how chaotic the reporting becomes, and how you tend to focus on what is happening to you in the act of reporting. I think every reporter does this, but it's intensified in a time of conflict. But at the end of the day, readers don't really want to know about that. That's not the reader's problem, the reader's concern. So trying to get past all that and bring some kind of order, some kind of intimacy to a story, that was a real tough challenge.

That's an interesting point and something that has a lot of meaning for people who are not necessarily in places where things are blowing up, but maybe in a

city hall somewhere in the Midwest just trying to negotiate through the process of translating the bureaucracy and dealing with people who don't want you to know things. We sometimes do get so wound up in our own process.

And it's often thought that the only way to bring that through a story is to introduce yourself into the story. But that's the last thing I wanted to do during the war because I didn't feel I was part of the story. I never got the sense that was what readers wanted to know about.

As a reader, Anthony, I can always feel you there in the story, but I feel you there as the eyes of the reader and not as a character.

Yeah. I really feel strongly about keeping myself out. We're not the story and that is something you always keep in mind, especially in a time like that.

Writers' Workshop

Talking Points

1) Anthony Shadid talks about how important it was for him to build trust with those he was interviewing—and to do it quickly, in a war zone. In the story of the family, for instance, he spent several hours talking to the family and listening to them before he took out his notebook. How important do you think it is to build trust with those you are covering? What methods do you use to build trust with ongoing sources? With people you interview during breaking stories?

2) Shadid did his reporting in a war zone, where physical danger was always present. But every journalist has to face some kind of fear at some point. What are the things that scare you as a reporter? Why? How do you conquer the fear?

Assignment Desk

1) Even in a war zone, Shadid took time to outline every story before he wrote it. Sometimes, he said, it took longer to outline the story than it did to write it. Before writing your next deadline story, prepare an outline. How does outlining change the writing process for you?

2) Shadid's stories are rich in images and detail. He says he tried to think like a photographer, capturing scenes as he reported. Sometimes, he said, color is more important to a story than capturing a good quote. Are you observing as you report or listening for the quote? Experiment with writing descriptions of scenes and individuals that show what is happening rather than telling through quotes.

3) Shadid had worked for the *Post* for only a short time before he went to Baghdad. He was dealing with editors he did not know well. Yet he says his relationship with his editors contributed strongly to his success. Before your next assignment, sit down with your editor to talk about your story. What are your editor's expectations? What questions would she ask if she were the reporter? After the reporting, debrief with your editor. Ask her what you are missing. Does she have ideas for how to write the story? How does working with the editor before and after reporting the story change the editing process for you?

Somini Sengupta

Finalist, Deadline Reporting

Based in Dakar, Senegal, Somini Sengupta covers 22 countries in West and Central Africa. She was born in Calcutta, India, in 1967. She was raised in midwestern Canada and southern California and graduated with honors from the University of California at Berkeley with degrees in English and development studies. She is the winner of the 2003 George Polk Award for foreign reporting.

Sengupta was a finalist in the inaugural year of ASNE's Distinguished Writing on Diversity category in 2000, writing about Chinese mothers in New York who send their children back to China.

In her story, "The Haves and Have-Nots Reside on Both Sides of Liberian Capital," Sengupta takes readers on a jarring, matter-of-fact tour of the bloodshed, chaos, and complex realities at play in a Liberian city split down the middle by war.

The haves and have-nots reside on both sides of Liberian capital

AUGUST 6, 2003

MONROVIA, Liberia, Aug. 5—Rebel-held Monrovia's only hospital is inside a brewery. Its operating table is a long wooden desk. The surgeon, who cleans shrapnel wounds, extracts bullets and ties up intestines punctured by gunshots, is a nurse who used to work at a maternity clinic. This afternoon, a patient with a fist-sized wound in his arm was howling in pain. The hospital is almost out of painkillers, as well as medications for its 50 cholera patients.

Divided by a series of bridges, the rebel- and government-held halves of this capital compose a bleak landscape of haves and have-nots.

One side, controlled by the besieged Liberian president, Charles G. Taylor, has little food or fuel, but a sufficient supply of drugs and doctors, thanks to international aid agencies. The other side, held by the rebel Liberians United for Reconciliation and Democracy, has no drugs or doctors but plenty of food and fuel, with the Free Port of Monrovia under rebel control. (Journalists got a glimpse of the rebel half today by walking across a bridge, waving a white T-shirt.)

This afternoon, the commander of what is to be a 3,250-member West African "interposition force" sent here to stop the violence on both sides, crossed over to visit the rebel zone. The commander, Brig. Gen. Festus Okonkwo, said nothing about how quickly his forces would take control of the Free Port. The rebels invited aid agencies to remove their shipments from the port, but said they would not leave it until Mr. Taylor not only relinquishes power, but leaves the country.

"Resign and leave Liberia. Then we'll release the port," said the rebel chief of staff, Gen. A. Seyeh Sheriff, after meeting with the commander of the peacekeeping force.

Much of the rebel zone was a wasteland today. Grenades and bullets had punched holes in the buildings. Roofs were gone. A dry goods warehouse was still smoldering from a recent rocket attack. A bloated body lay in a puddle on the main road. The wind blew the stench of death.

And yet, at a roadside market in the rebel zone on this day, chicken and beef were for sale, luxuries not seen on the other side. Two cups of rice could be had for 15 Liberian dollars, or 30 American cents. On the other side, even when rice can be found, it costs 10 times as much. Spaghetti, canned meat, toothpaste and sodas— all shipped in to the port—were abundant at the market. On the government side, there is little more than potato greens, cornmeal and hot peppers.

Earlier in the day, as foreign journalists toured the area, people poured out into the streets, shouting and clapping. "We want peace, no more war," they chanted, just as their counterparts on the other side have been chanting.

At the sight of visitors, the rebel fighters could not stop firing their guns in the air.

"They are rejoicing," one of their commanders, Brig. Gen. Sekou Kamara, otherwise known as Dragon Master, said, in an effort to offer solace. He wore a United States Army uniform, with a name tag that read "Hage."

This afternoon, soldiers who had been tossing grenades and spraying each other with machine-gun fire for the last 16 days, met in the middle of the bullet-strewn Old Bridge. They shook hands. They chatted. The rebel boys returned to their side, Kalashnikov rifles dangling from their shoulders, smiles from their lips.

From rebel headquarters, meanwhile, came threatening words from Gen. Sheriff, the rebel chief of staff, a man missing a couple of teeth and wearing a red beret and gold-rimmed glasses. He said he would storm the Executive Mansion if Mr. Taylor, the rebels' sworn enemy, did not leave the country.

"I will move on him," Gen. Sheriff told reporters. "I will attack him militarily."

Bluster aside, his words pointed up the fragility of the so-called cease-fire.

From the rebel point of view, peace depends on what the Liberian president decides to do. Mr. Taylor, who waged a seven-year rebel insurgency before becoming president in 1997, has vowed to step down Monday at midday, but said nothing about when he will leave Liberia.

His aides have suggested recently that he would not leave, unless a war crimes indictment against him was dropped; an independent United Nations-backed tribunal has charged him with crimes against humanity in connection with the war in neighboring Sierra Leone.

Mr. Taylor has already accepted an offer of asylum in Nigeria. The Bush administration, which has allocated $10 million for peacekeeping in Liberia but stopped short of promising troops, has made his exile a condition for any direct military involvement in Liberia. The Pentagon has sent three ships to the coast of Liberia, but many Liberians, on both the government and rebel sides, have all but given up on American assistance anyway.

Rebel commanders today shepherded visiting journalists through their territory, eager to show off their magnanimity. They brought out refreshments by the caseload and crowded into a small office in their headquarters to present their top officers, among them an assistant chief of staff for planning, a logistics chief and someone in charge of records.

They showed reporters territory that their enemies had claimed to control earlier this week. They tooted their horns as they drove the journalists through busy neighborhoods, and people lined up along the streets to cheer.

"Are we harassing these people?" A. Sekou Fofana, the rebels' deputy secretary general for civilian administration, mused.

Asked about his group's political ideology, Mr. Fofana said simply, "Our intention is to clear the land, remove Taylor."

The rebel commanders said that they had no idea what was in the port and that their job was only to secure it. Curiously, goods normally stored at the port were visible all over the streets, including pickup trucks with United Nations logos, with standard relief blankets piled in the back.

The commanders made a show of disciplining their rowdy rank and file, at one point beating a soldier with the butt of a rifle for firing in the air, at another, trying to punish looters who were carting away cases of food from a shuttered store.

"No monkey," they yelled, issuing orders to behave. (They also politely requested that photographers refrain from taking pictures of child soldiers.)

Tempers ran high. All transgressors, including those blocking traffic or driving too slowly, had guns pointed in their faces.

Food was in abundance and at bargain-basement prices. Virtually nonexistent were medicines and medical staff members to care for the wounded and ill.

Patients lay on relief blankets on the floor of the makeshift hospital at the Monrovia Brewery. Since the July 19 attack by rebels, the nurses running the hospital said they had treated 189 soldiers and 950 civilians. Fifty-seven civilians and 7 soldiers had been dead on arrival, a stark snapshot of who pays the price of this power struggle.

A new volunteer organization had emerged, buoyed by the idea of swapping food from the rebel side for medicine from the other side. Most had family on the other side, and had only heard the worst about how people were faring there.

"People are dying of hunger, bombs and bullets," said C-Musa Sheriff, a church administrator in the rebel zone. "We can't control the bombs and bullets, but we can do something about the hunger. We can't be complacent."

At times today it was difficult to distinguish the fighters on this side of the bridge from those on the other side. They wore the same clothes, the same wigs. They carried the same weapons. (Fighters on this side have a penchant for spray-painting their guns.) Neither side seemed to have any purpose beyond defeating the enemy. Both sides said they were tired of fighting.

One soldier, Emmanuel Weah, wearing dirty overalls and worn soccer cleats, described how he came to this side of the bridge. Last February, he was captured by government forces and sent to fight. Then he was captured by rebels and sent to a training camp for three weeks and then sent to fight. He said he found his former commander and had him executed.

Lessons Learned

BY SOMINI SENGUPTA

Which bridge? That was the question on our minds. We were two reporters and four photographers from the British and American press. It was a gray, rainy morning, like every other morning in wartime Liberia. There was a lull in the fighting. The two bridges in the heart of the capital, Monrovia, were empty.

For more than two weeks, the foreign press corps had more or less been trapped inside the half of the city held by troops loyal to the beleaguered Liberian warlord-turned-president, Charles G. Taylor. It was time to see the other half, held by his rebel enemies. The only reliable way to do so was to cross, by foot, what had become the war's final front line.

The decision to be made this morning was whether to walk across the Old Bridge—shorter, narrower, easier to see from one end to the other—or the New Bridge—longer, wider, with a concrete barrier on each side to shield ourselves from bullets, should they fly by, which they did with unnerving frequency in Monrovia in the summer of 2003.

For no particularly good reason, the Old Bridge won. We persuaded Taylor's soldiers to keep their guns quiet as we made our way across a carpet of bullet-casings. I had already called a commander on the other side and asked him to ask his soldiers on the bridge to do the same. He offered his blessing, but whether it would actually reach them, or whether they would obey, remained a mystery: I had learned by now that the chain of command in West African warfare had some weak links.

The choice to cross that bridge that morning was a decision every reporter had to make for herself, weighing risks and rewards, consulting with colleagues, and most importantly, asking, "Does this make sense for the story?" It would be foolish and fruitless, in my view, to have made that decision simply based on the logic of being first. We are not cowboys.

Decisions like these must be made on the basis of the

facts before you. But there's also something less tangible: your own gut. If your gut tells you you shouldn't do it, you probably shouldn't.

When we crossed the bridge that morning, we saw that the gunmen were just as skinny on the rebel side as they were on the government side—and, apparently, just as stoned. One of them silently sucked anchovies out of a tin can as he led us past a bloated corpse and through winding, muddy alleys, en route to a meeting with his leaders.

The rebel faction, Liberians United for Reconciliation and Democracy (L.U.R.D.), was all too happy to see the foreign press. They led us on what Rory Carroll, a colleague from a British newspaper, *The Guardian*, aptly described as a *Mad Max* tour of rebel-land.

We would see only what they wanted us to see. If there had been rebel atrocities, no civilian with any sense of self-preservation would talk to us about them. We would be chaperoned through the neighborhoods by L.U.R.D.'s self-described administrator for civilian affairs, a man who honked his horn to encourage the onlookers to cheer and clap, which they did, perhaps for our benefit, perhaps out of heartfelt desire.

Our visit that first morning seemed to enliven the L.U.R.D. rank and file, too. High as kites, they gleefully shot their rifles in the air. One of their commanders told us it was a gesture of welcome. Another asked us, politely, not to take too many pictures of the child soldiers. I made sure to include these details in the story. Sometimes our presence changes the dynamics altogether; it makes people do or say things they otherwise wouldn't. It would have been misleading to suggest that we were simply flies on the wall recording life in the rebel zone.

We marched back across the bridge before sundown. The story poured out quickly that night at the hotel.

One final note on making choices. One can be rightly criticized for covering conflict in Africa at the expense of other kinds of stories. And yet to not cover conflict—and later, its aftermath—would be to ignore an elementary fact. Those places we Americans can barely identify on the map, those places we grow weary of associating with famine and frightful wars—people live there. People who eat and defecate and make love and have dreams. People like us.

David Sanger, White House correspondent

The New York Times
Team Deadline News Reporting

The space shuttle *Columbia* blasted into the Earth's upper atmosphere in the lazy hours of a Saturday morning in February 2003. Within minutes, its fragile outer shell, having suffered a devastating breach upon takeoff, peeled away. Then *Columbia* disintegrated, showering the southwestern United States with circuit boards and rivet-studded panels, with engine parts and the battered remains of seven astronauts.

It would be the second loss of a shuttle in 17 years, and *The New York Times* had an experienced reporting team to cover it. Led by White House correspondent David Sanger and veteran science writer William Broad, part of the team that helped the *Times* win a 1987 Pulitzer Prize for coverage of the investigation into the space shuttle *Challenger* explosion, the *Times* set about understanding the cause and impact of the tragedy.

Reporters were dispatched to Nacogdoches, a Texas town near the Louisiana border where much of the debris landed, and to central Florida, where the *Columbia* crew had planned a safe return. The *Times* also brought to bear on the story what Sanger called "the great university of *The New York Times*," writers and editors with deep expertise in matters of science, space, and the oft-embattled NASA.

Sanger wrote the lead story, presenting a picture of human loss, a troubled space agency, and a shocked and jittery nation coming to grips with new grief. Broad, working with veteran reporter James Glanz, called upon sources he built covering the *Challenger* investigation and NASA. They pieced together the possible causes for *Columbia*'s breakup and offered a prescient analysis on deadline.

Atlanta bureau chief David Halbfinger and reporter Rich Oppel Jr. wrote from Nacogdoches. Their story told of a small town thrust into an international spotlight when tragedy rained down on a sunny winter morning. It captured the confusion and dawning horror as people heard the boom of re-entry, saw the debris, and came to understand what it all meant.

Together, the stories combine to tell a political, scientific, and mechanical story that never loses sight of the people who died in the sky and those on the ground who mourn them.

—Keith Woods

[*The Jesse Laventhol Prize for Deadline News Reporting by a team, given this year to The New York Times and The Boston Globe, is funded by a gift from David Laventhol, a former Times-Mirror executive, in honor of his father.*]

Shuttle breaks up, 7 dead; 'Roger,' and then silence

FEBRUARY 2, 2003

By David E. Sanger

WASHINGTON, Feb. 1—The space shuttle *Columbia* broke up this morning on re-entry into the earth's atmosphere, killing all seven astronauts on board and sending fiery debris over Texas in the second loss of a space shuttle in 17 years.

There was no immediate explanation of what caused the disintegration of the oldest shuttle in NASA's fleet, but there were some tantalizing clues. By late this afternoon, space agency engineers were describing a cascading series of failures of sensors on the left side of the craft.

That led to speculation that some kind of structural damage took place—perhaps caused by insulation that fell loose when the *Columbia* lifted off 16 days ago, perhaps from some other cause—that triggered a catastrophic failure about 9 a.m. Eastern time. But at a news conference, NASA officials said that had been analyzed and found not to be a concern.

The disaster occurred roughly 40 miles above Earth as the shuttle slipped into the netherworld between outer space and the upper atmosphere, just as it was slowing to 12,500 miles an hour and was minutes from its destination, the Kennedy Space Center in Florida.

Yet as the countdown clock at the landing site in Florida reached zero at 9:16 a.m., with an eerie silence and no sign of the shuttle, flaming debris was already falling in East Texas, and then in Louisiana.

Just minutes before the spaceship was lost, flight specialists in Houston had been communicating with the crew, talking about tire pressure on the *Columbia*. Nothing appeared wrong. Then Mission Control in Houston said, "We did not copy your last."

"Roger, uh ____" came the reply from the shuttle, then there was silence, and then just static.

The loss revived a long-simmering debate in Congress about the space program and is certain to lead to new hearings. It also renewed questions about whether cost-cutting and management problems at NASA may be compromising astronauts' safety.

President Bush, informed of the disaster at Camp David by his chief of staff, Andrew H. Card Jr., rushed back to the White House, his motorcade speeding down the mountain and then racing through suburban Maryland. He appeared drawn and stricken as he addressed the nation five hours after the shuttle broke up.

"The *Columbia* is lost," he said from the cabinet room. "There are no survivors." But as President Ronald Reagan did 17 years and four days ago, when the shuttle *Challenger* exploded, Mr. Bush vowed that the American space program would go on.

"The same Creator who names the stars also knows the names of the seven souls we mourn today," he said. He told the nation that while the astronauts had not safely returned to Earth, "we can pray they are safely home."

By the time Mr. Bush spoke at 2 p.m., the nation knew the fate of the crew. Much as viewers around the world knew the meaning of the terrifying images they saw on Jan. 28, 1986, when the *Challenger* exploded, they understood instinctively that there was no chance any of the five men and two women aboard the *Columbia* could survive a disintegration so high in the sky.

The silent confirmation of their deaths came around noon today, as the White House lowered its flag to half-staff.

The best-known member of the crew was the first Israeli to go into space, Ilan Ramon, a colonel in the Israeli Air Force who more than two decades ago participated in Israel's attack on a nuclear reactor in Iraq, and has long been a national hero.

Because of Col. Ramon's participation in the mission, security was extraordinarily tight. Experts said it was extremely unlikely that the shuttle had been deliberately struck, noting that it was so high in the atmosphere that it was out of range of anti-aircraft systems and missiles. A review of satellite data, administration officials said, detected nothing untoward.

Mr. Bush called Prime Minister Ariel Sharon of Israel this morning, and the two men—friends from before either took office—grieved together, as did their nations.

Other world leaders, including several Mr. Bush has been at odds with over Iraq, called to express condolences.

The flight was under the command of Col. Rick D. Husband of the Air Force and piloted by a Navy commander, William C. McCool. The mission was an unusual one for NASA these days in that it was intended purely for scientific experiments, more than 90 in all. More commonly, the shuttle is used to transport crew, equipment and supplies to the International Space Station, and to support military missions.

The scientific payload was overseen by Lt. Col. Michael P. Anderson of the Air Force; Dr. Kalpana Chawla, an aerospace engineer; and two Navy doctors, Capt. David M. Brown and Cmdr. Laurel Salton Clark.

The re-entry began about 14 minutes before the breakup. Re-entry has long been considered one of the riskiest moments in space flight, when a spacecraft is subjected to temperatures in excess of 2,000 degrees as it speeds through the atmosphere. But there is always a risk of structural failure—this was the 28th mission for the *Columbia* and the 113th shuttle mission to date— and, however remote, the risk of damage from meteoroids or space debris.

In past space accident investigations, early theories often proved wrong. But several days ago, NASA reported that a piece of what appeared to be foam insulation had fallen from the shuttle's left tank during the launching and hit its left wing. A similar shedding of debris occurred in a previous flight, but did no major damage.

Ron D. Dittemore, the space shuttle program manager, told reporters this afternoon that "we don't believe, at this point" that the debris caused the disaster.

Seeking the cause will be the subject of two investigations, one conducted by the space agency and another directed by someone outside NASA—a quiet acknowledgment that the agency has been accused of cover-ups in past disasters, including the *Challenger* accident.

"We will find the cause, we will fix it, and then we will move on," said William F. Readdy, a former astronaut who now runs the agency's manned flight operations.

NASA will activate a board of independent outside experts to oversee parts of the investigation, according to people involved. The board is led by Harold W. Gehman, a retired admiral who was the co-chairman of the independent commission that investigated the attack on the destroyer *Cole*.

Other members include James Hallock, chief of the Aviation Safety Division at the Volpe Research Center, part of the federal Department of Transportation, and Steven B. Wallace, who is in charge of the accident investigation branch of the Federal Aviation Administration. There are several military members, including Maj. Gen. Wilbert D. Pearson, commander of the Air Force Flight Test Center at Edwards Air Force Base, and Rear Adm. Stephen A. Turcotte, commander of the Naval Safety Center, in Norfolk, Va.

Whatever happened to the *Columbia* seemed unrelated to the causes of the *Challenger* disaster, which was triggered by a failure of seals in a booster rocket as the shuttle was in its ascent. Those rockets are shed minutes after launching, and the orbiter falls back to earth with only minimal power, moving in S-like patterns to skip off the atmosphere and slow the craft.

The space agency, which spent tens of millions of dollars improving safety after the *Challenger* accident, has estimated the risk of a calamitous event on re-entry as 1 in 350.

There is no escape from the shuttle, either on liftoff or on landing. Extensive studies of the possibility of placing an escape pod on the orbiter, to be used either on liftoff or on landing, concluded that there was no practical or safe way to design such a system.

It was difficult to assess how large a setback the loss of the *Columbia* would pose for the shuttle program. The *Challenger* accident resulted not only in a redesign of the booster rockets, but also in a major shake-up of the space agency, which had covered up evidence of longstanding problems in the shuttle's design.

The shuttle did not fly again for nearly three years, until Sept. 28, 1988, when the *Discovery* lifted off with a crew of five. With today's loss, the shuttle fleet stands at three: *Discovery*, *Atlantis* and *Endeavour*.

The biggest impact now may be on America's contribution to the International Space Station. Aboard the station now are three astronauts, two Americans and a

Russian, who will be directly affected by any delay in shuttle launchings while the accident is investigated. The station crew has completed three months of a scheduled four-month tour and was to be picked up by the shuttle *Atlantis*, which had been scheduled for a March 1 launching.

The station has a large stock of food, water and other supplies that would allow the crew to stay aloft for several months.

In addition, the Russian Space Agency was scheduled to launch an unmanned cargo ship with equipment and supplies to the station on Sunday. On Monday, the station's crew held a brief conversation with the crew of the *Columbia*—who could see the space station in orbit as they spoke.

There was no evidence today of any advance warnings about unusual risks in the shuttle's re-entry phase. But because the orbiter is studied with great care after each landing, there is an extraordinarily large amount of data about the shape of the *Columbia* after each mission.

Cameras trained on the skies for the first sight of the orbiter caught what appeared to be a normal re-entry. But the signals being received in Houston suggested, in retrospect, that trouble was building. At 8:53 a.m. Eastern time, a sensor for the left-side hydraulic systems fell to zero. Five minutes later, another temperature sensor failed.

"It's as if someone just cut the wire," Mr. Dittemore said.

Two minutes after that, all communication was lost, and optimism about a smooth landing on a beautiful day turned to fear, then panic.

NASA declared a "mission contingency," but the truth was evident to anyone looking at the live footage: the *Columbia* had broken up, and pieces were flying away from the body as it whipped, in a terrifying arc, across the sky.

But there was none of the immediate drama of the *Challenger* explosion, because this disaster took place so far in the air, near where the upper atmosphere peters out, and not in full view of an assembled multitude at Cape Canaveral.

Hundreds of square miles of Texas and Louisiana

were littered, however, with debris from the shuttle. In Hemphill, Tex., a driver came across what appeared to be part of the remains of an astronaut.

The space program today carries none of the political import it did 17 years ago, when it was still a symbol of America's status in the cold war. Nonetheless, it is a symbol of American scientific achievement, and the inclusion of foreign astronauts—from former enemies as well as allies—became a piece of American diplomacy.

That was evident on Jan. 16, when more than 300 dignitaries and guests from Israel watched as Col. Ramon became the first Israeli in space. "It was so moving," said Danny Ayalon, the Israeli ambassador to the United States. "The skies were colored blue and white; these are our national colors. We are privileged to join this very prestigious club of nations who have had astronauts in space."

Col. Ramon had little room to take personal items on the flight, but he did lift off with a piece of Holocaust-era art: a small black-and-white drawing called "Moon Landscape" that he had borrowed from the Yad Vashem Art Museum in Israel. The drawing, by Peter Ginz, a 14-year-old Jewish boy killed at Auschwitz in 1944, was a picture by a child who dreamed of faraway places and sketched what he thought the Earth would look like from the mountains of the moon.

This morning, nearly 60 years later, it was incinerated over the skies of Texas.

First the air shook with sound, and then debris rained down

FEBRUARY 2, 2003

By David M. Halbfinger and Richard A. Oppel Jr.

NACOGDOCHES, Texas, Feb. 1—It sounded like a freight train, like a tornado, like rolling thunder—and then a gigantic boom.

It fell from the sky in six-inch chunks and seven-foot sections of steel, ceramics, circuit boards and who-knows-what.

It tore holes in cedar rooftops, scorched front lawns, ripped a streetlight from its pole and littered the parking lot behind the Masonic hall downtown.

But miraculously, officials say, the countless bits of debris from the disintegration of the space shuttle *Columbia* that rained down on hundreds of square miles of East Texas and western Louisiana this morning injured no one on the ground.

There were horrifying discoveries, nonetheless. Officials confirmed tonight that human remains were found in Sabine County; there, in Hemphill, Tex., a hospital worker said he found a charred torso and skull near debris on a rural road.

The grim fallout scattered along a path at least 100 miles long and 10 miles wide, officials said. Here in Nacogdoches County, more than 1,000 reports of debris had come in by early evening, covering 500 square miles, more than half the county's area. But it seemed likely that there was more than one track of debris: fragments of the shuttle were also discovered some 80 miles north in Shreveport, La.

John Hughes, 34, was at work at his fiberglass factory when he was stopped by the noise. He walked outside to watch contrails corkscrew overhead, heard his uncle say "God Almighty," and turned to see a giant ball four feet across float to the earth like a parachute.

"I was telling everyone who was with me, 'You know, we really shouldn't be touching it,' but I just couldn't stand it," Mr. Hughes said. "Like curiosity killed the cat.

It wasn't hot, there were no heat shimmers, we put our hand above it and then we touched it and there was nothing. We kicked at it a little bit. The thing doesn't weigh as much as four gallons of milk.

"At first I was saying this is probably the coolest thing I have ever seen. Then we found out what it was and it was like, this is not the coolest thing I have seen anymore. It's too sad."

Across Texas and Louisiana, witnesses told of curiosity at the sound, at the "sparkles" they saw in the sky, and then of horror—of a sickening feeling as they learned of what had just happened, of what it was that was landing all around them.

Don Redfern, who lives in Palestine, Tex., said he saw the explosion out his car window. Mr. Redfern said he saw a glare first and thought nothing of it. Then he started to hear repeated sonic booms. "It was flopping back and forth across the sky, so I knew it was something out of the ordinary," Mr. Redfern said. "The contrails, as it went by, were zigzagging. It's not like anything I've seen before, and I don't want to see it again."

East of Toledo Bend, La., Pat Breaux found wreckage not far from her brick, tin-roofed home. "It was horrible, it was just devastating," Mrs. Breaux said. "We got a little bit shook."

NASA and local emergency officials warned residents to stay away from the debris to avoid being exposed to toxic materials carried aboard the craft.

Along with the vast stores of solid and liquid fuel that boost it into space, a shuttle carries propellants and fuels that help it stay precisely positioned in orbit and provide power for hydraulic systems. Some of these are extremely dangerous and carcinogenic substances, including hydrazine and nitrogen tetroxide.

On the ground, hundreds of local, state and federal law enforcement officers raced to locate, cordon off and guard debris against theft as officials told of scattered instances of souvenir-scavenging. Some homeowners even barred investigators from their properties in hope of keeping debris for themselves but then relented, one official said.

At the center of Nacogdoches, crowds of onlookers thronged around one roped-off hunk of metal, laying bouquets, joining in prayer circles and gaping at one another. "Everybody's treating this like it's an alien crash," said Phillip Russell, 17.

A detachment of 180 military police officers from Fort Polk, La., were en route here tonight, even as the county sheriff, Thomas Kerss, told of unconfirmed reports of people offering bits of debris for sale on eBay. Officials said the Federal Bureau of Investigation was to take jurisdiction over all debris eventually, and they warned that scavengers would be prosecuted.

Helicopters, F-16s and soldiers hunted for debris, marked it with global-positioning devices and left it in the care of National Guardsmen and volunteer firefighters. Officials said NASA was particularly eager to find pieces of the control panel.

But the scientist in charge of mapping Nacogdoches's debris locations, Dr. James Kroll, said most of the debris had probably ended up in the vast unpopulated pine forests near here. "People will be walking in there 10 years from now and find debris pieces," Dr. Kroll said.

Just what was recovered was up to the inexpert to describe: a big metal cylinder with jagged, burnt edges, spewing yellow smoke on Highway 155. A long metal shard embedded in the dirt of a cemetery. A pair of big tanks on the runway of the city airport.

John Anderson, 59, found close to 80 pieces of debris on his 14-acre patch of grass and woods, mostly pieces of tile, from postage-stamp-size to two feet long.

He said he saw the one that landed on his front porch first, recognized it and knew what had happened before he turned on the television.

"We heard this low-frequency, high-energy sound, an enormous release of energy, sort of a ragged boom," Mr. Anderson said. "I hadn't even remembered that the shuttle was landing today. Unfortunately we have gotten to the point of thinking of them as completely safe and commonplace. Then I remembered it was landing today, and I was afraid maybe something happened.

"Then I went outside and I recognized the tile. I've seen them on display at NASA at the Johnson Space Center. We went around and planted surveyor flags next to them."

The awful thing, he said, was "the realization that what you had thought possibly could be the case from what you had felt, was obviously the case. We had the TV on, and by that time they were reporting there had been no communication. But we already knew."

Inquiry putting an early focus on heat tiles

FEBRUARY 2, 2003

By William J. Broad and James Glanz

Although it could take months for NASA officials to learn what caused the destruction of the shuttle *Columbia*, they focused yesterday on the possibility that some of its protective tiles had failed, dooming the craft.

A small piece of speeding debris hit tiles on *Columbia*'s left wing during the shuttle's blastoff, space agency officials said. Though the incident was analyzed at length and dismissed as insignificant, they and other experts said it might have set off a train of problems that ended in the destruction of the spacecraft and the death of its seven crew members.

Ron Dittemore, shuttle program manager, said today at a NASA briefing that the impact had been analyzed by experts nationwide, who concluded that "it did not represent a safety concern."

"The technical community got together and across the country looked at it and judged that to be acceptable," Mr. Dittemore said. In hindsight, though, he added, the impact was on the left wing, and "all the indications" of trouble seemed to emanate from the craft's left wing.

The experts cautioned that it was too soon to draw firm conclusions about what went wrong. Even if the wing tiles failed, they said, some other factor might have turned this problem into catastrophe.

"There are a lot of things in this business that look like the smoking gun but turn out not even to be close," Mr. Dittemore said.

Eugene E. Covert, an aerospace expert who helped investigate the *Challenger* disaster for the federal government, said, "It's foolish to speculate."

He added, however, that engineers might never learn exactly what went awry.

While experts regard damage to the protective tile heat shield as the likeliest culprit, they said there were at least five other possible causes, in this general order of decreasing likelihood:

- An explosion of the ship's fuels and oxidizers, which are kept under high pressure;
- Collapse in the shuttle's structure, which is aged;
- Faulty navigation setup for the fiery re-entry, caused perhaps by a computer problem;
- A collision with a speeding meteoroid or piece of space debris;
- Terrorism, perhaps by a technician at the launching site.

The operation of all of the shuttle's myriad systems is monitored constantly and streams of data flow into NASA computers. Scientists will mine this trove in the days and weeks ahead, sifting for clues. "You can look at the data bank in Houston as the biggest black box in the world," Dr. Covert said.

But it will take time. The final report on what destroyed the *Challenger*, which exploded in flames minutes after launching on Jan. 28, 1986, was issued nearly five months after the disaster, and experts still debate details of how a leaky booster rocket turned the shuttle into a ball of flame.

Also, *Challenger* blew up while still within sight of the Florida launching pad, where long-range cameras recorded many details of its destruction.

By contrast, *Columbia* experienced its problem high in the atmosphere, and though amateur observers reported seeing debris falling from the shuttle, government cameras were not tracking it.

NASA officials discounted reports that the shuttle was following an unusual re-entry course for security reasons because the Israeli astronaut, Col. Ilan Ramon, was aboard. "There was nothing unusual about this trajectory at all," said Rob Navias, a NASA spokesman at the Johnson Space Center in Houston. "It was a standard re-entry profile."

Mr. Navias declined to speculate on causes, saying only that "the computers were perfect all the way down" and that NASA was impounding all mission data for the investigation.

But private experts said one of the likeliest causes of the *Columbia* disaster was faulty protective covering or tiles, which cover the shuttle's nose, wings and belly and protect it from the intense heat of re-entry.

On Jan. 16, as *Columbia* lifted off, a piece of insulating foam on its external fuel tank came off and was seen apparently hitting the left wing of the shuttle. Leroy Cain, the lead flight director in Mission Control, assured reporters on Friday that engineers had concluded that any damage to the wing and tiles was minor and posed no safety hazard.

"We took a very thorough look at the situation with the tile on the left wing and we have no concerns, whatsoever," Mr. Cain said.

But experts say a loose tile or protective surface might have started burning that triggered catastrophic failure during the fiery heats of re-entry. "It could have started as a wing problem," said James E. Oberg, an expert on the shuttle program and a former NASA engineer. "Wing problems quickly become whole spacecraft problems."

Mr. Oberg said flight controllers might have been able to compensate for the tile problem by having the shuttle turn slightly—no more than 10 degrees—to shift some of the brunt of re-entry to the undamaged right wing.

Instead, the craft began losing tiles over California, he said.

Mr. Dittemore said at the news conference that the first indication of trouble came shortly before 9 a.m. Eastern time when the flow of data from temperature sensors in the hydraulic systems of the left wing abruptly ceased. A series of other data failures occurred seconds and minutes later.

Around the same time, astronomers at the California Institute of Technology say, *Columbia* was trailing fiery debris as it passed over Eastern California, sending out flashes and pieces, as if dropping flares.

"I saw a bright spot in the sky and then a tail," said Dr. Carmen Sanchez-Contreras, an astronomer at Caltech. "The other thing I saw was a second bright spot, much smaller, separating from the shuttle."

In past shuttle missions, NASA has used long-range cameras on the ground—and perhaps had access to images from space-based spy cameras—to examine the winged spaceships for signs of damage.

Whether such precautions were taken on this mission

is not known, though it is likely to be a point of investigation.

Also, experts said, *Columbia* on this mission was not carrying one of NASA's robot arms in its 60-foot payload bay. In the past, astronauts have used cameras mounted on a robot arm to look for tile damage. It was not clear whether any of *Columbia*'s astronauts had undergone training for a space walk, which would have let them visually inspect the ship for damage.

But even if *Columbia* astronauts had spotted the problem, it is not clear whether they could have done anything, beyond tweaking their re-entry path and hoping for the best, to save themselves.

Another possible explanation for the disaster is a chemical explosion, experts say. The shuttles are loaded with hydrogen, oxygen and exotic fuels to power their many engines. Just before descent, a shuttle starts three extra power units, which run on hydrazine, a highly volatile fuel.

These so-called auxiliary power units run the shuttle's hydraulic system, which moves the spaceship's body flaps and rudder and deploys the landing gears. Temperamental and high-tech, these units have a history of woes, including outright failure. But none have ever exploded.

Another possible cause is structural failure. *Columbia* was the oldest orbiter in the nation's fleet, having first blasted into space in April 1981.

Robert Weatherwax, an analyst who in 1983 did a classified study of shuttle risks for the Air Force, said that *Columbia*'s failure during re-entry appeared to be near the point where the shuttle was undergoing the maximum buffeting as it pounded through the high atmosphere. The old craft, he suggested, might have suffered from the high stress.

"If there was going to be a problem on re-entry, that might be where you would see it," said Mr. Weatherwax, president of Sierra Energy and Risk Assessment, a company in Roseville, Calif.

But Mr. Dittemore discounted that possibility. "A lot of tender loving care goes into the care of our vehicles," he said.

Another possibility is a computer or navigation error that subtly changed *Columbia*'s angle of descent, increasing the re-entry pounding and heating. Ed Crawley, head of the department of astronautics and aeronautics at the Massachusetts Institute of Technology, said something like that might have turned a minor wing problem into catastrophe.

"There could have been a computer glitch that changed the shuttle's attitude slightly, which could have caused more heating than there should have been, which then could have caused the structural failure," he said. "Even if we know that the left wing started to overheat, that may not be the root cause."

A remote possibility, experts say, is that a piece of space debris or a speeding rock hit *Columbia*.

Another possibility, which they regard as even more remote, is that a terrorist managed to strike. Experts say no terrorist on the ground could have used a missile to strike the shuttle, which was moving at almost 20 times the speed of sound at an altitude at 207,135 feet—almost 40 miles—when its sensors failed, suggesting it was breaking up. But, however unlikely, a terrorist might have managed to infiltrate the shuttle operations and sabotage *Columbia*'s gear.

"The risk of terrorism is low but you can't rule it out," said Dr. John Tylko, a space shuttle expert at M.I.T. "Something might have been placed on board."

Experts said the federal investigation would look closely at all these possibilities, and perhaps others.

"It's easy to seize on the most recent tidbit we've heard on a day like this and extrapolate," said Dr. Crawley of M.I.T. "But realistically, there's not enough data. We have to be cautious."

Recalling deadline with
The New York Times

KEITH WOODS: How did you hear about the shuttle breaking up?

DAVID SANGER: I heard about it in a phone call to my house. I think I was feeding breakfast to my kids. At the first signs on TV that there were pieces breaking off the shuttle, I got a call from Jack Cushman, our weekend editor at the *Times* Washington bureau. Jack knew that I had been part of the team that had worked on the *Challenger* explosion. He told me the shuttle was breaking up and basically said to get down there as fast as I could. At the time I got to the bureau, you could still see on the television those streaks across the sky, but they didn't yet know what had happened to the main orbiter.

What did you do first?

I tried to come to some preliminary assessment about what could cause a breakup on re-entry. We still had a lot of both our mental and our physical database of shuttle problems, even though the *Challenger* explosion had been in 1986. On my way out of the house, I grabbed the NASA handbook on the construction of the shuttle that was left over from 1986.

Now, you say "we." Were you working at that point with somebody?

At that point, we were just gathering our people together and trying to deploy people into the area around Texas and west of it where there were shuttle parts coming down. We knew that we were under great time pressure. The Sunday paper has a bulldog edition that closes at noon on Saturday, and this was already around 9:30, so we knew that we had about two and a half hours to completely rip up the front page. What we determined fairly quickly was that I would put together a lead-all based on what we could get from other members of the *Times* staff and wire reports and so forth, and then keep rewriting that lead-all between all editions, knowing that we had another edition at 3 p.m. and another at 8.

It would not be determined for months that it was an insulation panel that was behind the shuttle's disintegration, yet you hinted at that in the lead of the story. What gave you the confidence to do that?

Two things. One, you're seeing parts fly off of the shuttle, and you knew that came from the heat of re-entry, so we had that. Second, fairly high up in the lead in the story we alluded to a problem on take-off of this loose piece of foam. We still didn't know whether that was a leading suspect, but we raised it as a possibility. But, of course, you always want to be cautious in writing these because, in most accident investigations, your first theory is wrong, and in this accident investigation, the first thought, of course, was about the tiles on the underside of the shuttle.

Did you have this information in your head from having done this once before?

Yes, I did. Now, the *Challenger* accident was an entirely different set of causes. That was an accident on take-off. This was an accident during the re-entry process. So the forces at work against the shuttle were completely different. But we knew enough about the system that we understood the basics of where the problem could be. I very quickly got into a conversation that morning with Bill Broad, who's in our science department and whom I had worked very closely with during the *Challenger* investigation and who understands a lot about the systems of the shuttle, and we have other people in the newspaper as well.

There are details in the story that clearly come from several different places. What was the process of collecting that information?

We had memos coming in from the people we had put out in the field. We had memos coming in from people who were at Mission Control in Houston. We had phone calls going out to NASA officials. We were, of course, watching what was unfolding on television. And by later in the afternoon, we had accounts that turned into separate stories about what was happening on the ground.

Were you using your position as White House correspondent to gather information about what was happening with the White House at the same time?

I was, and that was helpful for figuring out what the president was doing. The people in the White House probably had not as much information as NASA or perhaps even what we had. They were largely watching it on television.

How were you physically managing the information as it came in to you?

I moved over to the editing desk we have in the Washington bureau, wrote there, and one of our crack clerical staff was going through the memos as we printed them out, categorizing them by type—what was found on the ground, what the president was saying, what we were hearing from NASA—marking those up with markers, and I was organizing those by subject matter on the right side of my keyboard and writing the story through.

There are places in this story where you write with a distinct voice of authority, some places where you are attributing greatly, and some places where it's clear you know this material. Talk about that.

I'm not sure how authoritative it sounded, but that voice comes from the experience of covering the *Challenger* investigation for a year. At that time, I was a technology reporter in the business section. It turned out the *Challenger* was more than just an accident. It was the result of a major cover-up of well-known problems by people who had been responsible for building and designing the shuttle. So we had spent an awful lot of time with engineers involved in the shuttle's design and then its construction to understand its vulnerabilities, to understand how the systems came together, to understand what worked and what didn't. And it was that very intensive, yearlong seminar in the workings of the shuttle that gave me whatever little knowledge I had to put into this event some 17 years later.

There's a passage that gets right to the matter of what you knew going into reporting the story. You talk about "a quiet acknowledgment that the agency has been accused of cover-ups in past disasters, including the *Challenger* accident." That came in reference to the decision to have two separate investigations. Once again, it seems that you are writing as someone who knows this information firsthand.

Well, we were quite sensitive to the fact that we had gone through months when engineers had fundamentally understood what had happened and yet did not want to acknowledge it publicly and certainly did not want to tell the presidential commission in 1986. It took our stories about what had happened in the case of the *Challenger* and particularly with the design of the O-rings to force many of those issues into the public realm. Prior to that, of course, there had been the 1967 accident in which three astronauts were killed. In that case as well, there was a significant question about whether NASA told everybody all that it knew about the causes. So we understood a little bit about the bureaucratic dynamics of NASA.

Did you and your colleagues talk at all about how to handle some of the more gruesome information that you would get regarding the astronauts' remains?

We did, and we wanted to handle it tastefully because, first and foremost, this was a great human tragedy. It wasn't until much later in the day for our later editions that we began to hear some of the more gruesome details, mostly the recovery of some of the helmets of the astronauts, and we tried to allude to those without providing great graphic detail. It was a day or two later before we understood the full nature of what had been recovered.

What do you mean by that?

We didn't have the details ourselves of what kind of great trauma the astronauts' bodies had suffered on the way down. We could imagine it, but we didn't have the evidence of that for another day or so after the recovery of the parts of the shuttle all over the Southwest.

There are several places in the story at which you add context, political and historic, that expands on the meaning of the disaster. How important was that to you as you wrote?

That was very important. When you are writing about a major event in the history of the country, I think you always have a sense that you are writing stories that will be read the next morning. But they may also be read 50 years from now so that people can understand what we were feeling and thinking and seeing at that moment. I had the same sense only six or seven weeks later, when I was writing with a colleague of mine in Baghdad about the opening moments of the war in Iraq.

In both cases, you want to, of course, convey what's happening today, but you also want to put it in the grander scale of the questions it raises about, in this case, the future of our space program and whether or not the cost of human space flight, the human cost of it, and the risks of it are worth the return. You don't want to answer those questions, but you want to raise the big issues that are likely to unfold in the coming weeks to the greatest degree that you can predict them.

You make use of language in some interesting ways in the story. You referred to "tantalizing clues," the "netherworld between outer space and the upper atmosphere," and you use the word "incinerated" in the final sentence. How conscious were you of making those choices?

Very conscious. "Tantalizing clues" was intended to show the reader that we had hints of what was going wrong. And all of the early theories in the *Challenger* case that we had dealt with in the opening days in 1986 were wrong. It took a number of days, maybe even a few weeks before we got to what the correct cause was. The "netherworld between outer space and the upper atmosphere" was an effort to try to show the reader that where this trouble happened was in an area of the atmosphere we don't think about very much: Where you are out of the outer limits of the Earth's atmosphere, but you are not yet in outer space. And the third phrase about how the shuttle was incinerated was to try to convey a sense of the huge and fearsome natural forces that come to play on the shuttle if those heat protector shields fail.

I can imagine a writer being fairly uptight and, therefore, not making use of more lyrical language on deadline. Were you loose enough in writing that you could think about language in that way on deadline?

You're writing for history when you're writing a story like this, and you want to make sure that you are descriptive but that you also are descriptive with a great economy of words. You don't have many words that are going to be on the front-page portion of that story, and you have to be able to get the reader who only makes it through the first few hundred words on the front page a broad overview of the most important events of the day.

You write that spectators would know instinctively that the astronauts were dead, then you speak of what you called a "silent confirmation" that came with the lowering of the White House flag. Why did you choose to deliver the information about their deaths in that way?

Well, I thought that it was interesting that the White House chose to convey the information that way. No one at NASA wanted to admit in public what everybody had known, which was that the astronauts did not, and probably could not, survive re-entry like that. The White House flag came down to half-staff before the president spoke, and we felt in watching that flag come down that we had official acknowledgment of what seems obvious to all who were watching these horrific events unfold on TV.

What steps did you take to sharpen the writing as the day was going on?

I went through it sentence by sentence, but you know, I found that with events like this, the biggest fear is not that the writing needs sharpening as the day goes on but that you don't dull it down as the day goes on; that you end up getting such a flood of new facts, many of which are important, some of which are not, that you can load up the top of the story with the latest to the detriment of some of the emotional impact of sketching out the totality of the day, which you had earlier. So I went through it with the sense that we needed to fill in detail but to do so without trying to jam up the full story. And to tell you the truth, I think I prefer some of the early and middle versions of the story to the last edition's version of the story.

David, is there anything I've failed to ask you about the reporting and writing of this project?

I think the impact of the paper that day had very much to do with the other stories that were there apart from the lead-all: the remarkable reporting that was done on the ground; the very good scientific explanatory pieces that we had by the later editions. A wonderful news analysis that Todd Purdum did caught the emotion of the moment more vividly than anything I could do in the lead-all. A newspaper is not a single story; it is the whole package that you put together, and what never ceases to amaze me about *The New York Times* is the way that it rises to the occasion at moments of great national tragedy.

William Broad, senior writer

That morning I was at home playing around with my kids and doing the usual Saturday morning routine. David Corcoran, one of our science editors, called and said, "Bill, the shuttle has disappeared in a radio blackout and they don't know what happened." My smart-aleck answer was, "Oh, don't worry, that happens all the time. They always have a period of radio blackout when re-entering the Earth's atmosphere."

He quickly let me know that it seemed to be worse than that, and I threw on some reasonable clothes and hopped on a train. I did a bunch of downloading into my computer at home of things to read on the train and was tapping away writing the story as I rode in.

I've been at *The New York Times* for a little more than 20 years, and I've covered the space program for a lot of that time. I was a veteran of the *Challenger* disaster along with David Sanger. So I came in with all kinds of knowledge of shuttles and sources.

The shuttle is an immensely beautiful, immensely complex thing. When you kick the tires, you start to get some feel for the awesomeness. It's huge and extremely complex, and it's a miracle, to me, every time it takes off and returns safely. So I knew lots of stuff, I knew lots of people, and, therefore, I was a logical person to be involved in the reporting.

I went back and examined overall stuff I had on vulnerability. I had written a lot of stories on single-point failures and what the odds of catastrophe are. I don't know if any of that language appeared in this report, but it's a little sub-specialty in the space agency to study the odds of disaster that may have changed over the years. I recall looking for those kinds of files and that kind of information and trying to piece together what could have gone wrong.

I called Eugene Covert. That's one of the cases where old sources paid off. He was a member of the previous investigation. I had spoken with him repeatedly during the *Challenger* investigation, and all those people were logical people on my list. I don't remember if I got any others, but he was definitely one I connected with.

I was going down the list of all the former investigators from the *Challenger* investigation. Jim Oberg is an old source who is a former NASA engineer. He's done a lot of stuff there and knows quite a bit about the shuttle and NASA operations, so Oberg is definitely on the A list.

Many of them I didn't get. People who I did speak with over the years and who I had up-to-date numbers for I was able to get to quite quickly. It's a scattergun approach: You dial 30 numbers or you have a list of 30 names and maybe you get seven.

The debris hitting the left wing was an obvious thing that people had seen and worried about, and you sure want to take note of it. But then, you also want to bend over backward and go to guys like Covert and some other guys who are really deep into the complexities and the difference between causation and correlation and the intricacies of science and get them on this stuff, because what's obvious is often wrong. But we'd be fools not to mention the debris and to get it high in the story.

You always do your best, and you always wonder if it could have been better. Always. I'm a defensive writer. I don't ever feel real confident, especially because I'm a science reporter. I have some of the smartest people in the world reading over my shoulder, and they don't hesitate to write and tell me about the mistakes that I made or the stupidities in my interpretation.

Still, under the constraints of the day, I think Jim Glanz and I did a pretty thorough review of the possibilities and maybe played a hunch a little bit in the lead. But you always worry, and that confidence is pretty shallow, especially on a breaking story like this because there's so much to absorb in such a short period of time and so technically complex a story to tell.

Deadline Tip:

Never panic. Your computer can crash, you can lose everything, and all you have to do is just stay calm. You might not know what structure to use. You might not know what the lead is. It's a process, not a product. That's what this whole story was; it was a process. It's just digging and digging and going where the story takes you. Don't worry about the lead; don't worry about the package. Just stay calm and keep digging and usually in the end it works out.

David Halbfinger, Atlanta bureau chief

I remember being awakened by a phone call that Saturday morning from Lawrence Downes, who was then the weekend national editor. He said it looked like the shuttle was missing. I just said okay, hit the floor, ran downstairs, and turned on the TV to watch CNN. Lawrence's phone call was just to wake me, apprise me, and let me know to hold for orders, that I'd be dispatched somewhere soon. Like many Americans, I wasn't even paying attention to the fact that the shuttle was in the air.

A call came maybe half an hour or an hour later, to get to Cape Canaveral in Florida. Then this fluke thing happened. I got to the Atlanta airport very quickly with a ticket arranged over the phone with our travel service.

I got to the gate, and it was for Dayton, Ohio, not Daytona Beach, Fla. I freaked out and went to the ticket counter and called the desk and one of them said, "Well, it's just as well. Don't worry. We need to get you to Texas. That seems to be where the wreckage is." So I got on the next plane and flew to Shreveport.

I remember driving 90 miles an hour down two-lane roads all the way to Nacogdoches. There was a strip in town and there was already a media gaggle of trucks and reporters and photographers in the center of town.

At this point it was a matter of sitting through the first news conference, finding people who had experienced the debris landing, and getting them to talk.

I got Ariel Hart to go into the Atlanta bureau and make a lot of calls and basically search the wires and work the phones to find people.

I interviewed some people at their homes, saw the holes in their attic, saw the light coming through where the debris had penetrated, saw the stuff on the lawns, and talked to people about what they had heard and what they had seen and what they felt.

It was eerie. It was not the worst thing I've ever seen. It was very strange, and I remember it was a quiet, really sunny day. It was a little unearthly. None of the things I saw were grisly. They were all just bits of charred metal, things that looked vaguely industrial. They were small, and they were all over the place.

This is a small town in east Texas that was showered with this debris. They had to process the idea of what this debris was while the entire national media descended upon them, creating the usual media circus. It was that ghoulish kind of specter—all these different things happening. And yet you couldn't lose sight of the fact that there were people who had just died in the skies above, which was why this was such a horrible story.

I didn't stay out there reporting for very long. I went to a news conference and drove around town finding debris and people for about an hour, getting some color.

Then I sat down to write. I may have contributed one quote. I may have gotten some information firsthand from a news conference that anybody could have gone to. In a way it was really just to inform myself enough and to soak up enough to be able to write it in the right way.

I was joined at some point in the writing by Rich Oppel. It was all e-mail after that. Phone calls and e-mail. Ariel really was like an all-star. She got amazing stuff on the phone. I just put it together. In the end, I don't know how much of that story was my reporting—very little of it I think.

I suppose you could have written a story that conveyed some of the human drama without having been there, but you couldn't have had a feel for it. I'm not trying to make a big deal about having been on the ground—this is not about ownership of the piece. But having been there, you had a sense. The circus environment, the ghoulish stuff, the eeriness of it all—I don't know if any of that made it into the piece. But it informed me. It was from having been there that I was able to write the story in the dramatic way that I did.

You never could have written a story in this voice off rewrite. You never could have written a story with the confidence of having seen it and driven around the town and smelled the air and walked into somebody's home, and seen the officials and their news conference, sounding the way they sounded. They came together, and they were moved, rattled, concerned, and earnest, and, like everybody else, a little psychically wounded.

None of that comes out in the piece. But to see it, it gave you the idea that everybody was working from the same emotional starting point, and it allowed you to put it in the voice of the regular people. It enabled you to set the point of view from people's doorsteps and windows, not from the town square where the scrum was, not from the two-lane highway where people from out of town were already pulling over to traipse through the fields and look at the junk.

After the third or fourth person told me that it sounded like a freight train or a tornado, I think the lead was writing itself. The feeds bore it out, the feeds and wire stories were referring to the sound. It was universal, and universality is a good thing.

Like rolling thunder. And then a gigantic boom. That's how it differed from all those other things. That's why people knew it wasn't an act of nature. And it was after the boom that things started raining down and people couldn't really make heads or tails of what these things were. They could tell it was steel, they could tell it was some kind of manmade material, they could see circuits and electronic shards and stuff, but they had no idea what they were looking at.

They just knew that it came from something up there that had people on it until moments earlier.

There are some stories in which you write about the juxtaposition of the sunny day and you write about the leafy, tree-lined suburban town that's confronted with a murder or whatever. This was not one of those stories.

Deadline Tip:

In terms of useful advice or lessons, I think one of them is: Move your ass and get there. Now, I can't claim credit for the decision to send me there, and I wouldn't advise anybody to break speeding laws, but every minute counts. The clock tells you when to stop.

Writers' Workshop

Talking Points

1) *The New York Times* team credits a depth of expertise on staff for the newspaper's ability to speak with such an authoritative voice in the lead stories on the *Columbia* disaster. How might a newspaper staff with fewer "expert" reporters and less familiarity with the space program have done a credible job covering this story on deadline?

2) In the lead-all story, written as the magnitude of the shuttle's disintegration was still coming into focus, David Sanger told readers about NASA's past troubles investigating itself and about the clamor likely to begin about whether the shuttle program would even continue. How important was it to introduce those controversial issues in the first-day story?

3) There are some powerful quotes in the stories by William Broad and David Halbfinger. Which ones stood out? Why? Consider those you didn't mention and discuss how the stories would have changed had an editor deleted those quotes.

Assignment Desk

1) Sanger and Broad got help from other *Times* reporters and editors who knew critical information about the space shuttle. Choose another topic—rapid transit, for example—and research the kinds of things you'd need to know that would give your stories the kind of heft found in the *Times* pieces.

2) Halbfinger says he drove around Nacogdoches, Texas, just long enough to get a feel of the place before sitting down to write. Sanger said he walked over to the White House just to see whether it felt the same as the last time there was a shuttle disaster. Spend some time on your next story soaking up the atmosphere of a place—a politician's office, a police officer's beat—and see how much your insights add to the story.

3) Review your notes from the biggest story you've covered. How well are they organized? Sanger and Broad went back to old notes for help in identifying sources and angles. Look through your notes and index names and telephone numbers you would need if such a story were to happen again.

Top: Thomas Farragher, Peter Canellos
Bottom: Michael Paulson, Ellen Barry

The Boston Globe
Team Deadline News Reporting

The fire had taken nearly 100 lives on a Thursday night before anyone outside even knew. Reporters would learn that the heavy-metal fans at The Station nightclub in West Warwick, R.I., had just three minutes to escape the inferno that tore through the club, ignited by a band's stage pyrotechnics.

Editors and reporters at *The Boston Globe* were on the story early. Those who could, went immediately to the scene. Others began putting into place a structure created just for such an event; one that would split the tasks of reporting, writing, and editing in a way that muted the effect of the miles between Boston and West Warwick and gave the writing a seamless coherence.

Peter Canellos, now deputy managing editor in Washington, orchestrated the coverage, and Thomas Farragher,

Michael Paulson, and Ellen Barry were tapped Friday morning to write the main stories. Paulson and Farragher had to be summoned from a corporate gathering where they were being honored for previous outstanding work covering the Catholic clergy scandals. The three lead writers would remain in the newsroom and construct stories based largely on the reporting of others.

Several reporters gathered information at the scene or kept an eye on news conferences and other breaking events as the dimensions of the tragedy—and the controversy it created—came into focus. Researchers tracked down names and telephone numbers. Some people watched television coverage and shared what they saw with the writers.

Farragher, a projects reporter, wrote the lead-all and concentrated on the investigation that immediately sprang from the ashes of the fire. Paulson, the *Globe*'s religion reporter, focused on the agonizing minutes and hours after the fire as people tried to figure out what had happened to friends and relatives. Barry, who covered mental health for the *Globe* before becoming Atlanta bureau chief for the *Los Angeles Times*, used interviews with survivors to reconstruct the scene inside the nightclub as fun turned to panic and panic to tragedy.

They combined for a package of stories that covered the breadth of a historic fire, an event rife with anguish, pain, indignation, and huge questions about who was dead, who was alive, and who was to blame. Raja Mishra, Doug Belkin, and Michele Kurtz shared bylines with the three lead writers, but help poured in from many quarters. Others who had a hand in producing the winning deadline package included:

Anne Barnard, Scott S. Greenberger, Geoff Edgers, John Ellement, Tatsha Robertson, Christopher Rowland, Jonathan Saltzman, Megan Tench, and Joanna Weiss of the *Globe* staff, and correspondents Heather Allen, Peter DeMarco, and Jeff Nilsen.

—Keith Woods

[*The Jesse Laventhol Prize for Deadline News Reporting by a team is funded by a gift from David Laventhol, a former Times-Mirror executive, in honor of his father.*]

Death toll reaches 96 in fire at R.I. nightclub; 187 hurt

FEBRUARY 22, 2003

By Thomas Farragher and Douglas Belkin

WEST WARWICK, R.I.—A rock band's explosive light show ignited a lightning-quick blaze, a curtain of blinding smoke, and a panicked stampede to escape a hellish inferno that killed at least 96 people in one of the deadliest nightclub fires in U.S. history.

Scores of Great White fans trying to save themselves Thursday night were trapped in doorways, squeezed so tightly that few could slip out as the fire, fueled by the acoustic insulation behind the stage, consumed the crowded building.

As emergency crews searched the ruins of The Station nightclub yesterday for bodies and evidence, state and federal authorities opened a criminal investigation that initially focused on who was legally responsible for the indoor fireworks at the wooden, one-story building.

"I would say to let off pyrotechnics in that building you were asking for trouble," said Rhode Island Governor Donald Carcieri, adding, "If there's criminal wrongdoing, believe me, it will be pursued."

At least 187 people were being treated for burns and other injuries. Thirty-five of them were listed in critical condition last night with severe burns and smoke inhalation.

The nightclub owners said the band did not have permission for the theatrical fireworks that signaled the opening of their late-night set around 11 p.m. The band said it had received that approval from the nightclub.

Authorities, who interviewed band members and club owners, said neither had the state and local approvals required for a pyrotechnics display. Approval would have been "absolutely" denied if it had been sought, officials said.

Carcieri said investigators, led by the state attorney general's office, would seek to assess blame after the remains of all victims had been recovered and their families—some of whom searched frantically for loved ones at area hospitals yesterday—had been notified.

"This building went up fast. Nobody had a chance," Carcieri said. He said officials believe the bodies of all victims have been found.

Scenes from the fire—whose chaos and carnage was reminiscent of Boston's Cocoanut Grove blaze that killed nearly 500 in 1942—were captured by a Providence television station that employed one of the nightclub owners, TV reporter Jeff Derderian.

Derderian, at the club with a cameraman, escaped the fire and later was questioned by law enforcement officials.

The television images, broadcast worldwide by early yesterday morning, showed nightclub patrons cheering with pumped fists and longneck bottles of beer as Jack Russell, lead singer for the band Great White, began his set singing "Desert Moon."

As guitars wailed, pyrotechnics similar to Fourth of July sparklers exploded on stage, and the pumping fists turned to frantic hands pointing to the fire.

Almost immediately, flames licked acoustic material behind the stage and danced across the nightclub's ceiling.

Fire officials said the club was fully aflame within three minutes.

"I saw a wall of flame going up to the ceiling and it was just mayhem, panic," said John Reagle, a drummer for Great White's opening act. "As soon as we made it out the side door, everything went black inside."

Joe Barber, who lives near the club, said he escaped by climbing over victims at a side door. "It was terrible, terrible," said Barber, who burned a hand helping others to safety. "People just clawing, scratching, punching—anything they could do to get out. You feel so helpless."

Some patrons at first believed the fire to be part of the act, then described a chilling tableau of fear as patrons rushed for exits in smoke so thick they couldn't see. Exits were quickly blocked by patrons felled by fire, smoke, or chaotic trampling. Some broke a window and jumped through to safety.

West Warwick Fire Chief Charles Hall said the club's fire alarms were working, its fire extinguishers were workable, and its exit signs were lit. But he said the club was not required to use a sprinkler system because it was in operation before that requirement was adopted, and because of its relatively small size.

"If there were sprinklers in this building, we wouldn't be standing here right now," Hall told reporters. He said "any pyrotechnics in the interior of a combustible building is unsafe."

As crews raked through charred timbers, a sometimes emotional Hall described a macabre scene inside The Station. He said in the "panic and chaos," about 25 bodies ended up stacked up at the nightclub's entrance.

Others were found near the club's three other operating fire exits, near the stage and the bar. Some, he said, were found in the club's restrooms.

Fire officials, he said, have a copy of the WPRI-TV tape of the fire's beginnings. "Any video or any evidence that we can get is important," Hall said.

Russell, whose heavy metal band was nominated in 1990 for a Grammy, said the group has used the pyrotechnic displays "four or five" times since they began their most recent tour last month in Chicago.

"There's also been occasions when we've gone to the club and they said yes, we can use it, and we said, 'No, it doesn't look safe,'" he said. "It's like sparklers. You can put your hand over them. I stand there every night with my arms over them and I don't get burned."

Russell's contention that he has always asked permission to use the pyrotechnics and received that approval for Thursday night's show was immediately contested by the club's owners. Michael and Jeffrey Derderian, who own The Station, said the band did not seek or receive that permission.

"At no time did either owner have prior knowledge that pyrotechnics were going to be used by the band Great White," they said in a statement issued by their lawyer, Kathleen M. Hagerty. "No permission was ever requested by the band or its agents to use pyrotechnics at The Station, and no permission was ever given."

The owner of a nightclub in Asbury Park, N.J., said Great White used the theatrical pyrotechnics during a performance last week without giving club managers advance notice. "Our stage manager didn't even know it until it was done," said Domenic Santana, owner of the Stone Pony.

One patron recalled a small fire during a show at The Station a year ago, but officials said there was no record of it.

Paul Woolnough, president of Great White's management company, said he did not know details about the approval process for Thursday night's show. "Part of this tour, they have been using those effects," said Woolnough. "And it's always done on a case-by-case basis....I would presume that permission was granted."

Hagerty said the Derderians, who purchased The Station in March 2000, are "devastated and in shock over these events, which have claimed the lives of so many, including their friends.

"Jeffrey Derderian was in the club at the time the fire broke out, and assisted in helping to evacuate the building during the fast-moving fire. Mr. Derderian was interviewed by state and local authorities [Thursday] night on the scene and provided all information as requested."

The capacity at The Station, built around 1950, was 300. Fire officials said they believed there were fewer than 300 patrons there on Thursday night. But Carcieri, compiling figures of those dead, injured, or safe, said there may have been as many as 350 people inside.

"There seem to be more people than we had been led to believe," the Rhode Island governor said.

Investigators are examining additional pyrotechnics found on the site, but did not assess their significance.

Carcieri said seven bodies had been identified by last night. Eight more are expected to be quickly identified by "visual inspection." Five teams of forensic pathologists from around the country are headed for Rhode Island to help state authorities identify remains using dental records and DNA.

Emergency crews adopted a somber ritual at the burned-out wreckage. Firefighters removed their helmets and paused for a moment of silence when a body was discovered. Fire chaplains said prayers over the remains. Officials said the club's 1,700-square-foot basement was badly flooded and would have to be pumped out to determine whether more bodies are there.

"This is really a tough, tough day," said Carcieri, who spoke with a couple who escaped the club through a rear entrance. "Their description to me was that in 30 seconds, if you weren't out of that building in 30 seconds, you didn't have a prayer."

The scene was bathed in floodlights last night as work continued. During the day, a large section of the busy thoroughfare was closed as a large construction excavator knocked down remaining support beams and helped clear rubble. Fire trucks were positioned to block onlookers' view of the recovery effort.

The blaze at the nightclub 15 miles southwest of Providence was the deadliest fire at a U.S. nightclub since 1977, when 165 people died at the Beverly Hills Supper Club in Southgate, Ky. And it was the second deadly episode at a U.S. nightclub in four days.

Twenty-one people died in a Chicago melee early Monday after a security guard used pepper spray on patrons after a fight broke out.

"An investigation has begun," said state Attorney General Patrick Lynch. "The investigation will continue. But now is not the time to discuss the investigation. What is most important is notifying the victims' families and offering support to the many Rhode Islanders who are suffering at this time."

As rescue workers raked through the wreckage, Julie Belson, 31, struggled to recover from the shock of surviving a fire she watched unfold.

"I was in the front row with my boyfriend and I saw it catch fire," said Belson, a dental assistant from Rowley. "It was growing. It was really hot. The heat was like crazy. It burned off my bangs. My instinct was to grab my bag."

Belson was briefly lost in blinding, black smoke. Then she found a window. But not her boyfriend. "I don't remember if anyone helped me and I don't remember landing," she said. "I just remember turning around and he wasn't there."

Outside and badly shaken, Belson stumbled into her boyfriend, who was covered with soot and was listed last night in serious condition at Rhode Island Hospital with burns to his face and hands. "I couldn't believe how fast it all happened," said Belson, who said she could spot herself and her boyfriend in the television tape of the fire.

"I thought, 'Oh, my God. I'm going to die.' I couldn't see anything. We were all holding our breath."

Geoff Edgers, John Ellement, Christopher Rowland, Jonathan Saltzman, Megan Tench, and Joanna Weiss of the Globe staff contributed to this report, along with Globe correspondents Heather Allen, Peter DeMarco, and Jeff Nilsen. Material from the Associated Press also was used.

As hopes wane, families keep looking for answers

FEBRUARY 22, 2003

By Michael Paulson and Michele Kurtz

Early in the day, they arrived at the charred remains of the West Warwick, R.I., nightclub, pressing against the police tape, begging the firefighters for shreds of information.

Throughout the afternoon, they called, faxed, e-mailed, and visited a dozen area hospitals, offering photographs and descriptions to doctors trying to identify the sometimes unrecognizable victims.

But by evening, many family and friends of concert-goers were losing hope that their loved ones might have survived the inferno that destroyed The Station just as the headline act, Great White, was finishing its first song.

The missing were people like Robert Croteau, a 31-year-old Great White devotee, who enthusiastically followed the band from gig to gig and who proudly had the band's logo, a shark, tattooed into his left shoulder. Croteau's family members fanned out to area hospitals, hoping against hope that he had survived.

There was the band's 28-year-old guitarist, Ty Longley, who has not been seen since the ill-fated opening song. His website was updated yesterday morning with a plaintive appeal from his friends, "Come Home, Ty!"

And then there was Michael Gonsalves, a 40-year-old Providence disc jockey known as "The Doctor," who claimed to be the host of the country's longest-running heavy metal show, and who introduced Great White on Thursday. Six employees of WHJY-FM in Providence attended. Five came out alive, but Gonsalves remained missing.

"We're frustrated and we're broken-hearted, and we're just hoping he's still alive," said Bud Paras, WHJY's general manager.

Hospitals were deluged by family members trying to locate the missing. At Massachusetts General Hospital, which was treating about a dozen victims, family members looking tired and scared paced the hospital lobby, while others talked in hushed tones to medical officials.

"My heart really goes out to the families who have a relative who they think was involved in this fire," said MGH's Dr. Alasdair Conn. "They have no idea where they are."

Barbara Kulz of Warwick, R.I., said she was sure her 30-year-old son Michael was at the Great White show because she spotted him in video from the concert that was shown on television. Kulz said she and her husband have notified the Red Cross that Michael is among the missing, and they are frantically calling anyone who might be able to help find him.

"So many were lost in that fire, and so much time has gone by and most of [the injured] have been identified," she said. "With so much time, we really don't have any hope. I know he was in the fire—that's definite. His friend wound up in the hospital. We're hoping for a miracle."

Last night, Michael's father, George, e-mailed a photograph of his son to Mass. General, where there was still one unidentified male survivor. After that, he planned to stay home and wait—he said there was nothing left to do.

"Him and I used to go to breakfast on Saturday morning," Kulz said. "It's going to hurt."

For several hours yesterday, Patricia Belanger tearfully toted a picture of her 30-year-old daughter, Dina Demaio of West Warwick, to area hospitals. A legal assistant during the day, Demaio had been waitressing at The Station for several months to earn extra money as she raised her 7-year-old son.

Demaio normally waited tables on weekends, "but because of the concert they asked her to go in [Thursday]," said her sister, Kristy Garvey.

When Demaio didn't come home yesterday, Belanger drove to the club and found her daughter's car outside the charred building. Later that afternoon, Belanger drove to Mass. General hoping that one of the victims who had not been claimed by family members might be her daughter.

"She's not on any list that's out there," Belanger said.

Meanwhile, family members struggled with what to tell Demaio's young boy.

"If he asks any questions, we're just telling him she's

sick right now," Garvey said.

Many of the victims, according to hospital officials, ranged in age from their late teens to their late 30s. Most had one thing in common—their fondness for Great White, a metal band that debuted in 1982 and is best known for its Grammy-nominated 1989 hit, "Once Bitten, Twice Shy."

The audience included men like Kevin R. Washburn, 30, and Michael Stefani, avid fans and best friends planning to move in together. Stefani, of North Kingstown, R.I., had seen Great White at least six times before.

Inside the club, the two split up. When Stefani emerged from the men's room, he watched the flames in horror. Unable to find Washburn, a forklift driver from Franklin, Mass., Stefani fled out a back door and then ran to the front where he tried to help pull people out.

"I pulled one guy out. That's it," Stefani said.

Washburn was nowhere to be seen.

Among the missing were some of the people who helped organize and promote the show.

Gonsalves, a New York City native and a longtime fan of heavy metal, began his career while at Rhode Island College working at the school's radio station.

"He was somebody who really loved what he was doing, and was just a good fellow," said Gary Penfield, vice president for student affairs at Rhode Island College.

Longley was born in Sharon, Pa., and joined Great White in 2000. He began his career playing clubs in Sharon and is well-known in the small town, according to Sarah Adams, a news editor of *The Herald*, a local newspaper. According to his website, he loves rum and Coke and pizza and jogs as a hobby.

Yesterday, Nicole Fusco of Coventry, R.I., arrived at the club looking for her uncle, Tom Medeiros of Coventry, a 40-year-old worker at Bradford Soap in West Warwick who took a day off to make the concert.

She said she learned from one of his co-workers that he went to the club with his girlfriend, Lori Durante of West Warwick. Neither of them had been heard from since.

Medeiros's maroon pickup truck was still parked in the club parking lot.

"We checked all the hospitals and he isn't on any of

the lists," Fusco said. "We haven't heard anything."

As the day wore on, family members grew ever more anxious. By last night they decided to gather for solace.

"He was a big fan of the band," said Andrea Silva, Medeiros's niece. "We're just together now."

Some families were frustrated by conflicting information. Relatives of Steve and Andrea Mancini of Johnston, R.I., were losing hope even as a friend said she had heard that the Mancinis had survived. With no certain word, family members faxed to Mass. General the couple's wedding photo, taken just 15 months ago.

"The doctor on the phone said it doesn't match the description," said Dino Jacavone, one of Andrea's 10 brothers and sisters.

"Some people said they saw them get out," Jacavone said, his voice cracking. "But no one can find them. So we're just waiting."

The Mancinis worked the door at the club, he as a bouncer and she taking money; Steve, 39, also runs the fish department at a Stop & Shop in Providence, and Andrea, 28, helps direct her family's garden center in Johnston.

Steve has a third occupation: guitarist for the band Fathead, which opened for Great White on Thursday night.

John Ellement, Scott S. Greenberger, Tatsha Robertson, Christopher Rowland, and Megan Tench of the Globe staff contributed to this report.

In seconds, elation turned to horror

FEBRUARY 22, 2003

By Ellen Barry and Raja Mishra

WEST WARWICK, R.I.—Before the smell of burning flesh, before his knuckles were bloodied by scrambling feet, before the yelling turned into inarticulate screams, before he saw people with flaming hair and half-melted faces, everything was different.

Christopher Travis was singing in his pick-up truck.

For the last month, in preparation for the show, Travis had been playing his Great White compact discs at top volume on his way to and from the construction site where he works. He had first seen them live in 1986, when he was a hard-partying 20-year-old, and despite the changes that followed—a marriage, a divorce, sobriety—few things make him pump the air in wild joy like the opening chords of "Desert Moon."

While Travis was shaving a razor-edge into his goatee, Erin Pucino was checking her watch at the Shell station cash register where she works, and 19-year-old Mike Ricardi was interviewing Great White lead singer Jack Russell for his college radio show, *Jim and Mikey's Power Hour.*

By the following morning, all three would be survivors of one of the deadliest fires in U.S. history, gazing into the smoking rubble where at least 96 people had died: They would be wrenched out of dense piles of bodies, having groped along the floorboards of The Station and seen charred bodies in the snow outside the nightclub. Mike's friend Jim would be missing. Erin's friend Tammy would be missing.

At 9 p.m., though, it was all anticipation. Travis, in a satin Harley-Davidson jacket and black jeans, offered up the ticket he had bought for $15 at Strawberries Records. Past a bald bouncer, he stepped into a smoky club whose floor was sticky with beer. It wasn't the type of place you would take a first date, said one musician who had performed there.

Waitresses mingled through the crowd with racks of beaker-shaped shot glasses. The crowd, Travis noticed, "had a good buzz going." Great White's guitarist played the first few chords of "Desert Moon" opening the 11 p.m. set, and Travis was elated.

"I pumped my hands in the air," he said. "I had been waiting for this for a long time."

The Station was a thicket of waving hands, dozens of hands curled into the heavy-metal "Devil's Horns" symbol, when the act opened with three fountains of sparkling fireworks. As the cones of fire grew behind him, Russell leaned into the microphone, silhouetted by flame. The stage was bathed in orange light.

There was a moment, a pause. Twenty-six-year-old Rena Gersheris, carrying a rack of shots, gazed at the sparks and decided they were part of the show. Travis, who said he had seen fire break out at The Station at another show last fall, waited for someone to spring forward with a fire extinguisher and put out the fire as they had last fall.

"But nobody did anything," he said.

Pucino's friend grabbed her by the hand and said, "We're going now."

As captured on film, the waving hands suddenly moved differently: They pointed urgently toward the back-right corner of the bar, where one exit is. The music stopped. One of the musicians said something into the mike; it sounded muffled and echoing.

A male voice said, "I'm just going to the door." A woman said, "I can't move." Her voice rises to a shriek. "*I can't!*"

Then the power cut out. The fire poured up the wall onto the ceiling.

As he fell out of a side window onto a deck below, Michael Ricardi, a sophomore at Nichols College, felt the presence of his grandfather, a Worcester firefighter who died in a burning building. "I went that way; you're not going to," Ricardi said he imagined his grandfather saying. On the deck, wandering among charred and unconscious bodies, he was unable to cry, he said.

Pucino, a baby-faced 25-year-old, grasped her friend's hands tightly and made it to the front door—but was crushed under 15 to 20 people who fell on top of her. Her arms flailed at the door's opening and her legs were crushed by the weight of human bodies, Pucino said. Then she felt a hand grab her hand. Two women and one man were pulling her. They pulled her for two minutes, Pucino estimates, and while the women lost their grip on her, the man was holding her tightly when she fell, free, to the ground.

"I'd do anything for that man," Pucino said later. "I don't know who he was. I saw his arms, but not his face."

For his part, Travis was knocked to the ground, and started crawling along a wall as people stomped on his fingers. Hands pushed him forward, and he burst out through a side exit. There were people with their hair burnt off, and people with chunks of skin missing, people with blisters all over. Some people were rolling in the grass. Some people were ripping their clothes off. Some people had puffy winter jackets burning. On all fours, Travis realized that the smell in his nostrils was burning bodies.

"I've never smelled it before, but I knew what I was smelling," Travis said.

Anthony Carsetti, who was driving home with a bag of dog food at 11:15, saw two people stagger out of the club's entrance. Then he saw a dozen, running. Some had hair on fire. Then their faces began to be charred. Some crawled out of the club on their hands and knees. Some of them walked around stunned.

"It looked like they were zombies coming toward us," said Kim Toher, a waitress at the Cowesett Inn.

At the inn, waitresses began filling bags with ice. The 130 to 140 people treated there were suffering from second- and third-degree burns and legs broken from being trampled. Those who escaped found, often, that the friend who had been right behind them had been scorched in the seconds after they jumped out. A 34-year-old Pawtucket man who identified himself only as John said he had let go of his fiancee's hand only at the last moment, when he jumped through the window. Yesterday morning, when John was talking to reporters near the burn site, his fiancee was in critical condition.

"She was only in there four seconds longer than I was," he said.

The patients were wrapped, mummylike, in gauze, and transported to area hospitals. Dr. Selim Suner, an emergency room physician, said about a dozen of the 60 patients brought to Rhode Island Hospital have life-threatening injuries. Many have burns on their hands, suggesting that they were trying to crawl out of the club over a burning floor.

"I haven't ever seen the number of burn patients so concentrated as this one," he said. "One by one, they just kept coming."

Shortly before dawn, a local pastor approached Russell, who was standing near the site of the fire answering questions from reporters.

"You could see he was just on the verge," said Dave LaChance, pastor of the New Song Christian Fellowship. "I just asked him if he wanted someone to pray with. We just held on to each other a little bit."

The smell of carbon came and went yesterday morning, sometimes mingled with alcohol and sometimes, people thought, with rubber. After all four walls had fallen, the entrance to The Station—a section of wall painted with a 6-foot head of Ozzy Osbourne—still stood.

Travis drove himself to Kent County Memorial Hospital. The first thing he did when he got in his truck was play "Desert Moon."

He has an upwelling of wanting for the band members, and wants to give them his condolences.

But he has decided not to go to any more live rock shows.

"Maybe it's time to grow up and move on," he said.

Christopher Rowland, Megan Tench, Tatsha Robertson, Douglas Belkin, Anne Barnard, and Jonathan Saltzman of the Globe staff and correspondent Peter DeMarco contributed to this story.

Recalling deadline with
The Boston Globe

KEITH WOODS: Take me step by step from the moment you heard about the fire.

THOMAS FARRAGHER: I was, coincidentally enough, upstairs at the *Globe* where one of the chief officers of The New York Times Company was giving us an award for the Catholic Church coverage. Immediately after that, [*Globe* editor] Marty Baron came up to me and said, "Congratulations, we need you downstairs on The Station fire." That was the end of my celebration.

So I immediately went into a meeting with the metro editor and the city editors. Some of the first things I asked were: Had we pulled the records for the club so we could find out who the officers were and begin doing some elemental work on who owned this place and who was legally responsible for what went on inside? I had the luxury of some time before I wanted to begin crafting my tops, so I began reading all our feeds. Anybody who's done this for any amount of time knows that sometimes these feeds are okay, sometimes they're mediocre, and sometimes they're gold.

This was a case where we had gold. We had reporters in the parking lot at The Station as the survivors were still there. We had the incredible good luck of having two of our reporters who are former *Providence Journal* reporters, Christopher Rowland and Jon Salzman. They live in Rhode Island, and they were there very early. John Ellement, who was a crackerjack police reporter for us, was there and was doing great reporting, and Doug Belkin, who shared the byline with me. I didn't see Doug until 8 or 9 o'clock that night, and he looked like somebody who had been swimming underwater with his eyes open all night—his eyes were incredibly bloodshot. He had not slept for a day and a half. The feeds were magnificent. They just knocked your socks off.

What was good about them?

Well, you were reading quotes from people who were describing this grisly death scene in the immediate aftermath of having seen it. So you're not sitting on a couch talking to these people. They still have soot on their faces. They still have singes in their hair and emotions in their throat and they're telling you, "I couldn't find my boyfriend...the lights went off...I was lost in the smoke...I jumped out a window." We had incredibly rich detail of the frantic effort to escape the flames from people who still had the cuts fresh from their escape.

As you can imagine, local TV and CNN were going wall to wall with this, so I was able to monitor news conferences as they were happening. This would have been from the governor of Rhode Island, from the local police chief, from public safety officials and rescue workers, and even, very early, the band members. So I was able to, by electronic extension, cover those news conferences, even though we had people there, too. Mainly my job was to cobble this together and make it sing.

So knowing that the [edition] I'm writing for is going to hit the front porches a good 20 to 30 hours after the flames broke out, I wanted to write something that was not telling people that a nightclub in Rhode Island burned down, but to give it the drama and to put into it the texture and the rich detail that were in the notebooks of reporters. That's what I tried to do: to put together this mosaic of the human emotion, the investigative effort, the criminal liability, and the psychological aftereffects that we knew this was going to have for the people who had to endure it.

What words, what verbs, what adjectives, what descriptions carried the things that you wanted to convey?

One of the things we wanted to do was to give readers a feeling that they had been there or at least had been in a club like that. We wanted to make them feel the pump of the music. There's a paragraph about pumping fists and patrons holding longneck bottles of beer as Great White takes the stage, and we tell them what the first song was: "Desert Moon." So there you are, you're telling the readers what it was like at the trigger point: People are happy, they're celebrating, they're watching this little obscure band from the '80s take its place, and then as the music starts—and this description was greatly aided by the WPRI tape, which we used as our time clock—you could see that these people who were pumping their fists to the music very soon were extending a finger from those pumped fists and they're pointing to the fire.

So this paragraph—"As guitars wailed, pyrotechnics similar to Fourth of July sparklers exploded on stage, and the pumping fists turned to frantic hands pointing to the fire"—is there to convey the sense of urgency at first and then ultimately the horror that unfolded as these unsuspecting fans are wondering, "Is this part of the show, or is this something more dangerous?"

What tone are you trying to strike, considering that the death toll is rising as you're sitting there writing?

Well, I think you want to convey the sweep of this event. There are, at this point, close to 100 people dead. This is one of the biggest things that has happened in Rhode Island ever, and one of the biggest things that has happened in New England in quite a long time. So you want to convey that sort of historic sweep.

As I was writing, I was also cognizant that my colleagues were working on a victims' sidebar. So I wanted to get a flavor of that, but not dwell on it. But I think you wanted to convey that what happened here was immediately at issue, that you had fingers pointing at each other right out of the box, and you knew that this would end up in court and people were going to be held accountable. So you wanted to get up top in that story pretty quickly that there would be a criminal investigation. Those are two things: the sweep and the criminal investigation. And then you want to set the scene about where it happened, when it happened. What kind of a place is this?

How are you handling the material so that you can write when it's time to write?

The good thing was we wrote through for all editions on this story. By the first edition, by 4 o'clock Friday afternoon, the meat of the feeds, the really good, on-the-scene impact stuff, was in my computer and on my desk. I had the luxury of having feeds early and I could do some journalistic triage about stuff I knew was going to make it in the paper, stuff I knew might make it in the paper, and stuff I knew would not make it in the paper. One of the things I think any rewrite guy who has done it for a while realizes is that you have to be somewhat brutal in your decision of what to use. You can't be concerned that, "Jeez, Johnny Jones has filed 120 inches here, and I'm only going to use an inch." Well, you only use what you should use, and if you don't do that, you get in trouble real quick, as I learned as a young reporter.

You've got very evocative words in this piece. In the lead of the story you talk about a "lightning-quick" fire and a "curtain of blinding smoke" and "panicked stampede" and, later, the flames "licked" the acoustic material and "danced" across the nightclub's ceiling. Writers always want to know how much time you spend thinking about that and how much of it just popped into your head as you were writing.

I knew the stakes were high here. This was a very big deal, a very tragic event, and we needed to convey it with all the verve we could bring to it. This was not a case of having an hour and a half to compile this. I did have the luxury of time. I did take some care to present it in all its hellish detail but also with a sense of tragedy that 100 people had been lost here.

Any other clues you want to give to a deadline reporter, particularly somebody who's doing rewrite?

Watch the clock. You don't want to be writing your lead on deadline. I would take some time to frame the first 10 inches of the story and get that right—again, if you have the luxury of time. Then let the story flow from there. Some people like to write sections of the story, and that's okay, but my advice would be to watch the clock and get the lead right. That's the pattern I followed on this.

Is there anything I haven't asked you that you think is important to say about the story?

Well, I hope that whatever you do write will convey the

fact that I was using the great reporting of the people who are credited at the bottom of the story, because they were there. I was sitting at my computer terminal writing. They were down there with mud on their shoes, and they deserve the credit.

Peter Canellos, deputy managing editor/metro

I found out about the fire at 2 in the morning, when I got a call from the deputy city editor, Bryan Marquard. He had heard about it through our night person, Mike Rosenwald, who did heroic work for us to get a mention of the fire onto the front page in the late-edition papers when some of our competition did not.

When I spoke to Bryan, he was already back in the newsroom and had arranged for two of our reporters, who had formerly worked in Providence and really knew the Rhode Island landscape, to head out immediately along with our regular night reporter, Doug Belkin, who went out on the scene when we first heard about the fire. So we had three reporters there, and they followed it all night.

I got in touch with all the people who were there, including the late-night person on the copy desk, to make sure we could get the story in as many papers as possible. Once that was done and it was clear that there was no way we were going to be able to get anything else into the paper that evening, I began thinking about our coverage for the following day. We already had reporters on the scene, but then we would have the luxury of maybe 18 hours in which we could pull the coverage together. I wanted to take full advantage of that time.

We had the luxury of having had a team of reporters and editors who had been working together for a long time on our metro staff. We had had a number of major breaking news stories and had developed a kind of unwritten protocol for dealing with these kinds of really big stories.

We tried to divide the staff into reporting teams and assign somebody who would be a writer for that team and the people who would be reporting and feeding to that writer. Then we'd have one editor, one member of the city desk, assigned to edit each story. So from early in the day, the reporters knew who they were feeding the information to and the writer knew which editor to consult, and then I, in overseeing the process, knew who to talk to about which issue.

We wanted to have a lead story that would serve the traditional straight-news presentation of what had happened. But we felt that with this number of victims and a certain appetite on the part of readers to know who these people were, we would also have a whole team researching basic biographical information about the people who were killed or injured.

Tom Farragher is an outstanding writer who has handled the lead-all story on a number of big events and is able to communicate news-related, basic information in a very graceful way. Doug Belkin was the reporter who had been working the night before and was our first person on the scene. So Doug was able to contribute a lot of contemporaneous observation and detail for the story.

I think the best lead-all writers have a superb and innate sense of control. These stories are fundamentally news stories, and people want to get a sense of what happened and what the important issues are very, very quickly. But you also have to make them see the event and feel as though they were there, and to do so in a way that will really stay with people. The difficult thing about a lead-all story is that you don't have paragraphs and paragraphs of exposition to spend on that, so it has to be done with a few bold strokes and small flourishes, and I think the best lead-all writers are able to utilize those skills very well.

Michael Paulson is our award-winning religion writer, and he has written about victims of past tragedies for us. Like Tom, he's somebody who's able to communicate a lot of information quickly and clearly but also in a graceful way. So Michael was the person we chose to be the writer for the victims' story.

Ellen Barry is just an outstanding narrative writer, and we wanted to try to capture a sense of what the event looked like from the eyes of those who did escape. We tried to paint as vivid a portrait as we could of what was happening inside the nightclub.

Anybody who's been involved in these kinds of stories knows that it takes a large number of people to develop a full picture of a multifaceted story, and there are often very tough calls about credit and who gets bylines and who doesn't. The general policy is that we gave the bylines to the person who was the lead writer, who often did reporting by phone as well, and the person among the other reporters whose work was used the most.

As it happens, we're talking right now about a writing award, but good reporting is the source of all good writing, and I think the reporters deserve a lot of credit, too. In this case, the whole staff did outstanding work, and I would not say that the people who got the bylines are necessarily that much more responsible than the people whose names were mentioned at the end of the stories.

Deadline Tip:

It's very important to have an organized response and to have a designated writer prepared to do the stories. In the past we ran into trouble when multiple reporters were sent out, came back in, and started writing their stories. Then the coordination happened at a very late hour and reporter X and reporter Y were asked to combine their stories, and you end up with this kind of giant tapeworm full of "meanwhiles" and "in additions" and other poor transitions. So my advice to papers that have the luxury of a little bit of time, which we had in this case, is to try to organize people in teams and make writing a high priority.

Michael Paulson, religion reporter

I learned about the fire when I woke up and heard about it on the radio and saw it on the Internet. The *Globe* also managed to get a story into the final editions of Friday morning's paper.

I'm a religion reporter and only get involved in general news coverage when there's a huge crisis. However, this was the fourth occasion in the last few years when I've been called upon to anchor our story about victims of a mass tragedy. So what do we do? The first thing is to come up with names of people who were at the concert. We had reporters at the scene who were able to gather names very quickly because family members of concert-goers had started to descend on the scene to see what they could learn. We were able to gather some names from wire service reports and some names from people who called us either to share with us what they knew or to ask us what we knew. One person leads to another, and you start working the phones.

At this time, Friday morning, there were a lot of people who were missing and it wasn't clear who might have escaped but not contacted family and friends yet, and who might have died. So on somebody like [Great White guitarist] Ty Longley, where we have a name, I would call the library and get them to do a clip search on him and see what had been written about him. The band had a website that had biographical information about him. We ran him through databases that had personal information, like Accurint and AutoTrack, to help determine where he lived. They're the two databases that I use most frequently to help track down people, addresses, and phone numbers.

Then we were able to talk to people who knew him growing up or knew him in the music business. With victims or potential victims who were less well known, we would try to contact people who knew them by using databases that have addresses.

We created one file in which very large numbers of reporters were sending whatever it was they were gathering from wherever they were. By mid-afternoon, I was talking to as many of the reporters as I could to tell them what we needed, to remind them to double-check the spelling of names, to get ages, occupations, hometowns, so that we would have as much consistency and detail in the information as we could. Everybody feeds in a slightly different fashion. Their writing styles are different, and the kind of information they gather is different. So I can't just cut and paste information from these different feeds into a story; I have to weave it together into a single story that has a consistent voice and theme.

My job in these kinds of stories is to add as much humanity as possible, which means I'm looking for detail, I'm looking for personality, I'm looking for description that helps people understand who the folks are who showed up at this concert. What were they like? Why were they there? I'm looking for information in what reporters have gathered that helps me paint a picture of the kind of folks who were affected by this tragedy.

These stories about victims are extraordinarily sensitive and difficult because they involve calling people who are distraught, in shock, panicked, uncertain about what has happened to people they care about, people they love. So it's a challenge both for the reporters and for the writers. On the one hand, you want to gather as much information as you can to share with readers. Bringing home the human element of these tragedies requires getting as much personal detail as possible, so this isn't just a story about pyrotechnics or building inspections, but a story about human beings who leave home one night to see a concert by a band they love and don't return.

But on the other hand, you need to respect people's shock and privacy and potential grief. So you call people up and give them an opportunity to talk, but you also respect those who don't want to talk to a newspaper—maybe just at that point, maybe ever. At the same time, you give them an opportunity to share information.

Some people, many people, really don't want to talk to reporters at this point. But many do for whatever reason—because they hope publicity about somebody who is missing will help them locate that person; they're fearing that the person is in a hospital somewhere but unidentifiable and that if they circulate the photograph or the description, their loved one will be identified.

In some cases, they talk because they do know that somebody has died and they don't want them to simply disappear anonymously; they want somebody to listen to their description about why they cared about this person.

Sometimes, frankly, you just don't know why people choose to talk at a moment of tragedy and shock. For some folks, a recognizable, almost ritual element of a big public tragedy is that reporters cover those tragedies and folks who are participants in the news sometimes see it as part of their role to describe what happened.

Deadline Tip:

Be persistent but polite. Take your cues from the folks you're talking to. Explain to them why it is that you're doing this story. Share with them what you know if you have information. Don't lead them to believe that you assume somebody who is missing is dead if you don't know that they're dead. If the person who answers the phone is not willing to talk, ask if there's somebody else in the house who is. If they're not willing to talk, ask if you can call back at a certain time and check in. Be sure before you get off the phone to leave them your phone number and e-mail address so, if at some point they want to talk to you, they know how to reach you with relative ease. Use the present tense when describing people in conversations. Start off by asking something fairly conversational, like, "Is so-and-so a big fan of Great White? How did they get to the concert? Who did they go with?" And then back into more biographical, characterological information about what a person is like.

Ellen Barry, mental health reporter

I remember driving into work that morning and hearing the number of dead. At first, it was 13, and as I was driving it just kept getting higher. By the time I got to my office, which would have been around 9 a.m., it was already clear that it was going to be an overwhelming event.

It was one of those days when the newsroom just worked with incredible focus. Peter Canellos decided he wanted a narrative to accompany the main news story. We decided it would be better to have one person thinking about the structure of the story and receiving feeds. I got tremendously strong feeds from the people who were out there.

I interviewed by phone one of the three people we focused on after Raja Mishra had already done the interview there. I think what I used for the story was largely Raja's feed. He just got incredibly strong detail.

What was difficult was trying to figure out how to build the story on deadline. I wanted to capture the quietness before anything happened, because I knew that the main bar was going to start with the horror and the roar of the event, the terrible loss of life. I thought the second story in the package should start out with this quietness.

The slug for the story was "tick-tock," and we knew we wanted it to be an evocative narrative, not weighed down with the facts of the case, but instead evoking what that evening was like and who those people were, as simply as possible. So if we had found one person, we could have done it that way. But in this case, because there are so many people out there feeding and the atmosphere in general was so chaotic, I got this dump of different people, and we were lucky that two or three of them were enough to structure the story around.

I was taking feeds from a whole lot of different people, using the details that seemed to be the most resonant. You end up using what seems to be the most powerful emotionally. The amount that ended up on the cutting room floor at the end of this story was just enormous. Some of it was very, very good. You just pare away everything that doesn't do something, that doesn't do a job in the story, and, hopefully, you make readers feel a little bit about the people who were going through it.

I was extremely worried about what was going to appear in the story. If you were reporting on a war or Sept. 11, this is the same sort of seriousness of suffering and human experience that you would have written about. Even after the story ran, there were some things I wasn't certain we should have put in. It was difficult to make those decisions with this story—how vivid to make it, how lurid to make it.

I think you probably know you should use a detail if it upsets you when you hear it. I'm thinking about Christopher Travis, who told us so much more than we asked him about giving up drinking and about the failure of his marriage. There's just something incredibly touching about these guys and how much they cared about this band, and I think, in the end, it tells you a huge amount about what their lives are like in this particular economy, in this particular town.

We wanted to perfectly evoke the quiet that preceded the fire and then perfectly evoke the frantic suffering—this three-minute, very short, very intense event. And then I wanted it to be quiet at the end.

Deadline Tip:

If you're doing write-through on something like this, the best thing is to have reporters out there who have very strong sensibilities and know what to look for and can give you the kind of detail that you need. I probably could have written three different stories from what I got from the reporters, and all of them would have been good ones. And then, just be calm. Just keep your cool and be prepared for when the information starts to roll in.

Writers' Workshop

Talking Points

1) *The Boston Globe*, nearly 100 miles from the scene of The Station nightclub fire, divided duties nearly completely between writers and reporters. What do you think of that approach? What are the benefits? What are the drawbacks?

2) Michael Paulson talks about how important it is to use the present tense when writing about people who are missing, even presumed dead, as was the case in these stories. What other ethical concerns should writers consider?

3) Both Ellen Barry and Michael Paulson said they were trying to establish a specific tone for their stories. Barry said she wanted to convey the "quietness" of life before the fire. Paulson said he tried to capture the unsettling feeling of those still trying to learn whether friends or loved ones were still alive. Did the writers succeed? If so, what details, quotes, or turns of phrase combined to deliver the desired tone?

Assignment Desk

1) Go through the lead story written by Thomas Farragher and highlight all the active verbs. Try replacing them with less vivid words. Consider how that changes the power of the sentences.

2) *Globe* reporters and researchers used database searches to chase down information on victims of the fire. Compile a list of such databases, complete with URLs. Use free search engines available on the Internet to see how much information you can collect on the Great White band.

3) Practice doing rewrite. Assemble "feeds" from a team of writers that include quotes, background, and some description. Write a story on deadline from those facts, then meet with the reporters and compare your story with their notes. Discuss how well you relayed the information gathered by others. Then switch roles.

THE WALL STREET JOURNAL.

Susanne Craig   Ianthe Jeanne Dugan   Kate Kelly

The Wall Street Journal

Finalist, Team Deadline News Reporting

When the wheels came off at the New York Stock Exchange, spelling the end of the line for NYSE chief Dick Grasso, *The Wall Street Journal* team of Susanne Craig, Ianthe Jeanne Dugan, and Kate Kelly was ready.

They had investigated questionable trading practices on the NYSE trading floor that led to a Securities and Exchange Commission investigation. Now they'd turned their attention to the rising discontent surrounding Grasso's massive compensation package. When Grasso and others tried to cut off communications, the *Journal* team found sources elsewhere.

The result was "Grasso Quits NYSE Amid Pay Furor," a breaking news story so well sourced that the *Journal* was reporting the news of Grasso's departure before the NYSE board adjourned the meeting seeking his resignation.

Craig, born in Calgary, Alberta, focuses on stories about the brokerage industry. She joined the *Journal* in 2001, having worked for various publications, including *The Globe and Mail* and the *Financial Post,* both based in Toronto. In Canada, she was part of a team that won a National Newspaper Award for a series on insider trading.

Dugan has covered Wall Street and the business world for *The Washington Post, Business Week* magazine, and *Newsday.* While at the *Post,* she won the Gerald Loeb Award for distinguished reporting for breaking the first stories on the emergence of day trading. A native of Manhattan, Dugan writes page-one features for the *Journal*, where she has worked since 2000.

Kelly, a native of Washington, D.C., covers the stock exchange, the NASDAQ, the American Stock Exchange, and other trading firms. She was a writer for *Time* magazine and the *New York Observer* before joining the *Journal* in 2001.

Grasso quits NYSE amid pay furor

SEPTEMBER 18, 2003

By Kate Kelly, Susanne Craig, and Ianthe Jeanne Dugan

The forced resignation of New York Stock Exchange Chairman Dick Grasso could usher in a new age for the world's largest stock market.

Yesterday, Mr. Grasso, 57 years old, was pressured to step down after a public outcry over a $139.5 million retirement-pay package that he had built up over 36 years at the NYSE. Late last night, the exchange's directors were discussing candidates for the job of interim successor in a conference call. It remained unclear who would take the post.

The resignation, after an emergency NYSE board meeting yesterday, followed calls for Mr. Grasso to resign in recent days by a growing chorus of Big Board directors, floor traders, institutional investors and politicians. Critics were especially furious over his pay package because the markets are just now recovering from an unprecedented period of corporate scandal that included shockingly high compensation for some executives.

But the furor masked broader, more fundamental issues facing the exchange. Mr. Grasso was a forceful proponent of the Big Board's 211-year-old auction system—where every trade still passes through at least one live trader on the NYSE floor—despite a host of technological improvements. He has favored the Big Board's position as a secretive club run by Wall Street insiders—and has had his pay set by directors whose firms Mr. Grasso regulates. In 1999, he scotched plans for the exchange to go public, which some traders say could help the NYSE better compete with rivals. And Mr. Grasso has argued that the Big Board, to operate effectively, needs to remain both a market and a regulator. Skeptics see conflicts inherent in that arrangement.

Now all those issues are in play. Indeed, Mr. Grasso's ouster could force historic governance changes on the Big Board, reducing the power of industry insiders to rule the NYSE. And it could even put more pressure on the NYSE—and Wall Street, more broadly—to dilute or give up its self-regulatory powers. That would be a big blow for the securities business.

In his eight years as chairman and chief executive, Mr. Grasso steered the exchange through the rise of competition from Nasdaq and electronic-communications networks. He did that by grafting new technology onto the old system, while maintaining one of the last human-dominated exchanges in the world. Mr. Grasso also has brought in new stock listings, kept NYSE market share high and marketed the exchange effectively.

But he became a casualty of the public's revulsion over 1990s-style corporate excess. He was paid like a big-time Wall Street chief executive, rather than a regulator. The National Association of Securities Dealers, by contrast, pays its CEO about $2 million a year. And Securities and Exchange Commission Chairman William Donaldson—whose total annual pay when he served as Big Board chairman in the early 1990s was about $1.5 million—now makes $142,500 a year.

Mr. Grasso's pay package—he received more than $30 million in 2001 alone—also became a flash point because it came amid a weak market that squeezed many NYSE members. Mr. Grasso pushed the exchange to computerize some of its operations, so that some orders could be routed around brokers. That resulted in slashed commissions at a time when broker paychecks were already being hurt by the market slump.

Some floor traders were livid when Mr. Grasso's pay was disclosed because they had been asked to pay a total of more than $80 million in new fees since 2001 for technological improvements and regulation at the exchange. And the pay disclosures came on the heels of a continuing NYSE investigation into the practices of the floor's elite "specialists," which match buyers and sellers of stocks. The exchange is examining whether some specialists stepped between valid buyers and sellers of stock to make trading profits for themselves, rather than for investors. The specialists say they have done nothing wrong.

SPECIAL MEETING

Yesterday, at a two-hour special board meeting, NYSE directors voted 13 to 7 in favor of Mr. Grasso's resignation, according to a director. Among those who voted for Mr. Grasso to leave were several powerful Wall Street chiefs, including Henry Paulson Jr. of Goldman Sachs, Philip Purcell of Morgan Stanley and William Harrison of J.P. Morgan Chase, according to the director. Mr. Harrison kicked off the conference call, arguing that the integrity of the exchange was damaged and couldn't recover. Several of Mr. Grasso's supporters rallied around him. One director argued that the entire NYSE board should quit, and that Mr. Grasso should stay.

"For the past 36 years I have had the honor and privilege of working for what I believe is the greatest equities market in the world," Mr. Grasso said in a statement issued late yesterday. "Today, I shared with the board of directors in a conference call that, with the deepest reluctance and if the board so desired, I would submit my resignation."

Even before Mr. Grasso's ouster, some NYSE insiders were pressing for change. Some Big Board directors, under pressure from regulators, now are preparing to propose changes to how the exchange's board operates. These include barring the chairman from having input into the nomination of new directors. The preliminary proposals are scheduled to be discussed by the NYSE's special committee on governance at a meeting set for Sept. 29 and are expected to be presented to the full board three days later.

Some NYSE seat owners, frustrated over disclosure and governance at the exchange, are pushing for the Big Board to consider an initial public offering of its own shares. That would resurrect a popular idea that Mr. Grasso killed four years ago without ever publicly making his reasons clear.

The Big Board IPO plan will be aired at a special exchange-member meeting scheduled for today. The NYSE is owned by 1,366 people and institutions that hold "seats" at the exchange. The members, or their representatives, work on the exchange floor in one of two capacities: Traders buy and sell stock for themselves or for customers. Specialists also may trade for themselves, but they have an obligation to ensure the market's smooth functioning by buying stock when others want to sell, and buyers aren't stepping forward.

It was the governance issues raised by Mr. Grasso's pay package that took center stage in recent weeks. Critics from a number of the Big Board's constituencies were aghast that a regulator could be paid so much—and have his pay set by those whom he regulates.

On the NYSE floor, traders were circulating petitions, agitating for new blood in the exchange's boardroom and calling for Mr. Grasso to step down. They were angry that their fees had risen in the years Mr. Grasso received his lofty pay. Some NYSE directors, upset at not knowing the full size of his retirement nest egg, were quietly discussing whether to ask him to leave.

In Washington, the SEC's Mr. Donaldson, a former Big Board colleague, was crying foul over the exchange's governance. The pair are old rivals, dating back to 1990, when Mr. Grasso was passed over for the NYSE's top job, which went to Mr. Donaldson instead. For the next four years, Mr. Grasso privately campaigned to succeed Mr. Donaldson, according to a director who was there at the time. In 1995, Mr. Grasso persuaded the exchange's board that he should take over. Now, Mr. Donaldson was in a position to criticize the man who helped maneuver him out of a cherished Big Board role.

Yesterday, Joe Lieberman, the Democratic presidential contender and senator from Connecticut, called on Mr. Grasso to leave. "Instead of setting an example of ethical leadership for the market he oversees, Mr. Grasso's behavior has shaken the faith of investors and the foundation of the stock exchange," the senator said. Another Democratic presidential hopeful, Sen. John Edwards of North Carolina, also said Mr. Grasso should resign.

For weeks, Mr. Grasso, who has declined repeated interview requests, hung tough. And until earlier this week, some at the Big Board believed he would be able to survive the storm. An adept politician, Mr. Grasso wielded significant influence on the NYSE floor, as well as at major securities firms, which he regulated. Despite its aches and pains, the NYSE remains the most prestigious exchange around.

In recent years, however, dissent has mounted on the

trading floor, as some smaller firms got pinched by the bear market and saw technological changes eat into flow of orders. These firms also saw their profits squeezed when the exchange switched to decimalization, or trading in penny increments, instead of 12.5-cent increments. At the same time, members had no idea how much money Mr. Grasso was accumulating in his own pay package.

His highest point as exchange chief came after the horror of Sept. 11, which tore a hole in lower Manhattan's financial district. Markets were shuttered. Sleeping nights on the couch in his office, Mr. Grasso worked to ensure that his trading floor and the brokerage firms connected to it could begin trading again on Sept. 17. Joined by Sen. Hillary Clinton and New York Governor George Pataki that morning, Mr. Grasso recast himself in a more political light. He adopted a patriotic tone in exchange advertising, displaying an enormous American flag over the NYSE's Broad Street entrance and on the Big Board's 2002 annual report.

But as the months went by, attitudes toward Mr. Grasso shifted. Many exchange members were outraged to learn that he accepted a $5 million bonus for his work in the wake of Sept. 11. It was that special award that lifted his pay for 2001 to more than $30 million, nearly equaling the net income of the entire exchange.

This year, things got more rocky. The exchange was embarrassed late in March when an attempt to nominate Citigroup Inc. Chairman Sanford I. Weill as a director representing public shareholders on the board was foiled. Critics said it was preposterous to appoint Mr. Weill after his company had just paid $400 million to settle government allegations that its stock analysts issued misleading research to investors. Mr. Weill withdrew his name.

Soon after, Mr. Donaldson, the SEC chairman, asked the Big Board to begin a review of its own corporate-governance practices. Then *The Wall Street Journal* disclosed that the NYSE had launched its investigation of specialist firms.

Mr. Grasso went on the defensive. In an interview on CNBC, he said any such trading infractions were akin to "jaywalking," not "mass murder." But investors and some board members were concerned. And when the

Journal disclosed in May the existence of Mr. Grasso's pay-and-retirement package, some floor traders and directors became more restive.

In a compensation-committee meeting around this time, new members Henry Paulson of Goldman Sachs and James Cayne, chairman and CEO of Bear Stearns Cos., gathered with the group's other directors to review Mr. Grasso's contract. The two directors were privately incredulous at the size of Mr. Grasso's retirement package, according to people familiar with their thinking. But his 1999 contract guaranteed him the $139.5 million, which he will get to keep.

But the board was split on whether to draw up a new pay pact—Mr. Grasso recently had been re-elected to another term as NYSE chief—and whether to disclose the details of the old one. In an August board meeting, Mr. Grasso argued that he didn't think "it was wise" to proceed with a new pay agreement, according to minutes. But director Laurence Fink, chairman and CEO of BlackRock Inc., argued that the NYSE should provide Mr. Grasso with a new pay pact and release it to the public, according to minutes. The board decided to wait.

Regulators in Washington soon stepped in. On Sept. 2, Mr. Donaldson wrote a strongly worded letter to H. Carl McCall, the former New York State Comptroller who had been appointed compensation-committee chairman in June. In the letter, Mr. Donaldson demanded that the NYSE provide a detailed accounting of its decision to approve Mr. Grasso's pay package, saying it "raises serious questions regarding the effectiveness of the NYSE's current governance structure." A week later, NYSE directors dialed into a conference call to discuss when and how Mr. McCall should respond to the SEC's information request.

BOMBSHELL

Then, a bombshell: Mr. McCall told directors that in addition to the $139.5 million, Mr. Grasso was entitled to another $48 million in deferred pay over the next four years.

A number of directors were taken aback. One director urged Mr. Grasso to give back the $140 million, a person familiar with the matter says. Mr. Grasso argued that to return the money would invalidate the process by which it had been awarded. Several directors countered that they were willing to call a vote to keep Mr. Grasso from receiving the $48 million, even though they knew the move would be disruptive, directors say.

Mr. Grasso stepped off the call, telling directors he needed some time to confer with his advisers, including well-known Wall Street lawyer Martin Lipton, a partner at Wachtell Lipton Rosen & Katz, according to those who were on the call.

Ten minutes later, according to several directors with knowledge of the call, Mr. Grasso returned to say he thought he should give up the money. The directors voted unanimously to support him.

The NYSE announced the additional $48 million on Sept. 9, and Mr. Grasso's decision to forgo it. But divisions in the board persisted. An exchange spokesman asked NYSE compensation-committee members to stand behind Mr. Grasso in the news conference that day. But several balked, leaving Mr. Grasso and Mr. McCall to face the media alone.

Meanwhile, critics erupted. Several floor traders who own NYSE membership seats put together a petition calling for new management, a highly unusual move. One trader, Patrick J. Collins III, made an unusual appearance before a Sept. 5 meeting of the NYSE's special committee on governance. According to a transcript of his remarks, he told directors that many brokers on the floor were "shocked" when they heard about Mr. Grasso's pay and retirement package. "One board member thought it was a typo," Mr. Collins told them. "I think the trust of the membership has been damaged. I think the public trust has been shattered. You men held very important jobs. Did you ever make this amount of money?"

The exchange, in a statement, said, "Every member of course is entitled to express his or her viewpoint, and the special committee on governance invited members and a variety of other constituents to offer their views" during the governance-committee meeting.

The pressure kept mounting. The *Journal* disclosed this week that several NYSE directors—including Mr. Paulson, Morgan Stanley's Mr. Purcell, Credit Suisse Group Co-Chairman John Mack, and J.P. Morgan Chase's Mr. Harrison—privately were discussing options to quell the furor, including calling for Mr. Grasso's resignation.

In Sacramento, Calif., state treasurer Philip Angelides says he began agitating to take action. On Friday, he called Sean Harrigan, president of the California Public Employees' Retirement System. "Sean, I want to speak up on this issue," he said. "I'm inclined to write a letter, and I want to know if you'll join me." Mr. Harrigan agreed.

Two days later, Mr. Angelides drafted a letter to Mr. Grasso and the board. The pay disclosures, he wrote, had "set back critical efforts to restore the public's faith in our financial system." On Tuesday, Messrs. Angelides and Harrigan, along with Jack Ehnes, CEO of the California State Teachers' Retirement System, publicly asked for Mr. Grasso's resignation. They were joined in short order by officials in New York, North Carolina and Iowa.

Until yesterday, Mr. Grasso tried to put on a brave face. He still made public appearances, including ringing the opening bell, a tradition he has popularized since becoming chairman. On Tuesday morning, he was flanked on the balcony overlooking the trading floor by senior executives of Shinhan Financial, Korea's largest financial-services company. A smiling Mr. Grasso then joined the group on the floor, where they observed the day's first trade.

Lessons Learned

BY SUSANNE CRAIG, IANTHE
JEANNE DUGAN, AND KATE KELLY

Our coverage of the New York Stock Exchange taught a daunting lesson in tenacity: No matter how tough things get, never give up—on your own sources, on the story, or on your own reporting.

For years the NYSE had received mostly positive media, thanks to one of the longest bull markets in history and an incredible marketing effort. Former Big Board chief Dick Grasso turned the ringing of the morning bell into a nationally recognized event. Writing stories that raised questions about the NYSE wasn't easy.

In April 2003, the *Journal* broke a front-page story on allegedly illegal trading practices on the floor of the NYSE. This story led to a Securities and Exchange Commission investigation that resulted in five firms agreeing in early 2004 to pay $240 million to settle the charges. While the reporting ultimately turned out to be correct, the exchange excoriated our coverage. The week after our first story ran, the NYSE issued a press release saying our stories contained "substantial erroneous reporting." Its then-chairman, Grasso, went on TV to advance the NYSE case that our reporting wasn't accurate.

But we did not recoil. The *Journal* stood by our reporting. We continued to dig. NYSE officials, upset by this story and others that had preceded it, were no longer speaking to Kate Kelly, who covers the exchange. Her calls through the switchboard were redirected to corporate communications. NYSE asked that questions be submitted in writing.

Even as the NYSE did all it could to shut down Kate, we knew that finding a way to talk to exchange executives was important. After Grasso refused to speak to Kate, *Journal* editor Dave Kansas negotiated a compromise. We would have a conference call in which Grasso and Susanne Craig, our Wall Street reporter, could speak. Kate and Robert Zito, the NYSE public relations man, could be on the call, but would mostly listen rather than talk. It took two days to negotiate, but we got the interview.

With the NYSE proving tough to crack, we focused on non-staff sources such as the NYSE board of directors. The directors, who approved Grasso's $187.5 million retirement and deferred compensation nest egg, were largely high-powered CEOs who didn't take kindly to reporters questioning their actions. In early May, Kate and Susanne, along with colleague Charles Gasparino, were the first to report on Grasso's multi-million-dollar pay package. For months, most directors refused to return our calls, hoping the issue would go away. We kept calling.

Throughout the months we worked on this story, Michael Siconolfi, the veteran *Journal* editor who championed our coverage, always reminded us to "never leave anything on the table." With that in mind, we split up the names of board members and other key sources and called each of them every few weeks, even if the messages went unreturned.

In early summer, Ianthe Jeanne Dugan was assigned to the story. She concentrated on building relationships with exchange members. We made a pact never to call one another's sources, knowing we needed to build individual relationships with each one. It paid off. In late August, the Grasso pay flap began to heat up and the sources we had slowly developed over the summer began talking. By now, a number of directors were under attack for approving Grasso's large pay package. This gave them an incentive to talk, and we took advantage of that. But knowing that everyone had an ax to grind, we double- and triple-sourced every piece of information.

This reporting effort, which happened over the course of several months, made it possible for us to assemble on deadline the front-page story "Grasso Quits NYSE Amid Pay Furor."

The coverage really threw open the doors of the Big Board to public view for the first time since its founding more than 200 years ago. That exposure rapidly began to change the way stocks are traded at the world's biggest stock exchange. How those changes play out remains to be seen.

Dan Neil
Commentary

There is an outlaw quality to Dan Neil's life story that makes the reading of his brilliant and eccentric work as an automotive critic for the *Los Angeles Times* even more intriguing. Divorced twice, a recovering alcohol and drug abuser, a lover of fast cars from boyhood, fired from a newspaper job for writing about lust by the dashboard light—all this misrule belies the rigorous discipline and intellectual dexterity that mark his work as among the most distinctive in American journalism. If William Faulkner had run off with Daisy Duke, they might have produced Dan Neil as their love child.

His authorized biography goes like this: Born in Pennsylvania, he grew up in New Bern, N.C. His father was an engineer with Stanley power tools, his mother a private investigator. By the time he had graduated from high school, Neil had picked tobacco, cleared timber for

Los Angeles Times

the U.S. Forest Service, clerked at a record store, and worked as a lifeguard.

Neil attended East Carolina University and graduated in 1982 with a degree in creative writing. He entered the graduate English program at North Carolina State University in 1984, where he worked as a teaching assistant for two years.

Neil's first job in journalism was a classic: part-time obituary editor for the local newspaper, *The News & Observer* in Raleigh, N.C. Neil finished his master's degree in English literature and began working as a copy editor at *Spectator*, a weekly arts and entertainment journal. In 1989, he returned to the *N&O*, where he worked as a copy editor and began freelancing arts and entertainment features and reviews. In 1991, he moved to the classified advertising side of the paper, producing the weekly advertorial real estate and auto sections.

On his own initiative, Neil began writing reviews for the auto section and continued to do so for six years, without benefit of an editor. During this time Neil's often outrageous and frequently eloquent writing became a reader favorite. The paper's publisher, Frank Daniels Jr., often remarked that the best writer at the paper worked for the classified advertising department.

In 1997, his account of a backseat tryst with his fiancée prompted the *N&O* to rein him in, insisting that he begin running his columns past the director of automotive advertising. This Neil declined to do, and he was fired in May 1997 for what he likes to call "principled insubordination."

He then began work for *Car and Driver* magazine, the world's largest automotive enthusiast publication. His work has appeared in *Popular Science, Condé Nast Traveler, Robb Report*, and *The New York Times*.

In 2003 the *Los Angeles Times* recruited him to be the automotive critic. Along with winning the ASNE award, Neil won the 2004 Pulitzer Prize in criticism for his column, "Rumble Seat."

—Roy Peter Clark

[*Read two more of Neil's automotive commentaries on the CD-ROM included in this edition of Best Newspaper Writing.*]

BMW's bigger, better Rolls

SEPTEMBER 17, 2003

Not since torch-wielding peasants chased Frankenstein's monster through the town square has such a noble spirit been so mercilessly taunted. One critic compared the new $320,000 Rolls-Royce Phantom to a coffin maker's "Executive Slumber Series"; another called it the world's most majestic air conditioner.

Allow me to pile on.

Man, this thing is ugly.

Yet from the driver's seat, the Phantom is a sensational automobile. There's magic and mystery here, fistfuls of romantic motoring. I could drive it to the crack of doom.

Like Shelley's maledicted hero, the styling of the 2004 Rolls-Royce Phantom is something of a cut-and-stitch job. Rolls-Royce's chief stylist for exterior design, Marek Djordjevic, scoured the company's picture books for design cues and proportions that he considered elemental to the marque—a visual vivisection, if you will. The long hood, the short rear deck, a rising sill line, the convergent hood lines, all poised over a long wheelbase and fronted by a chrome rictus of a grille. These elements he sewed together to form the Phantom, the first new Roller produced under BMW's ownership.

For example, Djordjevic lifted the massive "blind quarter" of the new Phantom—the broad sheet-metal pillar aft of the rear window—from the Hooper-bodied Phantom limousines of yore (in the glory days of Rolls-Royce, buyers would send the bare chassis to coach builders such as Hooper to be fitted with a custom body).

Djordjevic also decided that the new car needed classic coach doors, hinged at the rear. The blind quarters and coach doors combine to create one of the new car's signature pleasures: Open a rear door, which feels as heavy as one of Ghiberti's *Gates of Paradise*, and step easily into the spacious rear compartment, barely ducking your head, then settle back in the leather banquette, secluded in aristocratic privacy behind the blind pillar. So, point to Rolls-Royce. Jolly good show on the coach doors.

Other quintessential double-R design elements in the Phantom are the blade edge of the front fenders; the headlight assembly set high in the "catwalk" between the Greek temple grille and the fenders; and the round fog lights situated just above bumper level (the simulacra of polished Lucas lamps).

But certainly the features that have most thrown viewers are the car's oppressive bulk and its crazy face. This new slab-sided Phantom is more than 19 feet long (longer than a Ford Excursion) and well above 5 feet tall, possessing something of the visual grace of a container ship. Djordjevic based his design, and its scale, on Rolls-Royces pre-1972. These were some awfully big cars, and in the current context, the Phantom reads almost comically big.

And then there's the car's front. It looks like the face of one of those robotic pet dogs they sell in Japan.

What could have possessed Djordjevic? I spent an evening with the young designer in Santa Barbara some months ago, and he seemed to have had all his marbles. What gives?

To begin, ask what exactly did BMW buy when it purchased the rights to the Rolls-Royce name from Vickers (the parent company of Rolls-Royce Motor Cars Ltd.)? Rolls-Royce was a shambles by the time BMW came along in 1998. The Museum-of-the-Industrial-Age Rolls factory in Crewe, England, was dirty and dim. The cars were awful. The only thing in the pipeline was soot.

Rolls-Royce's single salable asset was its history, its book of myths and legends lavishly illustrated with gorgeous cars dating to Edward VII. For the Phantom, BMW built a brand-new factory in Sussex, on the Earl of March's Goodwood property, and started from scratch. In fact, there is no "Rolls-Royce" in the sense of a continuous business enterprise started by Hank Royce and Chuck Rolls. To think of the new Rolls-Royce as anything other than the high-tech, super-luxury brand adjunct to the Bayerische Motoren Werke is to willfully suspend disbelief.

But some fictions are fun, even necessary. And for the fiction of Rolls-Royce to remain operable, BMW needed to make the car more British than King Arthur Pendragon, more aristocratic than Lord Mountbatten, more Rolls than Henry's dear old dad.

My guess is that the styling was driven over the top by the design team's anxiety over authenticity. What began as a paean to the past wound up looking like it had bolts in its neck.

What's it like to drive? I'm tempted to say it drives like a Rolls-Royce, but that too may be a sort of wishful back formation, a trick of memory. No Rolls-Royce of the former regime was half so luscious or so purely seductive.

The pleasure begins with the way the car situates itself around you. The driver's seat is more like a driver's throne, with a commanding view outward, the long reach of the hood stretching into the scenery. The eye position is as high as in many SUVs. The central console between the seats pairs with the door bolsters to create armchair-like support at the elbows—though it is easy to inadvertently pop open the console's compartments. Also, the power-seat controls are secreted in the console, so adjusting the seat position takes some attention.

One of the direct drafts from parent BMW is the Rolls "Command" panel, a dumbed-down version of the notorious I-Drive system operating the navigation, DVD and telephone systems. The rotary controller deploys from a compartment at the base of the seat console, while the white-face analog clock on the dash slips away to reveal the display panel. Mercifully, the basic climate and audio controls are available as rotary dials flanking the dash-mounted units.

The new Rolls carefully observes the tactile proprieties of tradition. The dashboard vents are opened and closed with sterling-silver organ stops, while the window controls are the classic violin key design. The large-diameter steering wheel is ultra-thin, like Brit cars of memory, and the steering wheel center has a glossy, piano-black roundel with the double-R emblem. The starter is a push-button affair. The woodwork is orchestra-instrument quality, with a buyer's choice of figured woods, from burr walnut to black tulip. Cabinet-style marquetry, inlays and crown-cut veneers are optional, but the lambs'-wool rugs and cashmere headliner are standard.

The rear compartment is likewise luxe, with lots of welcome extras, including adjustable ambient lighting,

Jazz Era-style reading lamps and umbrellas hidden in compartments in the doors. Even so, the Rolls is not so thoroughly accessorized as the rear compartment in DaimlerChrysler's Maybach 62, which is nothing quite so much as a corporate jet.

No, the Rolls is definitely a car, a motorcar, with all the stately advance the word implies. Rolls has long invoked the term "waftability" to describe the cars' effortless, nearly levitating acceleration and deep reserves of power. The word dates to 1907, from a motor journalist's happy phrase about a Rolls "wafting" down the road. But this powertrain—comprising a 60-degree, multivalve, 6.75-liter V-12 buttoned to a six-speed ZF transmission with shift by wire—has waft coming out its ears.

The stroked version of BMW's 6-liter V-12 features state-of-the art combustion technology, including direct injection, and infinitely variable valve timing and lift. Long gone are the days when an engine's inherent torque characteristics were fixed by metal parameters. The engine has been calibrated to produce an ocean liner-like 531 pound-feet of torque at 3,500 rpm, but 75% of that grunt is available at a mere 1,000 rpm, lending the Phantom a tsunami-like surge upon acceleration. Horsepower tallies a considerable 453.

It's enough to launch the 5,600-pound Rolls to 60 mph in less than six seconds; meanwhile, the thrifty direct injection gives the car an impressive fuel mileage of 14/24 miles per gallon, city/highway.

Over the road, the Phantom has all the glycerin smoothness and cathedral quiet you could hope for. The body structure is a space frame built up of aluminum and magnesium castings, riveted and glued alloy panels and exotic steel sub-frames. It is one of the stiffest chassis in production. The Rolls uses air springs at all four corners, double wishbones up front and multi-link suspension in the rear, all fastened to steel sub-frames.

There is no denying that this is a big car, and it drives big, particularly if you push it on a country road. There's a fair amount of body movement before it acquires its stance in a corner, and it feels a little ungovernable at high speed. But for the most part, the ride-and-drive is phenomenal. The Michelin PAX run-flat tires are—get this—31 inches tall, centered on 20-inch rims. That's 11 inches of sidewall, which makes for a pillowy soft, if predictably elastic, ride. The brakes are monsters, and then some, at all corners.

Rolls-Royce was once a kind of shorthand for excellence, for stately British cars with unsurpassed engineering, bespoke quality, craftsmanship and superb good taste. Now, in an odd quirk of fate, a big German company has rescued the marque—reanimated it, if you will.

Skeptics, put down your pitchforks.

Caught up in the Crossfire

OCTOBER 1, 2003

Like many great beauties—Marilyn Monroe, for instance—the new Chrysler Crossfire has a faintly tragic air about it. And like many consumers of beauty—Frank Sinatra, for instance—I'm only too happy to exploit it.

The 2004 Crossfire ($35,570 as tested) joins Chrysler's recent portfolio of low-volume, high-zoot production cars—including the PT Cruiser and the Prowler—that riff on the history of car design. The PT Cruiser and the hot-rod-inspired Prowler are not really serious cars but fun and frothy exercises in nostalgic styling, rendered with a kind of Toontown exaggeration that gives the viewer a winking nudge in the ribs. Alas, one's ribs get sore pretty quickly. These days, the PT Cruiser strikes me as insufferably twee. Both it and the Prowler look destined for the nearest Shriners parade.

The Crossfire, on the other hand, is deadly serious, a lighted fuse of polished elegance and high ambition. It's a small car, only 159.8 inches long sitting on a 94.5-inch wheelbase. But the Crossfire has tremendous visual presence, with its wide body raked over relatively huge 19-inch rear wheels and 18-inch front wheels. The glassed-in part of the car, the greenhouse, is low and narrowed, giving the car a sloe-eyed allure.

The most distinctive part of the Crossfire profile is its boat-tail hatchback, formed as the edges of the roof converge into a kind of teardrop shape, leaving the rear fenders to flare out over the rear wheels. It's a wonderfully organized form—romantic and rational at the same time. But what makes the Crossfire work is its surface detailing: the Art Deco fluting, polished strakes, raised spine and sculpted surfaces, which make the car look like a piece of precision-milled machinery.

This is the kind of car that makes you set your alarm clock early so you can go stare at it in the driveway. It's gorgeous.

As a "halo" product, the Crossfire is crucial to the Chrysler brand's effort to move upmarket, to be a premium brand in the same league as Lexus or Cadillac. This is not an easy thing to do. Consumers have a pretty definite idea of how much they are willing to spend on a Chrysler, no matter how swell it is. The Crossfire argues its case well.

So what's so tragic? Only that it's not really a Chrysler. Under the artful skin of the Crossfire is the running gear of a Mercedes-Benz SLK, right down to the crankshaft in its 3.2-liter V-6 (the car is assembled by Karmann in Germany). This is the first car to come from the DaimlerChrysler merger that gene-splices Chrysler design and Mercedes engineering.

Although few could complain about the results, I confess to a little wounded nationalism; it would have been great for such a wonderful car to be American to the bone. Chrysler, more than any other American car company, could justify a revival of streamlined, Deco-flavored styling. Chrysler's Airflow sedan in the 1930s was America's first streamlined mass-production car, and what it lacked in functional aerodynamics it made up for in the expressive, streaking styling of the Machine Age. The most exciting car of the year is made of leftover Mercedes.

And there is a degree of insincerity to the Crossfire. In the same way that Frank Gehry's Guggenheim Museum in Bilbao, Spain, is an elaborate titanium blossom surrounding more or less rectangular spaces, the Crossfire's exterior design, as beautiful as it is, isn't essential to the car.

Of course, a few laps around the neighborhood will wring such doubts from your mind. The Crossfire is wicked fun to drive. In the transition from the SLK's open top to a fixed roof, the chassis has become substantially stiffer. The car has all the flex of a cast-iron sink and that lovely feeling of deep soundness that Benzes, at their best, have. It feels as if you have a good leg under you at all times.

Commuters, be advised: The Crossfire's suspension tuning favors handling over comfort. The ride is pretty choppy in that short-wheelbase way, and there's a steady diet of zings transmitted through the steering wheel and seat from the huge Michelins.

On the other hand, the car handles far better than I

expected, with a nice even balance in S-curves that gradually and gracefully transitions to understeer. Toss it from corner to corner and the Crossfire recomposes itself without fretting, with little body roll or ungainly rebound.

Thanks to the car's low weight and its yards of high-quality rubber, the Crossfire has lots of lateral grip. The car has anti-lock brakes and traction and stability control, but on dry pavement these systems allow enough slip and slide to have fun.

Our test car was equipped with Benz's five-speed automatic transmission mated to the 215-horsepower V-6 engine. A six-speed manual is available, though most Southern California commuters will shun it. The car was pretty quick, returning zero-to-60-mph times in the neighborhood of seven seconds, though adding more power would be a beautiful thing.

It's expected that Chrysler will avail itself of the supercharged version of this engine, which in the SLK produces 349 horsepower—a lot of ponies, by anybody's reckoning. I just don't see where Chrysler will put the supercharger. The Crossfire's hood is practically on top of the engine cover.

One curiosity is the motorized spoiler that deploys from the cam-back at speeds above 60 mph. In mixed city driving, where one often goes above and below 60 mph, the spoiler cycles continually with a very low-tech-sounding motor whine. However, considering Audi's experience with the TT—the humpback car was quietly redesigned to include a spoiler after some Autobahn accidents revealed that the rear was lifting at high speed—the Crossfire's spoiler is probably a good idea.

Life inside the Crossfire would be cozy. Tall drivers may have a little trouble getting comfortable because the car has limited leg room and little recline available behind the deeply bolstered seats. Yet for a car so closed in, outward visibility is quite good (you are never far from a window in a small car), and the sculptured rear fenders create open sightlines through the side mirrors.

The car's instruments are sensibly arranged; indeed, given their vintage, they have a comforting simplicity: More fan? Turn the knob to the right. More volume? It's the knob on the left. Technophobes may like the car solely for its refreshing lack of digital interface. The central console and all the switch gear are coated with a shiny metallic finish, as in the less expensive Mercedes C-Series, a sort of acrylic that is strangely warm to the touch. The same material covers the shifter. The comforts of home include heated power seats, a 240-watt Infinity stereo with two subwoofers and six speakers, keyless entry and dual-zone climate control.

Composed and compelling, precise and polished, the Crossfire is a singularly appealing car. Unlike a lot of design-intensive cars, whose appeal is so perishable they ought to come with a "best-if-used-by" stamp, the Crossfire has a bearing that should hold up well over time.

The Shriners will have to look elsewhere.

What would Gulliver drive?

NOVEMBER 12, 2003

It has taken years of analysis and reverse engineering, but the Japanese automakers are now able to build vehicles just as big and stupid as the Americans.

This is a troubling development for Detroit, which has long had a lock on big and stupid. Indeed, the popular big-stupid segment has been a godsend to General Motors Corp. and Ford Motor Co.: Full-size sport utility vehicles, built on the same platforms as full-size pickups, offer the highest profit margins of any car or truck and represent more than 800,000 in annual unit sales in North America.

Toyota Motor Corp. was the first Asian automaker to pan for gold in the big-ute stream when in 2000 it began selling the Sequoia, built on the Tundra pickup platform.

Now comes the 2004 Pathfinder Armada from Nissan Motor Co., another SUV built on a big-pickup platform (namely, the steel ladder-frame underpinnings of the forthcoming full-size Titan) in the United States. Both Toyota and Nissan breed their Brobdingnagians at American plants: Indiana and Mississippi, respectively.

The Armada is the Double Whopper with Cheese of SUVs. Excepting the Chevy Suburban/GMC Yukon XL twins—and the Hummer H2, which is big-stupid *sui generis*—the Armada is longer (206.9 inches) and taller (77.8 inches) than anything else in its class, which includes luxury lorries like the Ford Expedition and Chevy Tahoe. It is as wide (78.8 inches) as the widest in the class (Tahoe) and has the longest wheelbase (123.2 inches) and highest ground clearance (10.7 inches) in its segment. The Armada's pricing is competitive with that of the domestic barges; our loaded-to-the-gunnels test vehicle priced out at $41,550 (a luxury LE edition with sunroof, power liftgate and DVD entertainment system).

But, clearly, Nissan's designers believed that gawdamighty size alone would not be enough to guile Americans away from their beloved domestics. It had to look scary. Thus the Armada's case-hardened styling—vast slabs of steel and glass soaring above the wheel wells, with fender flares punched out at discontinuous angles to give it a muscular look, though it looks to me less muscular than glandular. The chrome bumper insets look as if somebody swiped the doors off a Vulcan gourmet oven.

This isn't design, it's pornography.

The dimensions give the Armada a distinctly bus-like gestalt. Grab hold of the chrome door lever and pull. The door swings open like that of a side-by-side refrigerator (how long before the Armada is cheekily nicknamed the "Amana"?). The seat height is a pants-splitting 34 inches from the ground, and once you hoist yourself aboard you find yourself dwarfed by the Armada. Well, at least I did. I'm over 6-feet-1 and 180 pounds, and I felt as if I was wearing Shaq's warm-up suit. I dropped a piece of paper on the floor ahead of the front-passenger seat, and I could not reach it from the driver's seat.

The Armada, a seven- or eight-passenger vehicle depending on configuration, has vast amounts of room allotted to second-row seating with a full three inches more legroom than any of its competitors. Armadas with the second-row bench can be quickly configured in such a way that, when the second and third rows are folded, the cargo floor is flat from the liftgate all the way to front seat backs, creating 97 cubic feet of space. Vehicles with the second-row captain's chairs require you to remove the console.

As in the Toyota Sequoia, the Armada's second-row seats flip forward for easy access to the third-row bench seat, which is raised stadium-style to improve sightlines and reduce the consumption of Dramamine.

As all this suggests, Nissan is pitching the Armada as a family vehicle. Consider the tag line: "Liberate your family." I bet that plays well in Utah.

Consider, also, the various means available to distract the kids on the long drive from Provo to Orem. The LE model test vehicle was equipped with dual-media playback that allows the front-seat passengers—the adults—to listen to the stereo through the 10-speaker Bose premium sound system, while the kids tune to whatever CD-DVD-MP3 they desire with wireless headsets. A flip-down LCD monitor is situated in the ceiling for watching or video gaming.

In addition, the Armada is awash with cup holders, cubbies and bins, including an overhead console for reading lights, air vents and yet more storage.

The other thing the Armada has in abundance is power. Under the broad hood is a 5.6-liter V-8 with dual-overhead cams and four valves per cylinder—the same engine in the Titan pickup—producing 305 horsepower and 385 pound-feet of torque at 3,600 rpm. That is sufficient to give the Armada class-leading towing (9,011 pounds) and payload (1,949 pounds) capacity. My test model had two-wheel drive; a four-wheel drive model also is available.

Meanwhile, thanks to the Armada's five-speed automatic transmission—the only one in its class—the vehicle has unholy acceleration. *Car and Driver* magazine clocked an Armada from zero to 60 mph in seven seconds flat. The nearest class competitor is more than a second slower. A Mercedes-Benz E320 sedan requires three-tenths longer to reach 60.

So then, the ideal customer for this vehicle would be…who? A family of Masai warriors towing their 30-foot cabin cruiser to Lake Victoria for the weekend?

Unfortunately, this vehicle will find its way into the hands of too many suburban moms and dads who will use it as a short-range commuter and mall runner, tasks for which it is excessive. Even setting aside fuel economy (13/19 miles per gallon city/highway, according to the EPA), there is the Armada's sheer unfriendly bulk. You need the ground crew from Lakehurst, N.J., to park this thing. And every mall parking deck threatens to skim the roof racks right off it. The center of the Armada's headlamps is approximately 38 inches from the ground, which puts them at a perfect height to fuse the retinas of drivers ahead of you.

This is where SUV enthusiasts and I have irreconcilable differences: If you need such a vehicle—and that means you have five kids, live in Idaho and tow a boat the size of a Spanish galleon—fine, by all means. If you don't need one, what, pray tell, is the upside? And if you live in the Los Angeles area, may I mildly suggest you get out of my way?

It's not as if the Armada offers thrilling handling or a luxurious ride to compensate for these inconveniences.

I found the ride quality over anything but smooth pavement to be fretful, with lots of jostling over surface imperfections and fairly uncontrolled body movement as it thundered over uneven concrete and asphalt patches.

On California 2 heading north to Glendale, the Armada fairly bounded over the evenly spaced expansion joints in the highway. Over jolts big and small, the interior fittings rattled lustily. The central dash panel twittered. The rear bench shook. When I went looking for the source of the rattles, I instead discovered lots of shoddy upholstery stitching.

Sales of full-size SUVs are down 17% from a year ago, and this is anything but a growth market. In part that reflects automakers' offering crossover vehicles more finely tuned to the real-world needs of urban and suburban customers. Nissan's Murano and Infiniti FX45 are excellent examples.

It further reflects the rate at which people are abandoning full-sizers because of their wearying nuisances.

The Armada, as vainglorious as its name, is inanely bigger, when what the world needs now is better.

A conversation with
Dan Neil

ROY PETER CLARK: Does it bother you that I drive a PT Cruiser? Do you judge people by what they drive?

DAN NEIL: Not in a moralistic sense, but I believe that what people drive is indicative of the kind of people they are; more than that, the kind of background they have. I think that automotive choice is an extremely telling part of a person's makeup. There are two things. Vitruvius, the Roman architect, talked about what is volitional about design and what is obligatory about design. That same thing applies to car choice. There is what we have to have, what fits into our budget, and what fits into the number of people we have in our family and our "lifestyle." But then there's the volitional aspect. What is it about this car choice that speaks to me emotionally or speaks to me in some other way?

The PT Cruiser is a very evocative kind of car. It says that—well, okay, let's just do a little armchair psychology, except that it's in the driver's seat. A PT Cruiser is a sassy car. It has kind of a winking irony about it. It's style intensive. It has a need to be noticed. It's fun but practical. If you wanted to deconstruct it, you could say that the person who buys a PT Cruiser has certain obligations that he must fulfill, but he doesn't want to be defined or hamstrung or hemmed in by those obligations.

What kind of car do you drive, Dan?

Well, typically I drive test cars, but I own a 1960 MGA roadster with wire wheels, which I rebuilt from the ground up.

Are you an engineer by training?

No. I am at best a shade-tree mechanic. I know a lot about automotive engineering in a broad conceptual sense because of the beat I cover, but when it comes time to pick up a wrench, I would not say that I'm a working technician or a mechanic. The thing about working on cars is that it's like painting or pottery. It's really about manual dexterity. I can tell you exactly how to, say, port and polish an intake manifold. But actually doing it with my hands, that is something that only comes with a lot of time and a lot of practice, and working on cars is about knowing which tool will fit in that little spot and how to get your hand on it and how not to break off stuff. Great mechanics are extremely smart, dexterous, patient people.

Tell me the evolution of your passion for cars.

My father was an engineer. He worked for Stanley power tools. I grew up in North Carolina, so I was around machinery and cars and tools all the time. We had boats and cars, and the driveway was always full of some half-baked project that my father was working on. He was a very good engineer. I wouldn't say that Dad was a superior mechanic. He would occasionally tear stuff up, too.

My first experience with a car was my sister had a 1968 Pontiac GTO convertible with red-rim tires and a 440 engine and a Hearst four-speed shifter—this was basically the hot setup in 1968. She went to Hawaii on vacation to meet her husband. My dad and I took the car out, and Dad said he was just going to blow the carbon out, which, as I know now, was crazy talk. Dad was many things, but he sure wasn't the greatest driver in the world, because that was a very high-performance car for its time, on little, little tires. So we go hauling ass down this road and we're going—I don't know—a buck twenty, a buck thirty. It seemed like the speed of light at the time. That was my first experience with the exhilaration of being in a big, fast car. Then a couple of years later, a neighbor of mine had a '69 Dodge Charger, and this car would turn a 12-second quarter-mile pass, which was at the time very, very fast—it's still fast—and so we went out to the local drag strip and I sat in the car and we went and made a pass. Well, it was that sensation—the giddy, gossamer, in-the-gills kind of feeling—that exhilaration of acceleration that was imprinted on me pretty early from there. I was fascinated with cars, but I had other interests. I was interested in karate and girls.

What year were you born?

Jan. 12, 1960. So when I was 16 in 1976, I bought for $1,100 a Fiat 124 Spider, powder blue, proceeded to blow the engine up in that, put a new engine in it. I loved this car, and I worked on this car all the time. Then in a weird quirk of fate, a guy with the exact same kind of car, same year and everything, ran into me and totaled it in one of those *Magnolia* moments—you know, where life is stranger than fiction. So then the next car I got was a Fiat—for some reason I had this thing about Italian cars, so I was a masochist or something. But I bought a Fiat 131. It was a sedan, orange, and I drove that thing on two wheels most of the time. I really learned to drive hard in that car. And then after that, I had a Datsun B210.

I had one of those.

Well, the Datsun 510 was really the first tuner car, and it raced and won all over the place. Datsun made a good car. At the same time they were building the 240 and the 280Z, so Datsun had a performance background. I drove that car for a long time. Now, I started getting high in high school, about 1976 or '77, and I proceeded to develop just a sensational drug and alcohol habit up until 1989, when I got clean.

What are we talking about? Marijuana?

Yeah, we're talking about all kinds of stuff. We're talking about alcohol and drugs and whatever was available. You know, the party didn't stop when I got out of college, let's put it that way. So the car that survived my drug and alcohol years was the Datsun B210, and I can think of no greater tribute to that car than that it survived these years when I was really in my cups and it was a miracle. That car just wore like iron; I couldn't break it. Not that I was taking all that great care of it.

So I got clean in 1989. I went to work for the local newspaper in about the same year.

Whose paper would it have been?

That would have been the Raleigh *News & Observer.*
Marion Gregory, who was the managing editor, hired me
more out of pity than out of any sense of confidence that
I could do the job, which was basically copy editing the
calendar listings for the features department. I had
worked there while I was in school editing obits.

Where did you go to college?

I went to East Carolina University, 1978 to 1982. Actually, it's a funny thing about college. I don't actually remember going, but I remember so much of what I
learned. I mean, I kick ass in *Jeopardy.* I remember so
much stuff. I must have gotten a great education, though I
don't remember it. So I got a degree in creative writing at
East Carolina University, and then I went to North Carolina State University to get a master's in English, which I
did, '82 to '84. So by the time I came back to *The News &
Observer* in 1989, I was a recovering addict with a master's in English and those were my qualifications.

Where else did you work?

Well, in 1988, I went to work as a copy editor for *Spectator* magazine, which was a weekly arts and entertainment
journal, kind of the North Carolina version of the *Village
Voice.* I worked there for a year and a half, and that was
really when I was coming to the end of my tether, so I
didn't exactly distinguish myself as a writer. Although
there's one thing about the *Spectator* years, as I think
about it now, that resonates. A lot of people give me credit
for being broad in my learning, and at the *Spectator* I met
two of the most phenomenal autodidacts in the world.
One was a guy named Hal Crowther, who is Bosley
Crowther's son. Bosley Crowther was *The New York
Times* movie critic for many years.

The other was Godfrey Cheshire, who is now the
movie reviewer for the *New York Press.* These two guys
were just brilliant, learned men, and what I took away
from my experience with them is that you don't stop
learning when you get out of college. These guys were

learning, were studying things every single day of their lives. They read books, they took notes, they taught themselves. It was an amazing thing to see, and it was a habit I picked up that I try to do even now.

Your writing voice is so distinctive that I was curious about your influences. You've just suggested that these two men really helped shape your sense of what it means to be a writer who's learning all the time.

Yeah. Believe me, I came from a pretty impoverished intellectual background. Learning was not highly cherished, especially when I was picking tobacco. After I got fired from the *Spectator,* I went into rehab for obvious reasons. When I came out I didn't have a job. I was also married and had a 3-year-old son. So I went to work in this very low position at *The News & Observer* editing the calendar listings, which I confess I didn't do all that well. But I started writing stories for the paper on a free-lance basis, and the very first real newspaper story I wrote was about my counselor in rehab, a guy name Rob Martin, who is also still a very good friend. I wrote about his life, his adventures in alcoholism and sobriety, and what took him on his path to being a counselor.

Marion Gregory said she would read the story. She sat down with me on one Saturday afternoon, and she edited my story while I looked over her shoulder. Well, I didn't know this was possible. I mean she turned that story from straw to gold. She was so good. She was such a terrific line editor. And in that one session, she taught me so much about how sentences are structured, how stories are structured, how sentences have beats, the importance of euphony, the importance of bringing the reader from one paragraph to the other. She was magnificent. She was the best line editor I'd ever worked with, and, even to this day, she's the best editor I ever worked with.

In my life there have been these people who have given me this undeserved grace. Marion was one, and the other person who comes to mind is a guy named Mike Grimwood, who was one of my professors at N.C. State. This guy was the real deal. He had the classics, had the Greek and Latin, and had gone to Princeton. When I got to N.C. State, I had a degree in creative writing, which meant that I had spent two years of my college career sitting in little rooms listening to other people's bad poetry. It was not exactly the most useful curriculum. So when I got to N.C. State in the master's program, the truth was I didn't know anything about grammar. I didn't know anything about punctuation. I was the e. e. cummings of that class. I was lost. I couldn't tell you a subject from a verb. For that whole first semester, every Monday morning at 8 o'clock, Grimwood sat down with me and he taught me grammar, shoulder to shoulder for an hour every Monday for 15 weeks, and he gave me the tools to make a living. Every time I write something, I think of the debt that I owe him.

Let's honor his contribution to you by reviewing some of the most important lessons. What are some specific tools that you use on all of your stories now?

I try to create some fascination for the reader by linking seemingly unconnected ideas, bringing either a cultural or an engineering concept to bear that informs the story, so it's a surprise and delight in three words. A lot of my tropes are the wedding of unusual ideas and showing how they work together.

For example, at the beginning of the piece on the Rolls-Royce, you have what I would call an extended metaphor, a conceit in which monstrousness derived from the story of Frankenstein is applied to the understanding and analysis of a new kind of Rolls-Royce.

Is that an example of the kind of thing you're talking about, trying to take an image that the ordinary person could not imagine to describe what this car is all about?

Yeah. Readers love to learn. I think one of the most limiting ideas in journalism is this idea that you can only tell people what they already know, or invoke ideas that are so common as to already be clichés before they're even used in a newspaper. My experience is that people love to learn new things if you can give it to them in a way that provides context. For instance, years ago I wrote a story about sports cars versus luxury cars, and I talked about

Mani, a second century Persian philosopher from whom we get the word "Manichaeism," which means a kind of separate duality that can never be linked—either/or, yes/no. I was talking about how these opposing principles in the Western tradition are not reconcilable. However, there is no such tradition in Asian culture, and so the Asian car manufacturers have been able to wed sports and luxury in a way that seemed to be inconceivable to the Western carmakers who are coming at it with a Western tradition. And people were like, "Oh, yeah, hey, cool. I like that." And it helped them remember the story, and I think it made a good point about the car.

Let's talk about the range of allusions in your story. People probably would be surprised to see references in automotive journalism to the classical arts, to architecture, to philosophy, literature, the kinds of things that flavor and open up your stories. Talk about the high-level allusion. The criticism would be that those are too highfalutin', that you run the risk of losing the reader. Is this going to fly with Joe Six-Pack?

Not every joke is for every person. There are "two-per-centers," references that only 2 percent of people will get. One of the great tyrannies of copy editing in journalism is that "Oh, well, nobody will get it." Well, not nobody, but 5 percent will get it and 95 percent will go right past it and not think twice about it. But the 5 percent who get it will laugh their asses off because they'll have the delight of recognition. So that's huge. People laugh when they get a joke, and they laugh harder when they think maybe that the next person won't get it.

There aren't too many artists or authors who successfully refer to the high and the low end of art and culture, and then meld these things into one creative whole. It's like a writer has to choose between referring to Aristotle or to Hulk Hogan...

And it's a totally classist way to look at the world. It is a false choice. I have a lot of respect for people who work in this business, but there are certain ideas that are taught in J-school that are just flat-out wrong. And one of the most exasperating ideas is that the constellation of knowledge that we have, the things that we know, the words we can use must be snubbed down to this very limited subset for the reader of the daily newspaper. I don't know if you can quote me on this—"Bullshit." I will fight tooth and nail against this idea. Because people love to learn. There's this whole thing about a word being too rare, too obscure. If it's in the dictionary, it belongs in the palette of newspaper writing. This is our language, and the only way words stay current, stay vital, is if we use them in a modern context.

I had to look up "twee." It means "overly precious or nice."

"Twee" is a wonderful word. It's also very British. But let's savor the word "twee" for a minute. It means "over-refined."

You're talking about my damn PT Cruiser!

I know. I knew where you got that. There is kind of a preciousness about that car. But "twee" is such a great word, and why shouldn't we use that word?

I recognized not all but most of the literary or artistic or cultural references. But I found myself in the discovery mode when I was reading your technical descriptions of automobiles. So it was when you were describing certain parts of the car or certain design elements that I had to focus.

Is this the way you challenge readers, not just in terms of the things that are extra-automotive, if you will, but also in the way that you describe automobiles?

Right. In a very real sense, using all the cultural references is just a way to avoid writing the same story week in and week out. I mean, it's a car review, for God's sake. So primarily my job is to entertain; it is also to inform. And when it comes to the technicalities of automobiles, the technology of an automobile…

...for example, "The body structure is a space frame built up of aluminum and magnesium castings, riveted and glued alloy panels, and exotic steel subframes." I had to take your word for it, in the sense that this is a lexicon of special understanding in which I'm on the outside looking in.

It absolutely is, and you know what? There are a couple of things about this that make the job challenging. One is that the audience is very diverse. Some know everything about cars and so they know what an aluminum space frame looks like; and some know nothing about cars. You risk losing the ones who know everything about cars if you stop to explain every week, week in and week out, because these terms turn up week in and week out. One principle that's still kind of in development for me is this idea of the educable reader. Do I count on the fact that a reader is returning to the column over and over again and has built up a certain body of knowledge, or am I looking at a tabula rasa every time I write? Do I have to bring people along every single time I mention things like "oversteer" and "understeer"? This is a fairly difficult problem.

Would you be willing, Dan, to generalize about writing criticism in newspapers? What if you're the architecture writer, what if you're the classical music critic? They have similar challenges, no?

Right. It is a balancing act, and I think that it's all about percentages. If you're an architecture critic, you can count on 20 percent of people reading your story or maybe less, say 15 percent, know what an Ansonia house is, right? Or 25 percent might know who Tadao Ando is. So what do you do? Do you bring the entire narrative to a grinding halt while you offer some thorough explanation? You have to count on people bringing a kind of enthusiasm to the subject matter if they're reading the column. The thing about cars is that almost everybody who reads the newspaper has a car, and so it's an extremely diverse set of readers with very different needs and expectations. Now, I'll tell you what's cool about it, though. Sometimes I'll stop and I'll—like I wrote a story a few months ago about torque. There was this movie called *Torque*—I wrote this story about what exactly is torque, because this car, this Mercedes-Benz E55, has 550 pound-feet of torque, which to most people means zero. They have no idea what that means. What's a pound foot? What's torque? What the hell are you talking about? So I wrote this story about what exactly is torque, and people loved it. I got tons of e-mail from people who thanked me for that explainer. Basically, it's exactly what it is. It's an explainer as a genre of journalism, and people really, really thought that was cool.

You know it's an interesting term because the other technical place where torque is often described is in golf. "Tiger Torque" is now a term of art in...

Oh, I love it, I love it. I didn't know that. Use it in a sentence.

"Tiger Torque refers to the extraordinary twisting motion of Tiger Woods as he goes from his back swing to his follow-through."
I want to ask you a few technical things about the writing process. Do you work from a plan? Do you draft the first version of your reviews and stories from a plan?

I usually start with a phrase or with a single conceit that seems to open up the car to readers. Because cars are so rich in their metaphoric dimension, it's easy. People will buy into it. They'll go along for the ride.

I want to explore what you mean by conceit. Just by using one of the examples that won the prize, the one about the bigger and better Rolls-Royce. What I find interesting is that some journalists will give readers a single metaphor. How is this automobile like Frankenstein's monster? You answer that question not just in a sentence or even just in the lead. You answer it throughout the story.
You're giving us "torch-wielding peasants," "Frankenstein's monster..."

I like "torch-wielding peasants." I still laugh at that.

"Mercilessly taunted," "Man, this thing is ugly," driving it "to the crack of doom," "Shelley's maledicted hero," a "visual vivisection."

I had a bit of trouble getting "vivisection" in the paper.

Yeah, you have three v's in nine letters, so that's pretty good in and of itself. "These elements he sewed together." Now I'm well into the story, then another 500, 600 words into the story: "What began as a paean to the past wound up looking like it had bolts in its neck."

That killed me.

And then all the way down to "the brakes are monsters," and then, "Skeptics, put down your pitchforks." So this is an image that you will not give up. I mean, it begins in the first line and spreads like *The Blob* through the entire piece. So you have the basic image at the beginning, and then it kind of repeats itself as it ripples through the story.

Job one for me is to be entertaining. The service dimension of my work is, frankly, marginal. People who want to really know about the Rolls-Royce as a possible purchase would go to *Consumer Reports*. My job is to write about this thing in a way that is both entertaining and informative. Part of what's happening in that story is the silliness of the extended metaphor, and it's also fun to ding Rolls-Royce—you know? Talk about your free-fire zone.

If I could visit your workplace would I see something that looks like a plan or an outline, something that shows you have a sense of the whole before you write?

No, I don't have an outline. I do a lot of preparatory reading. I try very hard to have a good grasp of the car in terms of its mechanics and engineering, in terms of its market share and its market, and background of the brand, because brand really operates as metaphor in a consumer culture. So when I say "Rolls-Royce," you know what that means. So I do all this preparatory reading, and then I sit down in the morning, usually after my first cup of coffee, and I will work on the lead and I'll write the lead maybe 10 or 15 times in different ways. I'll try out different ways to open, to kick open the door, because, basically, if you can hook them early, you can keep them going, and typically that means that you make them laugh. But it's kidding on the square, right? There's a bigger point in play. So I'll write the first sentence 10 or 15 times, and it's almost certainly not the same sentence. Very often it'll be 15 different leads. I'll get to a lead that I think is funny or that I think is intriguing, and then as long as it's pointing me in the right direction, I'll start constructing it. My experience is that journalism is puzzle-solving. If I can just get them to the jump, get them past the jump, I have kicked ass, because that's not how people read the newspaper. Most people, when they read the newspaper, they get to the jump, boom, they stop.

Do you place a mini-cliffhanger or something right before the jump?

Yeah, ratchet it up just that much so that they have to take the jump. It's like catching fish, you know? You've got to reel them in, give a little slack—you don't want to lose them.

Then I'll write a story, and it usually takes me about eight hours to write 40 inches. I'll write a paragraph, I'll stop, I'll read it from the beginning, read it all the way through, write another paragraph, start at the top, read it all the way through. So by the time I get to the end, I've read it a hundred times.

I'm curious about your geopolitical perspective on the world of politics and automobiles and whether it precedes your arguments about individual cars or is shaped by it.

Well, first of all, I'm a raving liberal and unapologetically so. And why? Because liberals are right. Typically this is against expectations. Not everybody knows this, but car guys are a pretty conservative bunch. They like big horsepower, lots of gas burning. They think Ralph Nader is the devil and the EPA is taxing their gig. I don't feel that way. My view is that in order for the automobile to remain the sort of essential pleasure that it is in American culture, it needs to change, and we need to embrace change rather than run away from it, and we need to change the way we think about the automobile. I personally don't care if an automobile runs on turkey shit, as long as it goes fast. That's what I care about, because what makes me happy is a fast, fun car. I also think—I realize this could be perceived as grandiose—but I think the subject I cover is one of the most important subjects in American life. The automobile and our dependence on foreign oil, our dependence on fossil fuel. I mean when you think about the automobile, it is the nexus of so many pressing issues and insistent problems that we face. So in some ways I feel very privileged to be able to write about this.

I'm going to make you King of Newspapers. Improve newspaper writing for me by just telling me the kind of reforms that you would institute as king.

This is easy. I say this to people all the time when they start telling me I'm such a great writer. Almost anybody under this roof at the *L.A. Times* could do what I do if they were given the freedom to do it. If I'm going to reform newspaper writing, I'm going to open it up to a wider sensibility. I'm going to make it more challenging. I'm going to make it livelier. I'm going to make it less monolithic in tone and sensibility. I'm going to give my writers room to be outrageous. The rule is "get me to the next paragraph. Don't abandon me."

Writers' Workshop

Talking Points

1) Dan Neil expresses the opinion that too many newspaper writers and editors fail to challenge their readers. He argues that readers love to learn. There is much to learn from Neil, not just about cars, but about culture, politics, art, and literature. Discuss Neil's journalism and his sense of audience. What percentage of readers will recognize his cultural allusions? Does it matter? Does it affect his ability to engage readers?

2) Underline any word, allusion, or technical jargon in Neil's reviews that you don't understand. Now discuss the character of Neil's writing vocabulary. Compare and contrast it to other journalists and authors whose work you know. Discuss your own strategic decisions about the level of language and vocabulary. How do you imagine your audience?

3) Neil confesses to being a "top down" writer. He writes and rewrites his first paragraph until he is satisfied with it. Then he writes the second paragraph and revises and revises. And so on. Neil's method contrasts to that of Poynter's Christopher Scanlan, who likes to write drafts quickly to discover what he wants to say. Discuss where you fit as a writer on the spectrum between Neil and Scanlan.

Assignment Desk

1) Conduct 10 casual interviews with people about their cars. Get them to tell you stories about their cars and express their opinions or feelings about the cars they drive. If possible, have them give you a tour of the car, or ask them to drive you around the block. From this experience, write a brief column on what a car says about the character of its owner.

2) Listen to at least one broadcast of *Car Talk*, the National Public Radio program in which two brothers tell jokes and field questions from listeners about automotive repair and engineering. Write a brief reflection on the similarities and differences between *Car Talk* and Neil's columns. Consider writing issues such as voice, narrative, character, language, authority, audience, technical expertise, and utility.

Robert L. Jamieson

Finalist, Commentary

Robert L. Jamieson has been a reporter for the *Seattle Post-Intelligencer* since 1991, covering higher education, city hall, and general assignment beats. He became a full-time metro columnist in March 2001.

Having spent his 20s at the *Post-Intelligencer*, he has covered a wide range of stories, from Dennis Rodman's travails during the NBA playoffs against the Seattle Supersonics to the crash of Alaska Flight 261, to the fatal police shooting of David Walker, a mentally ill man whose death caused police to adopt less lethal weapons.

Jamieson is a 1991 graduate of Stanford University. His adviser, Condoleezza Rice, now national security adviser for President Bush, influenced Jamieson to become a journalist. His first jobs were at *The Wall Street Journal* and *The Oakland Tribune*.

He has won awards for his work from the Society of Professional Journalists and the Best of the West competition. He was a finalist for the ASNE Distinguished Writing Award for Commentary in 2003.

In "Store Owner Holds His Ground Against Ugliness," Jamieson tells a tale of hate, struggle, and redemption, adding clever turns of phrase to an already powerful story.

Store owner holds his ground against ugliness

APRIL 11, 2003

Business owners and neighbors comforted Yehya Omer Saleh, owner of Saleh's Delicatessen, after someone scrawled a slur behind his store.

"T-O-W-L," says the youthful-looking man with the permanent tan and milk chocolate eyes. "They forgot the 'E.'"

Using his index finger, Yehya Omer Saleh traces the neon-green letters someone spray-painted this week on the Dumpster behind Saleh's Delicatessen, the Ballard-area store that he owns: "Towl Heads."

Saleh sighs.

Hate stings, even when it's just an anonymous dart tossed by a coward—a spelling-challenged coward who likely knows little, if anything, about the travails of a business owner who is struggling to make it.

The coward may be unaware of the piercing glares people shoot daily, poking tiny, invisible holes in Saleh's soul, especially after 9/11 and the war with Iraq.

Some people glance at this man who looks like a grad student in his rumpled khakis and T-shirt, and they do not see the story of an immigrant from Yemen. Nor do they see an all-American guy who loves the Buffalo Bills, Rosa Parks and Philly cheese steaks, and tapes up handwritten notes as reminders to "Call Mom."

They see a terrorist behind the counter. A towel head.

So one can only wonder—why is this Muslim man still smiling?

"What I've gotten from all the hurt," Saleh explains, "is more than the pain."

* * *

The story of Saleh is one of those quiet tales that threads together a neighborhood—in this case, the Loyal Heights section of Ballard. What is happening in and around the shop at 24th Avenue Northwest and Northwest 80th Street shows how a caring community can forge a bulwark against ignorance.

A few days before the Dumpster incident, Saleh had

to deal with a bizarre case of apparent prejudice. A woman in a Range Rover roared into the parking lot and stormed inside the store.

She was mad because a sign in front of the store said Support Troops—Bring them Home. She blasted Saleh, lobbing piercing words that questioned his American-ness, his heritage. She threatened to call radio and TV stations to start a boycott. She marched out into the parking lot, pacing and huffing into a cell phone before thundering back inside the store—and getting in Saleh's face.

He kept his cool with the stranger, a human tornado who stayed until Seattle police came. She then got testy with the officers, though she wasn't arrested.

Store security cameras caught the March 31 episode, and three different angles composed one big picture: un-bridled ugliness. "I put the cameras in after Sept. 11," Saleh says. "Just in case."

* * *

Much of his 39 years has been about anticipation.

He jumped at the chance to leave Yemen in the early 1980s, when his father, a merchant marine and Ameri-can citizen, sponsored him to come to the United States.

Saleh's family lived in Buffalo, where his father owned a grocery store. In high school, he took the name "Steven" because kids butchered his birth name. Next up was university in upstate New York, where he stud-ied business.

Afterward, Saleh managed a liquor store in the Bronx and owned a deli in Rochester before he reached an epiphany: New York was too cold and snowy. A magazine touted Seattle as "a most livable" city, and in 1989 he packed his bags.

It turns out, he says, the people in Seattle were a lot warmer, too.

Saleh owned a 7-Eleven in the University District, figuring he would stay a few months, pool together some money and open a restaurant. A few months turned into five years.

In the mid-'90s, he split and opened the Ballard-area shop. "Great location," he recalls thinking. "Safer than the U-District. People are nice."

* * *

Saleh could never have fathomed how nice.

After the slur appeared on the Dumpster, the lady who runs the day care next door rushed over with open arms and tears in her eyes. Another woman dashed in and just silently held Saleh's hand.

A brute of a guy barged through the door and squeezed him in a bear hug. And the owner of Red Mill burgers dropped by with gift certificates. Even a Mr. and Mrs. Steele from the neighborhood brought over roses with a note: "Steven, we love you! Do not leave!!!"

Word got around town. Phone calls rolled in. From customers, strangers. "And my ex, of course," Saleh says with a chuckle.

The outpouring bowled him over.

In the past year and a half, Saleh, like many Arab Americans, has silently swallowed indignity after indignity. Like the time at the St. Louis airport when Saleh was stopped five times between the ticket counter and boarding gate to be searched or questioned. His 10-year-old daughter was with him.

Or the time at Seattle-Tacoma International Airport when a security official yanked him out of line as he was talking to a client. "Humiliating," Saleh says. And Saleh can't forget the drunk who stumbled in the store one day screaming about "the F-ing Arabs."

A soul can only take so many blows before it breaks.

Love helps. Love heals. "And people," Saleh tells me, "have been more than human after what just happened."

The owner of the corner store had considered packing it in. Instead he is holding his ground, standing behind the counter with a smile powered by all of this human kindness.

Lessons Learned

BY ROBERT L. JAMIESON

I tend to gravitate to quiet stories that speak to louder truths. By quiet, I mean stories that appear deceptively simple. Then you scratch a bit, and *voilà*—complex, universal themes emerge. Yehya Omer Saleh's story is about a hate crime that leads to an unexpectedly positive community response. We all can identify with the Manichaen struggle of good versus evil, love battling hate—so I suspected this story had legs.

The story presented itself during a casual conversation with a colleague. She mentioned that something "upsetting" had happened at her neighborhood store. She didn't have the details but figured I might want to check it out, provided I had the time. This brings me to the first lesson this story reinforced: Always make time to track down a tip, no matter how small. What Saleh, an American from Yemen, experienced wasn't the kind of hate crime that grabs the big headlines. It wasn't a cross burning on a lawn or a brutal physical attack. Someone had tried to write "towel head"—a derogatory term for Arab Americans—on the Dumpster behind his store and misspelled it.

Viewed through the normal news lens it would have been too easy to pass on this story. But I trusted the hunch of my colleague—as I do with many other co-workers and casual acquaintances. I nurture this network, which includes bartenders, hotel workers, secretaries—all people who see and hear things on the ground level. This brings me to lesson number two: the importance of having "listening posts" in the community, beyond the usual suspects. They are an extension of one's eyes and ears.

I eventually called up Saleh. He reluctantly talked on the phone a bit about what happened. I soon realized this was more than a story about one immigrant's pain. It was a window into our entire community and how it was both coping and not coping with post-Sept. 11 rage. Saleh was reluctant to proceed. He believed the perpetrator might retaliate.

And so the courtship—lesson three!—began. I referred Saleh to stories I had written to show him that I wasn't interested in a quick-hit, sensational piece. I told him that because America is a land of immigrants, many readers would identify with his story.

Saleh said he'd mull it over. I told him that I would be passing his shop later in the week and would drop in. At the very least, he could put my face with my name. When we did meet, Saleh really opened up. Which brings us to lesson four: When possible, interview people in person. The phone can—and does—create a huge wall between a writer and his or her subject. As journalists we know this, but sometimes we get lazy and resort to phone work. If I'd waited for Saleh to call back, I might be still waiting.

I would be remiss if I did not point out a final lesson. This story shows the importance of having editors who allow writers the freedom to pursue "invisible stories" that define the places we live. As a columnist, I often feel the pressure to come up with a fire-and-brimstone screed or undress a bumbling public official with sharp words. Thankfully my editors, assistant city editor Mark Waligore and managing editor David McCumber, loosen the leash, allowing stories such as Saleh's—about heart and hope—to see the light of day. For that I am grateful.

St. Petersburg Times

Howard Troxler

Finalist, Commentary

Howard Troxler is a metro columnist for the *St. Petersburg Times*. His column appears Sunday, Tuesday, and Thursday on the front of the newspaper's B section.

Troxler joined the *Times* as a columnist in 1991. He took a turn as the *Times*'s political editor from July 1995 to November 1997, serving as the lead reporter on national, state, and local politics. He returned to column writing in late 1997.

Before the *Times*, Troxler worked for nine years at *The Tampa Tribune* as a reporter, editor, and columnist. He came to Florida in 1982 after working as a reporter for *The News & Observer* in Raleigh, N.C.

In 2003, Troxler won first place in the serious commentary category of the Green Eyeshade competition sponsored by the Atlanta chapter of the Society of Professional Journalists. He had been a finalist twice before. Troxler has also won first place twice for column writing in the annual competition of the Florida Society of Newspaper Editors.

Troxler was born March 19, 1959, in Burlington, N.C., where he grew up and attended public school. He has a bachelor's degree in journalism from the University of North Carolina at Chapel Hill and is pursuing a master's degree in ancient history from the University of South Florida in Tampa. He and his wife, Lynn Casey, live in St. Petersburg.

His columns are funny, but his punch lines come with sharp, often stinging punctuation. In "Public Money, Private School, and No Answer for Tinkerbell," Troxler puts his sarcasm to work to take on not just a local private school with an odd principal, but the larger, more controversial matter of school vouchers.

Public money, private school, and no answer for Tinkerbell

AUGUST 6, 2003

Having a warped mind, I can think of only one thing while reading about the principal of Community Christian School in Largo, who took his schoolgirls on trips to Disney World, sometimes unchaperoned in the same hotel room, called them "Princesses," dressed them in his own personal collection of little swimsuits, took their photographs and liked to tickle them:

School vouchers.

That's right.

No matter what Dick Baker did or didn't do as principal of Community Christian, it doesn't matter. His school is still *automatically* declared to be a superior alternative to any crummy, lousy public school in the state of Florida. Your child is automatically better off with him. Your state Legislature says so.

Dick Baker's school, therefore, is automatically entitled to your tax dollars. And you in return are not entitled to know how his school spends your money. Nobody is. There is only a puny, non-specific requirement for audits in the state law, and the state Department of Education is not enforcing even that.

Community Christian School (before all this) had at least 16 kids under the state's corporate-tax voucher program, in which corporations pay their state taxes directly to private foundations that in turn give the money to kids. Since the lowest tuition at the school is about $3,500, that's a minimum of $56,000.

On top of that, some of the school's 245 students (at least, it *used* to be 245) are attending under the state's McKay voucher program for students with disabilities. According to the Pinellas school district, Community Christian had 28 such students last year. The total dollar figure is not available, but for the sake of comparison, the average McKay cost in the public schools is $6,000 a head. For 28 kids, that would be $168,000.

Mind you, if a Melrose Elementary School in the public system has enough troubled kids who score poorly on a standardized test, then that school is a "failure" and must be punished. But if a private Community Christian School is secretly whisking off its students to hotel rooms in other cities to play Tinkerbell and Ariel with a principal who calls himself "The King," that is just ducky by the state, and it will keep forking over the dough.

Now, listen. I am not trying to smear the entire universe of private schools with a single school's troubles. Most of them are good and caring. (So are most public schools.) Some private schools are much better than the public alternative. And yes, some of the kids in private schools are better off thanks to school voucher programs.

But why, oh why, is Florida so pig-headed about throwing the money around without any accountability? Why is this considered the "conservative" way to do it, and why is it "liberal" to ask for an audit, or a test score, or *something* to show in return for the cash?

The big untruth here is the claim that parents, not audits, will hold these private schools "accountable."

Oh, really? Look at the truth.

Look at the shocked parents at Community Christian School who are trying desperately, as hard as they can, to get some answers.

They have asked to see the bylaws. They have asked to see the budget. They have asked to see whether any of these little Disney trips came out of the school funds. They have asked to see—the nerve of them!—the academic qualifications of the remaining staff.

In response, the school's board has told them to get lost. Meanwhile there is a purge under way inside the school. Teachers and staffers who have spoken out are getting fired.

That's not "accountable."

Of course, what Gov. Jeb Bush, state education chief Jim Horne and voucher supporters mean by "accountable" is simply that parents can take their next voucher check to another school—*after* they find out they have made a mistake. How reassuring. Parents in such a system are mere check-passers, not stakeholders. Their only power consists of yanking their kid out and moving along.

Tell you what. I am willing to bet that not a single *public* school principal around here shared a hotel room last night with an unescorted student. But if he did, I am pretty sure the School Board would fire him. And if the School Board didn't fire him, then I am pretty sure the voters would fire the School Board.

So at least in the pajamas-and-tickling-little-girls department, we have a fair idea of which system is more "accountable."

Lessons Learned

I really, really hate doing the obvious column topic.

For example, the most useless columnist in the world is one who simply reads a wire story and dashes off:

Suing for spilling hot coffee? Why, our legal system is broken! Lawyers are greedy! Jurors are idiots!

(You know what a good column is? Go look up the *facts* in that hot-coffee case.)

I also hate a column that says:

Can you believe what an idiot (insert name of idiot currently in the news) is?

Or:

This latest murderer, he's a bad, bad man, and how do we know what monsters lurk among us, etc.

In the tale that led to this particular column, our reporters had written about a private-school principal in Florida who liked to take some of his little girl students to Disney World, dress them in costumes, tickle them, and, on occasion, share hotel rooms with them.

"Man, oh man," my editor says, "I bet you can have a field day with THIS one."

But, what's that column going to say?

That, duh, it's a bad idea for a principal to share hotel rooms at Disney World with little girls he has dressed in costumes and likes to tickle?

I thought briefly about *defending* the guy, but didn't get too far.

"Grr!" says me to my computer. "Once again, the important stuff happening to public education in this state gets brushed aside for the cheap and salacious. I wish I could get people to read THAT."

So I wrote this, and people liked it okay.

Tommy Tomlinson
Profile Writing

Tommy Tomlinson usually writes a three-times-a-week column for *The Charlotte Observer*, but that's about as predictable as things get for him. His columns, like the topics he chooses to write about, move around a bit.

"The *Observer*'s been really great about letting me roam around and try different stuff," including sports writing, he says. As evidence, you could find Tomlinson in late 2003 and early 2004 following the Carolina Panthers through the playoffs as they marched to Houston and Super Bowl XXXVIII.

In 2003, Tomlinson pursued two stories beyond the boundaries of a metro column. "A Beautiful Find" reconstructed the four-year quest of John Swallow, a young mathematician trying to solve a math problem that had eluded others for decades. "Michael Kelley's Obstacle Course" is a vivid, you-are-there account of a moment of truth (actually 7 minutes and 20 seconds) for a police rookie who must prove that the military accident that left him disfigured by near-fatal burns won't keep him from becoming a police officer.

Tomlinson was born in Brunswick, Ga., in 1964. He is a graduate of the University of Georgia who started his professional career at *The Augusta Chronicle* in 1986. He joined the *Observer* as a reporter in 1989 in the paper's York County, S.C., bureau and was made a columnist for the regional edition in 1991. He was the *Observer*'s pop music writer from 1993 until 1997 when he was given a metro column. He is married to Alix Felsing, the newspaper's national editor.

Tomlinson's detailed reporting and cinematic style elevate these profiles beyond the superficial "person in the news" to create layered portraits of two men confronting and overcoming insurmountable odds.

Mindful of *Wall Street Journal* publisher Barney Kilgore's memorable admonition that "the easiest thing for the reader to do is to quit reading," Tomlinson keeps our attention with concrete details, creative approaches to structure, and a narrative sense that anticipates and serves the reader's interest in news and stories.

—Christopher Scanlan

Michael Kelley's obstacle course: Part I

NOVEMBER 9, 2003

Nine years of healing. Six months of training. It comes down to this cold October morning. Michael Kelley versus the obstacle course.

He reaches down to take off his sweatshirt. The hand with the two missing fingers pulls the sweatshirt up over the missing ear.

He bends to touch the ground. The T-shirt sleeve draws back to expose a raw and twisted arm. The Band-Aid stretches across the elbow where there's not enough skin to cover the bone.

He braces both hands against a concrete pipe. Under the camouflage pants are the legs covered with skin grafts. Under the gray running shoes are the Achilles tendons that had to be split and the foot bones that had to be fused.

He looks out onto the obstacle course.

One recruit is sprinting across a field. Another is climbing slick stairs. Their arms hang limp with fatigue. Their sneakers are soaked with cold dew. The ones who went out first are crouched off to the side, sucking in air or heaving up breakfast.

There are 18 Charlotte-Mecklenburg police recruits out here this morning. They quit good jobs, worried their families, even moved from other states for a shot at wearing a badge. They gambled six months of their lives on the mandatory training.

Now they have to beat the obstacle course.

Its official title is the Police Officer Physical Abilities Test. Everyone who wants to be a law enforcement officer in North Carolina has to pass it. There are 11 tasks. You get seven minutes and 20 seconds. If you fail, you turn in your gear and go home.

The stopwatch doesn't care how bad Michael Kelley was hurt that day nine years ago.

The stopwatch doesn't care how long it took him to walk again, how much longer it took him to run.

All that matters is now.

He wipes the sweat from the side of his head.

Officer Bobby Buening, the head trainer, marks down the time for the recruit who just finished. Then Buening shouts:

"Let's go, Mr. Kelley!"

Michael jogs over to the starting point, stiff-legged, limping.

Buening pulls out a fresh score sheet, the one with Michael's name on it.

He sets the stopwatch to zero.

ONE: CRUCIFIED

If he had been standing in another spot. If he had been looking in the right direction. If they had trained another day. No sense dwelling on it. He was there, that spot, that day, that moment.

On March 23, 1994, Michael Kelley and 500 other Army paratroopers gathered at a staging area called Green Ramp on Pope Air Force Base. The group from the 82nd Airborne had come over from Fort Bragg. They were planning to jump that day.

Michael had 11 years in the Army and more than 60 jumps behind him. While he waited for a briefing, he practiced off a 3-foot-high platform. It was just after 2 in the afternoon.

He noticed an odd movement out of the corner of his eye.

A cargo plane and a fighter jet had tried to land on the same runway. They clipped each other in the air. The cargo plane landed safely, and the jet pilots ejected. But the empty jet crashed into a third aircraft on the ground—a C-141 transport that was waiting to take the paratroopers on their jump.

The giant plane had just been filled with fuel.

A ball of fire as big as a two-story house shot out from the explosion. No one in its path had time to move.

Michael got hit from behind. The impact knocked him down. As he got up and turned he could see over his shoulder. His back was on fire.

He spun, but the fire curled around to his front. He rolled, but the ground was soaked with fuel. By the time rescuers found him, he was burned everywhere but his left shoulder and part of his left side.

· Rescue teams had to deal with dozens of injured soldiers. In the chaos the medics hurried the soldiers into groups, depending on the level of injury and pain.

Military triage guidelines include a category called "expectant." That means the patient should be made comfortable, because he is about to die.

The medics took one look at Michael and moved him to the expectant group.

He was the only one in the group who lived.

Twenty-four soldiers died from the explosion. More than 100 were wounded.

Michael's wife, Lisa, saw the report on the news.

Those with the worst injuries were flown to the Army's burn center in San Antonio. Lisa caught a flight right behind Michael's.

She remembers being led into the intensive care unit. She thought the soldiers would be covered in bandages. But instead they were naked except for a square of gauze over their private parts. Their arms were stretched wide and strapped down to keep the muscles from drawing up.

She thought: *They've been crucified.*

Later on, the Army advised her to sign a paper on Michael's behalf, changing his status from active to retired. That way she'd get better benefits when he died.

She didn't sign.

Michael spent much of the next three years in hospitals.

He normally weighed 140 pounds. Fluid from the burns swelled him to 190. Then his withering muscles dropped him all the way to 83.

He went into surgery 37 times. Sometimes two or three doctors worked on different parts of his body while he was under.

For months he wore Ilizarov frames—metal cages around his legs attached with pins that went all the way through.

Skin from his thigh was grafted onto his neck. Skin from his hips went onto his shoulder. Skin from his back went onto his arms.

Back home at Fort Bragg, he crawled from room to room. He pulled a towel behind him to drag a snack from the kitchen.

It was nearly a year after the accident before he could walk.

Two years after that he put an end to the surgery. He didn't care about a new right ear or a reconstructed nose. He could get up and move around. That was enough.

In 1997 he took a medical retirement from the Army, leaving with the rank of staff sergeant. He had a wife, two kids, a full pension and no idea what he'd be able to do.

"But I did know what I *didn't* want to do," he said. "I never wanted to just glide through life."

Fort Bragg found that out. One day some paratroopers were going over the roster for an upcoming flight. One of them noticed a name he hadn't seen in a while.

On one of his last days on base, Michael Kelley came that close to sneaking onto the plane.

He wanted one last jump.

TWO: STAKES IN THE DIRT

Four years out of the Army, eight years after the crash, Michael was safe and healthy and restless.

By this point he had moved the family to Charlotte. He grew up here, graduated from Charlotte Catholic. His mom and dad still lived in town. He could hang out with them and know the accident wouldn't be the first thing that came up.

He had spent a lot more time with the kids, Michael (who's now 17) and Mary (who's now 15). They barely remember what their dad used to look like.

Right after the accident, they learned not to hug him hard. But as he got better they could tease him about the hairless patch on the back of his scalp. They think it looks like a cat.

He took classes at Central Piedmont Community College, then transferred to UNC Charlotte and majored in psychology. He got his degree in May 2002. He looked around at graduate schools. He realized he didn't care if he got into one or not.

He tried to figure out what he did care about.

Just about all the Kelley men were soldiers or cops. His brother had also been in the 82nd Airborne, and their grandfather had served in the 82nd in World War II. His other grandfather had been a U.S. marshal. His dad and uncle had been on the Charlotte police force.

Michael didn't like being compared to anyone else. But he couldn't deny the pull.

The same things he loved about the military, he saw in the police. He needed to serve. To be part of a team. To do something intense, even dangerous.

Most of all he needed to do something he thought was important. Something to say he did his part for the world.

One day in the fall of '02 he took Mary to the library. While she looked up things for class, he logged onto a computer. He called up the Charlotte-Mecklenburg Police Department's Web site.

He found the description for the physical skills pretest, a stripped-down version of the obstacle course. He'd have to do 30 sit-ups, 30 push-ups, 40 reps on an aerobic step.

He would have to run a total of 400 yards.

He hadn't run at all since the day of the accident.

A couple of days later he found his wife in her work room, where she teaches classes in doll making. He waited until she turned around.

Let's talk about me, he said.

A day or two later he stood on the street in his neighborhood off Albemarle Road. He had mapped out a route with his truck. Three-quarters of a mile. He figured he'd jog a few steps and walk the rest.

He was slow. His feet wouldn't bend and so he clopped like a horse. His elbows swung out high. Every step rippled with pain.

He ran the whole way.

The pretest required running between two cones 50 feet apart. Michael drove two stakes into the ground in his back yard. He had never heard of an aerobic step. He stacked two railroad ties.

Every day he ran between the stakes and stepped up on the railroad ties and did sit-ups until he couldn't move.

Michael took the pretest in December, after two months of practice. He passed with a minute to spare.

The Police Department gets 300 applicants for every 20 people selected as recruits. Michael went through the interview, the psychological exam, the polygraph test. He was accepted in April. He was 38 years old and starting over.

The application papers give fair warning:

Applicants should continue to prepare themselves to be challenged physically....

The 142nd Recruit Training Class gathered for the first time on May 19, a Monday.

By Thursday, someone had already quit.

THREE: FROM BUBBA TO STONEHENGE

They meet every morning in the same classroom and sit at the same desks with the same name cards.

But nobody uses the names on the cards. Everyone has a nickname.

Over here is Sean Parker, thick and strong. He's Bulldog.

Over there is Lisa Speas, the only woman in the class. She's Queen Bee.

Ben West throws up after long runs. He's Upchuck. Scott Zay moved from West Virginia to be here. He's Hardcore.

"The Fire Department is testing today," Bobby Buening says as the class does sit-ups in the grass. "Mr. Zay, you wanna go over there?"

"No, sir!"

"Why not?"

"I didn't move 400 miles to polish chrome for 30 years, sir!"

Michael Kelley has a reporter and photographer following him around.

He's Hollywood.

Even the landmarks have names. A steep hill on the way to the firing range is Bubba. The area scattered with concrete blocks by the pull-up bars is Stonehenge.

The criminals of the world go by one name: Joe.

"Joe's out there doing one-armed push-ups," Buening says as the recruits strain on exercise machines. "Joe don't care if you're tired. Joe hopes you quit."

It is Buening's job to make sure the recruits are ready for Joe. He's 44, a 19-year vet with the department, in triathlon shape.

He has known Michael since they were kids—Buening was a few years ahead of him at Charlotte Catholic. In his heart he roots for Michael. In his mind he knows it is up to the grade on the test and the time on the clock.

So he pushes. He makes everybody do 142 sit-ups in the wet grass because they are the 142nd Class. He takes them out to Stonehenge for round after round of dips—vertical push-ups on a set of parallel bars. The class does them until their arms tremble.

"Some of these guys, they think they're hurting after a five-mile run," he says. "I tell them, 'You think about what Mr. Kelley went through. You don't know what pain is.'"

On the first day of class, they all told their life stories. Everyone knows what happened to Michael. Most of the other recruits are younger. Several are ex-military. They treat him with respect.

"Mike, I'm telling you, the way you've turned your life around, the way you've made it back…," says Billy Kiley. "I'm so proud of you."

Long pause.

"You know, the six years in jail and all."

Chris Ireland jumps in: "Yeah, and coming out of the closet must have been hard."

Everybody laughing now.

"Well, there was the meth lab explosion," Kelley says. "I don't know if I mentioned that one."

They know one another's soft spots. They know that Quentin Blakeney would rather shrug than talk, that Ben West sometimes zones out in the middle of class.

They know that Buening makes Billy Vang yell "STOP! POLICE!" over and over because his Hmong accent makes it sound like "STOP! PLEASE!"

But Lisa Speas knows who's struggling with the classwork and she helps. Class president Jeff Williams knows who needs to be spotted on the bench press and he's there.

One morning they go out for a timed run, three laps around two cones set on the road, a mile and a half in all.

Williams is always the fastest in the class. He finishes in 8:18. A few others cross the line soon after. Nearly everybody has finished all three laps when Michael makes the turn on his second. He is fighting shin splints. The burn marks on his face are glowing red.

Michael runs around the curve, out of sight. Bulldog, next to last, is already coming back toward the finish. He finishes at 12:50. Michael doesn't appear for nearly a minute. He is alone on the road.

Jeff Williams turns to the other recruits: "Let's go get him."

They jog back down the sides of the road, spreading out until they make a human tunnel.

As Michael passes the first two, they fall in beside him.

Two more, two more, two more.

The ones up ahead shout as they wait.

"Hollywood!"

"C'mon, Mike!"

Fifty steps from the finish, the last two runners join the pack. They holler his name. They make a knot behind him.

The whole class runs him in.

FOUR: A CALL FROM SPRUCE PINE

In the old photos of Joe Kelley you see his youngest son.

His bucket-handle chin is Michael's chin. His thin lips, Michael's lips. His even stare, Michael's stare.

Joe Kelley joined the Charlotte police in 1961. He retired 30 years and 30 days later. After that he was head of security for the Bank of America building. As far back as Michael can remember, everybody in town seemed to know his dad.

He taught at the police academy for years. During training, Michael and Joe called or e-mailed almost every day. Nothing special. *How you doing, son? Fine. Hard work, but I'm OK.*

Back in the '80s Joe bought an eight-sided cabin up near Spruce Pine. Sometimes the whole family would gather up there. Sometimes Joe and his wife, Lani, went up alone. Joe would piddle around with wood carvings, go for walks, spend all day in a book.

On Sept. 7, seven weeks from the end of Michael's training, Joe and Lani were spending a beautiful day at the cabin. Joe cut up a fallen tree. He came inside for lunch and the second half of the Panthers' opener.

He sat down in his favorite chair and had a heart attack and died.

He was 63.

The funeral was three days later in Charlotte at Sacred

Heart Catholic Church. The pews were filled with police: officers in the honor guard, detectives on their day off, retired cops with gray hair and stories.

The night Joe died, Sgt. Dave Gehrke—the academy's training supervisor—told Michael he could have the week off.

Michael came back the day after the funeral. He figured his dad would have done the same.

"We didn't have deep, long talks about my going to the academy," he says. "But I know how he felt about what I was doing."

Michael leans back in his chair.

"I'm going to miss having a chance to get his advice about all this. But if there is a connection from that side to this side, he'll see how it turns out."

In the final weeks, Buening eased off on the physical work to help everyone heal. But every day he reminded them about the obstacle course.

The course simulates what an officer might have to do under stress. Run long distances. Drag someone to safety. Crash through a door. Crawl through a tight dark space.

It is designed to wear you out. There are two stops where the recruits have to do 20 push-ups and 20 sit-ups. Each push-up has to end with their chin touching a trainer's fist on the ground. Each sit-up has to end with their elbows touching their knees. If it's not done right, it doesn't count.

Everyone had practiced on the course a few weeks before. But that day the only obstacles were the ones they could see.

On test day, pressure becomes an obstacle. Anyone who fails the test gets one more chance. Anyone who fails again can't come back.

Michael Kelley's obstacles follow him around. The shins that won't stop aching. The ankles that won't get loose. The whole damn awkward apparatus of his body, all those muscles still withered, all that skin in the wrong place.

And now his dad.

If he fails, he doesn't know if he could go through it again.

All the way up to the day of the test, he swears he's not nervous. He watches the Panthers on Sunday, same as always. It's their first loss of the season.

He gets up at 5:30 on Monday morning, Oct. 20. Showers and shaves. Skips breakfast like he always does on physical-training days. Checks his bag to make sure he has extra underwear. He'll be sweating.

He flips the radio between NPR and "John Boy & Billy." *It's just another test*, he says to himself. *I've taken a million tests.*

But he knows better.

Nine years of healing. Six months of training. It comes down to this cold October morning.

* * *

The starting point is the driver's seat of a police car.

Michael buckles himself in. The first task will be to jump out of the car and run.

Recruit Kris Kodad gets in next to him. Kodad is the designated victim. Later on Michael will have to drag him away from the car, twice.

The running path is in front of him. The rest of the course is off to his right. Michael looks right, then straight ahead. He forces himself to breathe deep.

Buening comes up to the open window.

At the beginning of the test, the trainer calls out two street names. At the end, the recruit has to repeat them in order. Anyone who misses has to run 200 more yards.

"All right, Mr. Kelley," Buening says. "Maple and Monroe. Repeat it."

"Maple and Monroe."

Rush-hour traffic races by. A plane roars overhead. But between the two men there is a silent space. Buening waits. Kelley breathes.

Finally, Buening leans in. His voice is quiet now.

"Leave no doubt, sir."

Michael grips the steering wheel.

"You ready?"

Michael nods.

Buening checks his stopwatch. Puts his finger on the button.

"Go!"

Michael Kelley's obstacle course: Part II

Michael Kelley throws open the car door and takes off running.

His shoes leave tracks in the cold, wet grass. His duty belt sags on his hip. The orange cone is a hundred yards away. To him it looks like half a mile.

Behind him, in trainer Bobby Buening's hand, the stopwatch spins.

Michael aced the firearms tests. He's solid with the books. Through six months of training he has proved he can do everything else it takes to be a Charlotte-Mecklenburg police officer.

Now he must conquer the obstacle course.

He has to run, drag, climb, crash, push, bend and crawl through a course built to weed out those who lack the strength or speed or will.

And he has to do it in seven minutes and 20 seconds.

He rounds the orange cone now, heading back toward the rest of the course. From a hundred yards away he could be anyone. But with each step closer something new is revealed. The skin is seared. The feet won't flex. Pieces are missing. Two fingers. An ear.

Nine years ago, Michael Kelley was swallowed by fire. He went through 37 operations. He crawled through his house until he could walk. And every day he inched closer to the man he used to be.

He has seven minutes and 20 seconds to make it all the way back.

1:01, 1:02, 1:03...

Michael hobbles back to the car, opens the passenger door, pulls out the slumped-over body inside.

Fellow trainee Kris Kodad plays the victim because he's the right size—150 pounds. He makes himself dead weight. Michael reaches under his arms and drags him backward.

Buening shuffles beside them, right in Michael's ear: "Drive! Drive! Drive!"

Michael bends deep at the knees and rears back. Kodad's heels bounce along the ground. Buening holds his hand out at the 50-foot mark. Michael's shoulder touches.

"Stairs!" Buening shouts. Five steps up one side, five steps down the other. Up and down three times.

The bones in Michael's toes are fused. He can't spring up on the balls of his feet. So his shoes smack flat on every step.

Thunk.

Thunk.

"Six months, Mr. Kelley," Buening says.

Thunk.

Thunk.

"This is six months of training, right here."

Up and down three times. He spins to his left and runs toward a red door in a wood frame. The door is attached to a pulley with 50 pounds of weights.

He lowers his shoulder and lunges. The weights jerk up off the ground. The door flies open and Michael leans through it.

* * *

He had nightmares for a while after it happened. Dreamed the whole thing over again.

That day in 1994 at Pope Air Force Base, when a freak airplane collision caused a huge explosion on the ground. Michael was there with his fellow paratroopers from the 82nd Airborne. The blast let loose a fireball that ran right over him.

More than 100 were wounded, and 24 died. Of the survivors, Michael was hurt the worst. He was burned everywhere but his left shoulder and part of his left side.

Doctors and physical therapists worked on him for three years. He is covered with skin grafts, striped with scar tissue.

"I went through a lot of training in the Army," he says. "I never trained for having a plane crash on top of me."

But his training helped him heal.

And his training made him think he had a shot to make it through the police academy.

"I know this sounds strange," he says, "but I don't think there's any significant difference in me between now and back then. The accident didn't change my views on life. It didn't change whatever strength is inside me.

"I don't have the nightmares anymore. When I dream now, I never see myself the way I used to look. I am what I am now."

2:06, 2:07, 2:08…

"Don't do it fast, do it right," says training supervisor Dave Gehrke. "18…19…20. Good."

Finished with the push-ups, Michael flips over and starts on sit-ups. At the top of each one he shoots a plume of breath that fogs his glasses. Up, back. Up, back. A metronome. He does 20 in 20 seconds.

"Yeah, Mr. Kelley," Gehrke says. "Go get it."

Back to the steps. Three times up, three times down. He strains on the third climb. His mouth droops open. The other trainees have stopped warming up. Everybody watches Michael now. They pound their hands on the 40-foot-long concrete pipe in front of them.

Kelley jumps off the last step and makes a hard right. He unclips a flashlight from his belt and turns it on. The pipe is just big enough for a man to crawl through.

He drops to all fours and dives in.

* * *

On the fourth day of training he wrote:

My weaknesses would primarily be physical…I will need to put forth an extra effort to correct this.

The day before, as part of a routine physical-fitness check, Michael could do just 23 push-ups. After the bench press, the run, the flexibility test, the trainers put his results into their formula. He scored a 33 out of 100.

Six months later the class goes in for its last checkup, 11 days before the obstacle course.

Trainer Glenn Jones turns on a tape player with a recording of a metronome. The class has to do push-ups with the same *thock-thock* rhythm.

The tape runs for a minute. Michael does 42 push-ups without slowing down.

In six months he has gained 6 pounds of muscle, lost 4 percentage points of body fat, added 30 pounds to his bench press. He improved everywhere but the mile-and-a-half run. His final score is 56.

Still, that's barely average. A police officer has to be more than just healthy. Suspects run. Then they fight when you catch them.

"Look," Gehrke says one morning. "Michael is never going to be the guy who chases down the crook. But he's got stamina and he's tough. Our tests are set up to screen out people who can't fulfill the physical requirements. He's met every one."

3:42, 3:43, 3:44...

Jeff Williams, the class president, yells through a crack in the concrete pipe.

"Go on, Hollywood! Get on through there, Mike!"

Ten seconds later Michael eases out the other end. Two trainers are waiting with a mat. Twenty more push-ups, twenty more sit-ups.

This time everything is slower. On the push-ups his arms quiver. On the last few sit-ups he can barely lift himself.

Recruit Richard Jones runs over and squats next to him.

"It's all you, man. All day. One at a time."

Michael's arms are streaked with dirt and sweat. His lips are coated with white flecks. He breathes so hard his shirt comes untucked.

One last sit-up. He staggers to his feet. He has to run out to the cone again. But he heads in the wrong direction, way off at an angle. It takes him four steps to stumble back toward the right line.

Buening warned them weeks ago. The class had come out to practice the obstacle course. They didn't go full speed. Some in the class didn't think it was so hard.

Wait and see what it's like on test day, he said then. Wait and see when it's for real.

4:59, 5:00, 5:01...

The class started out with 20. One quit the first week. Another blew out his knee playing volleyball on the weekend. Williams came up with a slogan for the rest: *One machine, 18 parts.* They had it sewn on the class flag.

The slowest part of the machine has two minutes left. He trudges out toward the cone.

Jose Aguirre waves him in with both hands, like he's pulling a rope. Billy Kiley yells until his voice cracks.

Buening, the trainer, keeps checking his stopwatch.

Michael rounds the cone.

Kris Kodad takes his spot next to the police car. He gets to be dragged away again. It's the last physical task on the obstacle course.

Michael runs toward the car, and all of a sudden the shouting stops. No one says anything. The class leans forward in a line against the concrete pipe.

Thirty steps away.

Now 20.

Now 10.

He comes up behind Kodad, reaches under his arms again, stands there for a long second.

Then he pulls.

And the noise explodes.

"Straight back, Mike!"

"One more time!"

"Be strong, Hollywood!"

Michael doesn't hear any of this. Instead he hears a voice in his head:

Maple and Monroe?

or

Monroe and Maple?

At the beginning of the obstacle course, Buening told him two street names. At the end Michael has to repeat them in order.

If he gets them wrong, he has to run to the cone and back again.

If he has to go out there again, he'll run out of time.

Maple and Monroe? Monroe and Maple?

He resets his grip around Kodad. Pulls hard one last time. Backs into Buening's waiting hand.

"Gimme your street names!"

Buening holds his finger over the stopwatch button.

"MAPLE AND MONROE!"

Click.

"Wooooo!" Buening hollers, doing his best Ric Flair.

He looks down at the stopwatch.

6:14.

Michael pulls off the duty belt. The whole class crowds around him.

But after a second or two he walks off by himself, near the edge of the woods.

He leans over, hands on his thighs, and he stays like

242

that a long time.

Out on the obstacle course, Sean Parker struggles through the second set of sit-ups. He lies on the mat until he musters the strength. He finishes the course with five seconds to spare.

On this day Michael Kelley is not the slowest.

He walks back toward the obstacle course, over where Michael Davis is standing. Davis is a former Forsyth County deputy. Everybody calls him Sheriff.

"You OK, Hollywood?" Davis says.

Michael looks out at the obstacle course, draws in a deep breath.

"It's all over, man," he says. "It's all over."

* * *

Graduation day.

They spend most of it waiting. They had one last uniform inspection in the morning, when they all turned in their patches that said POLICE TRAINEE.

They split up to meet with the officers they'll be teaming with on patrol. Every new officer rides with a veteran for 14 weeks. Michael has been assigned to the Baker 3 district in east Charlotte.

Afterward, the recruits talk about cop shows.

"Baretta," Jeff Williams says. "He was the man."

"I liked *Adam-12*," Billy Kiley says.

"*S.W.A.T.*"

"*Starsky and Hutch.*"

"You know," Ben West says, "the sci-fi network is remaking *Battlestar Galactica.*"

Silence.

"Hang with us, Ben," Ron Webster says. "Focus, son."

Before long the families start to show up. The recruits mingle for a while, then go back upstairs to the classroom where they met every morning.

Buening stands in front of the group for the last time.

"What else is there to say?" he says. "I wish you all the best. Always be safe. Make the right decisions out there. Stay motivated. Do the right thing.

"In about 20 minutes here, we're going to be brothers and sisters. Be proud of that badge. Don't bring any disrespect to it.

"All right. Line up."

They go down the hall, wait in the stairwell, walk past the photos of the officers killed in the line of duty.

They sit in the front of the auditorium. They get three standing ovations.

The choir sings and the chief of police gives a speech and the chaplain says a prayer.

Then they are called up one by one.

When it comes Michael's turn, he climbs the stage and shakes a row of hands. Buening is the last one in the row.

"This is a real honor, for me to be able to give this to you," Buening says.

And he hands Michael Kelley his badge.

* * *

One other thing about that day on the obstacle course.

It happened after Michael staggered to his feet for his last run.

After the accident, he didn't run at all for eight years. Since he started back, he hobbled around every corner, limped with every stride.

But for a minute there that day, he caught a second wind, or something popped loose, or his body was too tired to hurt.

The awkward stride planed off. The clomping feet hit the ground smooth.

The obstacles were almost done with.

Michael Kelley ran free.

A beautiful find

NOVEMBER 16, 2003

Question One: You decide you want to solve a math problem that's so hard, no one's come close in 25 years. How do you begin?

John Swallow began four and a half years ago, 6,000 miles from home, staring out the window of a bus.

He's the guy you want next to you on the bus seat. Friendly but quiet. You might not remember him later, unless you glanced over when he'd just thought of something, and you saw his left eyebrow rise over the rim of his glasses.

Swallow started writing computer code when he was 7. He aced college calculus when he was 13. He entered grad school at Yale when he was 19.

But here he was at 28, in Haifa, Israel, with a problem that clogged his mind like kitchen sludge.

Swallow teaches at Davidson College. He went to Israel on a working sabbatical to trade ideas with a professor named Jack Sonn. Swallow and Sonn are two of maybe 100 people in the world who are experts in their particular side street of math.

They study algebra at its highest levels. They work with sets of numbers called Brauer groups, named for a Jewish mathematician who left Germany when Hitler took over. They apply ideas based on Galois theory, named for a 19th-century French mathematician who died in a duel.

The work has practical uses, such as cryptography— the making and breaking of codes. But to Swallow, it combines the things he loves about math: the beautiful patterns in numbers and the challenge of seeing how far his skill and imagination can stretch.

In Israel, Swallow and Sonn spent a semester warming up with some minor theorems. Then one day Sonn suggested a problem that other experts in their field had thought of back in the '70s. Many mathematicians worked on it into the '80s—Sonn among them—but no one ever came up with an answer.

In every branch of math there are problems no one has ever solved. They are numerical shipwrecks. If you dive deep enough you could find treasure. But you might spend years and come out with nothing.

The problem Sonn suggested involves analyzing two Brauer groups—huge algebraic structures, whole fields of numbers—and trying to show that they're the same.

The numbers in Brauer groups aren't just the ones you use to balance the checkbook. They're irrational numbers (like the square root of 2) that can't be reduced to a fraction. They're even imaginary numbers (like the square root of -1) that don't show up on a calculator.

Swallow came to think of his problem as comparing two forests. They look exactly alike. The heights of the trees match. But to prove that they're identical, you have to get down to every needle and every hunk of bark.

He had never worked on a problem that required so many techniques, so many new ideas, so much brainpower.

For months he sat in Sonn's office every afternoon, the two of them staring at the blackboard, sometimes for so long that Sonn would doze off.

At night Swallow rode home on a city bus. The other passengers chatted in Hebrew or Arabic, languages he didn't understand. Swallow thought about all the rest he didn't understand, the equations on the blackboard, the numbers skittering out of reach.

He wondered if he had come this far only to find something he had never run into: a problem that was stronger than his mind.

* * *

Question Two: You're struggling to solve a math problem that's so hard, no one's come close in 25 years. You also have a normal life. How do you balance the world inside your head with the one outside?

Cameron Swallow calls it "the math-problem expression." She describes it as "an abstracted gazing into the middle distance."

She first saw it in her husband half their lives ago. They met in choir practice at the University of the South in Tennessee. She was a freshman at 17. He was already a sophomore at 16.

They both loved math and music and English literature. They had long romantic talks about quadratic equations. He had enough credits to graduate early, but he stayed an extra year—partly to finish off a double major, partly to be with her. They got married in 1991, when John was at Yale.

In 1994 they came to Davidson. Soon they had a daughter, Ruth, and then another, Sophie. The talk shifted to whose turn it was to change diapers and when to buy the minivan. John became, as Cameron puts it, the Kitchen Spouse. He makes a mean Reuben sandwich in the Crock-Pot.

In Israel their kids were still small, so John and Cameron had time to talk about the math problem. But he and Sonn weren't getting far. They had spent six months digging and hadn't hit anything solid. And it was time for the Swallows to go back to Davidson.

Swallow resumed his regular life—teaching during the day, spending time with family at night. He worked on the problem in spare hours, between classes and church services and oil changes. He filled sheets of paper with equations next to phone numbers for the DMV.

Sonn had gone on to other projects. Swallow worked by himself for months. But he kept getting stuck. He thought of it like trying to lay carpet that was too small for the room. Every time he got one corner to fit, another would pop loose.

He worried that he had lost his confidence, lost his aggressiveness, lost his faith.

He put down the problem for nearly a year.

He taught, traveled, read to his daughters. He got in touch with a Canadian collaborator. They worked on a smaller problem that they wrapped up in a few months.

When they were done Swallow went back to the folder in his file cabinet, the one marked *"Current" Research*.

It was filled with copied pages from textbooks, scribbles on graph paper, half-finished thoughts on index cards. The Brauer groups, those two huge fields of numbers, ran all over the pages. He was sure they were the same. But he had to prove it.

He read the notes over and dug in again.

He spread out his work on a table at Summit Coffee across from the Davidson campus. He tried out theories in his head as he drove back from family visits, Cameron and the kids asleep in the minivan, a band called String Cheese Incident playing on the stereo.

Sometimes he forgot what he'd already done and repeated the mistakes he and Sonn made in Israel. Sometimes he worked for days and ended up back at the same wrong place.

But then he thought about the smaller problem he'd already finished. He realized that some of that work overlapped.

He still wasn't getting far. He wasn't even doing enough to call his progress slow and steady. Slow and unsteady, maybe.

Still, after two and a half years, the stubborn numbers in Swallow's head began to shift a little.

His eyebrow rose.

* * *

Question Three: You've spent countless hours trying to solve a math problem that's so hard, no one's come close in 25 years. What will it take to finally break through?

The speaker was boring. Worse yet, he was boring in French.

By now it was July 2001. Swallow had come to Lille, France, north of Paris, for a math conference. He knows French. But this guy at the front of the lecture hall was talking so fast that Swallow couldn't understand half the words, and didn't care about the rest.

Eventually he gave up. He reached over and pulled out his notes on the problem he and Jack Sonn had been working on.

All of a sudden a fresh thought flashed in his mind.

He grabbed a pen and wrote one word.

Suppose.

He followed that word with a string of equations that set new limits on the number fields.

Maybe if he put just a few restrictions on the problem, narrowed the scope just a bit, it would work. He went back to the idea of trying to lay a carpet that's too small for the room. Maybe the answer was to make the room a little smaller.

For the next couple of days he did calculations in every spare moment. The numbers were lining up, making graceful curves on his worksheets. But there were still places where the numbers strayed.

One morning Swallow skipped the conference and went looking for coffee. He ended up in a shopping center and found a table in a restaurant called Quick—a European version of McDonald's.

He doesn't remember much about the scene around him. The steam coming off the coffee. A woman pushing a baby stroller.

Then, another flash.

All along he had struggled with a few key places where the two number fields could have been different. If they were the same, he could apply an equation to both fields and the two sides would add up to zero. But one side always came up with the wrong result.

This time Swallow tried a new technique, something he'd never thought of before that moment in the fast-food joint in France.

It was as if he had been trying to train a dog for months, and the dog finally came.

Lots of dogs. Whole fields of them.

The numbers lined up and sat still.

Swallow applied an equation to both Brauer groups. Did the calculations.

They added up to zero.

Perfect balance.

He had made it down to the needle and the bark. The forests were the same.

Swallow still had to try his new thoughts on other parts of the problem. He still had to recheck his calculations. He still had to trust himself.

He went back to Davidson. His wife noticed the old "math-problem expression." Swallow ran through the steps of his solution over and over until he felt sure.

In the fall of '01 he sent Jack Sonn a draft of the solution. For the next six months they e-mailed back and forth, challenging each other's ideas, getting stuck and starting over. Swallow had to refine his work, make the path to the answer more clear.

The revisions took more than a year.

In November 2002, Swallow sent Sonn a draft that contained all the changes. Sonn spent two months looking them over.

And then Sonn e-mailed back with the words Swallow

had waited to hear for almost exactly four years:

"Looks good."

* * *

Question Four: You think you've solved a math problem that's so hard, no one's come close in 25 years. How do you know when you're done?

At the highest levels, every math problem is solved twice: once in private, once in public.

Swallow and Sonn agreed that they'd found the answer. But now the math world would get to check their work.

They typed up a formal version of the proof: "Brauer Groups of Genus Zero Extensions of Number Fields." It ran 22 pages.

Swallow sent copies to several other experts. He and Sonn posted their work on Web sites devoted to new research papers.

Based on the feedback, they made a few small fixes. Then they got the proof ready for the final step—submitting it to one of the academic journals.

The journals are the hockey goalies of math. If they think a paper is worthy, they send it to referees—other mathematicians who go over every detail. The referees are anonymous. If they agree with the proof, most mathematicians consider the problem solved.

Most journals get more submissions than they can publish. One journal decided not to look at Sonn and Swallow's proof. They sent their work to a second journal. It was now February 2003. Swallow thought it might be another year before they heard back.

Swallow picks up his office mail at the college union. In summer he goes by every couple of days. In early August he found a letter. It was from an editor of *Transactions of the American Mathematical Society.*

I am pleased to inform you that your manuscript… has been accepted for publication.

One referee suggested two tiny changes. The other didn't suggest any.

It had been four years and seven months since they started. Now they were officially finished.

Swallow sent Jack Sonn an e-mail. He said it was time for a drink.

* * *

Bonus Question: You've solved a math problem that was so hard, no one else came close for 25 years. What did you learn?

The first breath of fall is blowing across Main Street in Davidson. The folks behind the counter at Summit Coffee learned long ago what John Swallow wants. Regular latte if it's the morning, decaf latte if it's the afternoon.

They know what he wants to drink, they might know what he does for a living, but they don't know what he has accomplished. Not many people do—his family, a few other faculty members, maybe 50 mathematicians worldwide.

The problem he solved won't win any of the big math prizes or make it into *Newsweek*. It's not even necessarily the kind of thing that would earn him a raise.

But there are rewards.

He'll move up in the eyes of those who study top-level algebra. People will ask him to speak at conferences, publish papers, collaborate on new ideas. He's already got a textbook due in December.

He knows now that figuring out the mysteries of giant number fields isn't that different from working out the problems of everyday life. You break them down into small steps. You leave them alone now and then so you can come back fresh. Mainly, you trust what your instincts tell you.

These days Swallow is in charge of figuring out supper and hustling the kids to the car pool. Cameron has gone back to work; she teaches algebra at Smith Language Academy, a Charlotte-Mecklenburg magnet school. Ruth is 7, and Sophie's 5. They're ahead of their age groups in math.

Swallow is due for another sabbatical in 2005. He's thinking about taking the family to France. He's had good luck in France.

Meanwhile he daydreams about the next big problem, wonders what mental turn he'll have to take to solve it.

"There are lots of good ideas, but at first they are only ideas," he says. "They have this feeling of novelty and newness. But until you sit down and hack it out, look at the details, you're never sure what you've got. The idea can be beautiful. But only the work can make it beautiful."

And his left eyebrow rises up.

A conversation with
Tommy Tomlinson

CHRISTOPHER SCANLAN: How did you come to write these profiles?

TOMMY TOMLINSON: The John Swallow story had its origin first. I met John at a party, and he asked me what I did and I asked him what he did. And then I said something like, "So what are you working on?" and 30 minutes later he finished telling me. Immediately I thought that could be a good story because it's sort of a quest. This person's looking for some knowledge that doesn't exist right now or that humans have not been able to figure out.

I thought I would be able to explain in layman's terms what he was doing. That was the big hurdle for both of us. He was very interested in trying to explain to a wider audience what he was doing, trying to make sense of it, because when he talks about this, he's mostly talking to other math professors and they have this shorthand or jargon they use. They don't have to explain it to ordinary people. He was very interested in the prospect of trying to figure out how to put this into ordinary language and, of course, that was necessary for me if I was going to do the story. So we spent a lot of time at the beginning talking about that, talking about metaphors. "How would you describe this if you had to describe it in visual terms?" Or, "What does this mean?" So that's where we started.

Metaphor is a poet's tool. How did you come, in the course of an interview as a journalist, to say, "I'm searching not just for information but for metaphors"?

In this story, it was a very practical matter because I couldn't just describe the information. So what we were trying to do in terms of the metaphors was to give people some sense of the vastness of the problem and the complexity of the problem without getting into too much detail about exactly what the problem was. In one sense it was too complicated, and in another sense it really wasn't that important. The important part is, and I think what the reader would take away is, here's a guy who tried to solve a really hard math problem and here's how he did it. He came up with the best image in the story, about the problem being like a carpet that was too small for the room and trying to pin it down and it pops loose. I'm not sure the particulars of the problem are that important.

How did the Michael Kelley story come to be?

It came to our city desk e-mail tip line. The tip said, "Here's this great guy. He has a really good story. You ought to try to find out about it." So as happens every day, an e-mail went out to five or six people in the newsroom saying, "Anybody interested in this?" Thank God, I just happened to be here that day. I looked at it and said, "Yeah, I'll give this one a shot." I called to talk to his mom and dad, and then I think I talked to his wife next. Michael was not there, I think, at the time I called, and I just told her what I was interested in doing and asked if they would be interested in talking to me about it.

What did you say?

I made my standard pitch. I said, "I write a column for the *Observer*. I like to write about people doing extraordinary things. This sounds like an interesting story. Could I just come over and talk to you about it?" I never commit to doing a story and I never commit to any particular type of story because you don't know what it's going to be until you do the reporting. So, anyway, his wife said she'd talk to him and he said yes.

It turned out—I didn't know this at the time—that we'd written about him fairly extensively when the accident happened. The problem was he was in a coma for most of that, and so he really didn't get interviewed much. But she was used to having a reporter around and he was semi-used to it. All this had happened, I guess, nine years before, so it had been awhile, but they sort of knew what it was going to be like. So I wasn't coming in completely cold, which was a good thing.

How much time did you spend with them?

A lot. I don't know how many days I spent at the police academy. They met there every day. I tried to get there almost every day they had physical training, which was most days. There was a lot of class work, and I sat in on some.

How might the story have changed if he'd failed?

That was one of the things we talked about early on, not just with him and his family, but internally. Are we going to do a story if he doesn't make it? My thought from the beginning was that we would still do a story, because the real obstacle was just making an effort to do this and bringing himself all the way back to where he felt like a full human again. That was the big obstacle in many ways. Certainly it's better for him and better for me that he made it. But I think the story would not have changed substantially, except I would have emphasized more that what was important was that he tried. So I don't think the story would have changed a huge amount.

The story ran on a Sunday and a Monday. I came in on Sunday to check the proofs for the next day, and I had lots of e-mails from people saying, "Please tell me that I'm not reading this story to watch him fail on Monday."

How do you collect information, in a notebook or on a tape recorder?

You know how you hear a noise at night like your house creaking and it's all you can think about? All I can think about when I'm using a tape recorder is the tape recorder. So I use notebooks.

Let's talk about structure. In the John Swallow profile, you used questions. How did you come to use that organizational scheme?

I knew fairly quickly this was going to be a long story. Any time you have a long story, you need a way to break it up. I thought, "What structure would make sense with this story?" Part of it is that this guy was testing himself. He's taking his own test in terms of his skill and imagination and mathematical ability. So pretty early on, I suggested that maybe we ought to structure it as sort of a test.

And that did two things. One, it kept us from having to do subheads, which are pretty good but can sometimes not give you a whole lot of information. And, two, it provided an introduction to each section. I thought it was so easy and so obvious that I was sure it had been done before. Dannye Powell, who writes a column and who sits right next to me, often says that when you're thinking creatively, you think the first thing that comes into your mind is so obvious that it can't be fresh. But when you're thinking creatively, a lot of times your mind will do that work and will give you something fresh.

You use very few quotes. Why is that?

Well, I guess there are lots of reasons, but the simplest is that we're the storytellers, we're the professionals. Unless somebody says something really good or really compelling, we can probably say it better. And so over the years, I've gotten much, much more strict on which quotes I will use. The quotes really have to have some deep insight into the person I'm talking about or to the subject of the story, or it has to move the story forward in a really compelling way even better and faster than I could. That's my standard. In the Swallow story, a lot of the conversation was long sentences with long pauses. I'd say, "John, tell me about this carpet metaphor again." He would talk about it for a while and work it out in his own mind as he was talking, and then we would sit there and stare at each other for a couple of minutes, and he would start up again. That doesn't lend itself very well to quotes.

So what do you put in your notebook?

I'm putting paraphrases and I'm putting pieces of quotes that I might use—I had quotes in the notebook, I just didn't use but one.

Many reporters think that when we go to an interview, we're there to get quotes. What are you there for?

I'm looking for the story. I'm looking for that narrative thread, for the idea that pushes the story forward.

You write with so much authority. Is that deliberate?

Absolutely. I think part of that comes from being a columnist and your job, your duty, is to write with authority, and so it's comfortable having that voice. But the other part of it is getting to know your material. I felt comfortable saying everything that I said in the story because I felt like I knew the material pretty well.

I want to talk a bit about revision because I'm struck by how lean the prose is. How do you do that?

Well, I think a big part of it, especially on the Michael Kelley story, was figuring out in advance how I wanted the story to sound. These two stories are similar in structure, I think, but very different in the particulars. In the John Swallow story, almost all the action is in the guy's head. In the Michael Kelley story, almost all the action is out in front where you can see it. So at the very beginning I knew that this story was going to be almost all action. I don't think there are any metaphors in the Michael Kelley story. The whole notion of the obstacle course, of course, is this gigantic metaphor. But in the writing it didn't need any. The facts of what happened to him and what he was going through and the action of the story were enough.

So I remember sitting down at the very beginning and thinking, "Just write down what happened and don't doll it up." The narrative, the pull of that story, was going to be enough. There's no fancy writing in that story at all.

I wrote the beginning of that story, those seven paragraphs, probably a hundred times—literally. There were two roles that lead had to play. One, it had to introduce you to what was going on, and second, it had to say, "This story is so great that we're going to run it on two open pages for two straight days and you're going to want to follow it to the end."

The Kelley story reads like a script. Are you conscious of this, doing it deliberately?

Not so much in the sense that I want it to read like a screenplay, but I want it to feel cinematic because the story is cinematic. I mean, this would be a great movie.

When I'm talking to somebody at the beginning of one of these things and telling them what is going to be involved in me doing a story like this, one of the things I say is, "I'm trying to describe your story as if it were a movie, and I'm trying to get what's in the background, what music might be playing, what the sounds are, what other things might be going on in that frame, what might be inside your head," to prepare somebody for the kind of detailed questions I might be asking. Because most people, ordinary people I write about, they've never been interviewed like this. I think their idea of a normal interview is almost like an interrogation. And what I'm looking for are those details that make it cinematic, that make it into a little movie. You know, the great thing about books is that sometimes they're really good and you forget you're reading, and it's happening in your mind. So that's the ideal on any story—that you make it so good that people forget they're reading.

Is the *Observer* a good home for this kind of work?

It's a fabulous home. I'm astonished every day. I'm especially astonished when I look at other papers when I'm traveling. First of all, as a columnist, I can be anywhere in the paper. One of these stories ran on the front page two days; the other story ran in the Living section on a Sunday. I'm astonished at all the papers I've seen where the columnists are locked into that spot in the rail two times a week or three times a week or whatever and they're never not there. I know the theory behind that: that people get familiar with something being in a certain place every time and they come back to look at it.

I guess my theory is the main thing they come back to look at is good stories. If you've established over time that you can be a reliable provider of good stories, people will look for you wherever you are in the paper. So I skip around a lot. I get to write lots of different lengths. I'm not writing a 600-word column every time. So that to me is just an incredible tool for growth as a reporter. I learned so much from getting to do these two stories, and I got to apply so many things that I had learned over time and don't get to use maybe as often in a daily column, or things that I did use in a daily column and now I get to use in sort of an expanded format. I just wonder why more papers don't let their folks run free like that.

Did you think of these as profiles as you were writing them?

When I found out that this was the category I won in, I thought, "Oh, profiles. Well, that's exactly right." But it wasn't really how I was thinking about them. I was just thinking about them as good narratives.

Why are they good profiles?

Well, first of all, these are two guys who you have some sympathy for and hope that they do well. Second, I think there's a lot going on that people can identify with. In Michael Kelley's terms, people have been through horrible things in their lives. It doesn't matter what it is. It could be the death of a spouse or a child or something like that, and one of the things you have to do is figure out how to rebound from that, how to overcome that and try to lead the most normal life you can afterward.

I got lots of calls and e-mails from people who said, "I'm not going to complain about anything again after reading this guy's story." That's where the resonance of it comes in: Everybody has some hardship in their life, and we have to figure out how to get around or get over our own little obstacle course. The John Swallow story is similar, although his was more of an intellectual challenge, but also a test of confidence. "Do I have what it takes to solve this problem?"

These aren't traditional profiles on somebody who's in the news, where you talk about their background but there's no particular narrative other than this person is in the news. These are two people who are *not* in the news. Most of our readers would never have known about these guys unless these stories appeared.

These are two very long stories for newspapers and I hope they are evidence that people will read long stories. I believe people will read very long stories. What they *won't* read are boring stories. So the one thing above all else in these stories is I didn't want them to be boring. I knew from the material it was not boring and so the question was, "Can you make that person's interesting life translate into interesting writing?"

Do you outline your stories?

Not what I would consider a formal outline. The way it usually starts is going through my notebook and flagging things that I want to make sure end up in the story.

How do you flag them?

If it's a shorter thing where I don't have so many pages to look through, I'll just put like a big asterisk by it. If it's a longer thing, what I'll do is make little tabs. I take a Post-it Note and have it stick out of the side of the notebook and then write on that tab what it is—a quote about his dad or whatever. Then at some point, I'll get a sheet of paper and write down what I thought were the really good scenes of the story.

What's an example of what I might see on this page?

In the Michael Kelley story you might see the scene where they bring him in on his run, and you might see the scene where he sets up the stakes in his back yard. I do just four or five words, but I know in my head what that scene is. Then when I have them on a sheet of paper, I can move them around a little bit and they sort of make sense after awhile into which order they should be in. So once I get the scenes lined up, then I start figuring out the connective tissue. What needs to go in between these, how much of it needs to be straight chronology, whether there are going to be any flashbacks, and, if so, where they go. This is sort of where the magic of it is, I guess. I don't have a good sense as to why I put things where they are sometimes. I just do it until it feels right.

Did you know the Kelley story would end by returning to the scene where he's running the race?

No. But I knew when I saw it happen that that was a possibility, and the more I thought about it, the more I thought it had to be. I called that ending the "Schwab."

The what?

There's a guy named Gary Schwab who's a great editor here. I worked on a story with him many years ago about a guy who won a bass fishing tournament, the Bassmasters Classic. He was a rookie, and it was a huge upset. A few months afterward he died in a plane crash, and the tournament was coming back to the place where he had won the year before, which happened to be in North Carolina, which is why we were writing about it to begin with. So I went up—he's from Connecticut—and visited his family and talked to them and got a lot of great narrative material. At some point, his girlfriend and his sister took his ashes out to the lake that he grew up on when he was a kid and they poured the ashes in the lake.

As I was hearing this, I was thinking, "There's my ending." Gary was my editor on the story. We get through it and Gary says—and he's very gentle with all this—he says, "That's a great ending, but that's the ending I expected. Can you give me an ending that I didn't expect?"

So I went back and looked through my stuff. When I was meeting this guy's family, his mom and dad got out one of those 8mm films of this guy as a kid, and it just so happens—just a complete stroke of luck—that they have a film of the first fish he ever caught. They're showing it on the wall of the house, and his dad keeps rewinding this film and showing it over and over, and that became the ending of the story. I thought that was such a better ending to the story because it brings it back to the beginning, and it adds such a richness to what is going on, not only in this kid's life but in his family's life.

So any time I have a big story like this, I try to think, "Is there a Schwab ending that I could put on this story?" The natural ending of the Kelley story is the guy getting his badge, because that's what he's worked for this whole time, and I think probably five or 10 years ago, that's the ending I would have put on the story. But after this beautiful moment when I realized that there could be something else, I've always looked for that sort of coda, in musical terms, something that brings you back. You've got this guy who, for just this one moment, was sort of fully the person he used to be. As soon as I saw that, I knew that could be the ending, because it was this moment in the story where this weird thing happened. All of a sudden he was moving. He was really running. I asked him about it afterward, and what he told me was pretty much paraphrased in the story. He said, "I don't know what happened, if I just caught a second wind or something popped loose, but, yeah, I felt great all of a sudden." The more I thought about it, the more I thought that needed to be the ending.

You see it in movies all the time. The end of *Hoosiers* is not when they win the state championship. The end of *Hoosiers* is when you come back and see the old gym and this little kid dribbling the basketball.

Do you read aloud?

Not only do I read aloud, my editor reads aloud. Not everybody here does that, but I think it's a pretty well-developed practice here of reading stories aloud during the editing process with the reporter sitting there. So what I'll do is I'll be writing and I'll read stuff aloud. I may not read the entire story aloud top to bottom, but I will certainly read sections of it from time to time aloud, especially parts where I'm trying to describe something complicated or I'm using sentences that might not be your simple declarative sentence, to make sure it flows well.

Then during the editing process, Mike Gordon will read through the story and pick out things he wants to talk about. He'll call me over to his desk, and he reads the story aloud from the screen. That's excruciating and incredibly powerful at the same time because you immediately see all the places where you're slowing down because he can't read it well out loud. So if he's not reading it well, then I'm probably not writing it well. So you go back and try again until you get it to flow a little better.

You have a line at the end of the story about John Swallow: "He knows now that figuring out the mysteries of giant number fields isn't that different from working out the problems of everyday life. You break them down into small steps. You leave them alone now and then so you can come back fresh. Mainly, you trust what your instincts tell you."
Is that what writing is for you?

Absolutely. The more I thought about the story, the more I thought that it not only described what he was going through, it was in a lot of ways what I was going through trying to write the story. I had this big complicated thing that I was trying to figure out, and at some point I thought it was too much for me and I put it away. Then I brought it back and looked at it in a little different way. It's what I think about as I'm writing. If I have a complicated story, I need to do a small part of it first to prove to myself I can do it.

What's the hardest part of a story?

I think in some ways the hardest part is what I was just talking about. A big part of writing with authority is trusting your gut. You have to think, "I have a good handle on what's going on here. I know what the story is. I just have to write it." And I think that's a big leap to make. It's certainly a big leap I've had to make in realizing that I was capable of doing this kind of stuff, in capturing these complicated lives and trying to get them on paper somehow. You have to have faith in yourself that you can tell the story right.

For me, there's a whole lot of anxiety between the reporting and the writing. The question is always, "Can I rise to this material?" especially on stories like these where there's so much great stuff. Can I give these stories what they deserve? That, to me, is always a cause of anxiety when I'm writing. As a columnist, you're writing about a lot of big events, and you're writing about them often under tight deadlines. But oftentimes that deadline is a savior because you don't have time for anxiety. You don't have time to think because you've got 30 minutes and it's got to be done.

On these stories, where there was no particular deadline or particular space that you're writing to, lots of doubts crawl in, at least for me. Most of them have to do with whether I can muster enough skill to do right by this story, and that leads to a lot of staring at blank screens and writing stuff over and over and over and then getting up and walking away for a while. Or sitting there leaning, cockeyed, looking at the words to see if that could possibly be an acceptable sentence to put in our newspaper. That sort of thing. And so that to me is the hard part, and I haven't found that it gets easier—believing in your ability and believing in the material or believing in your ability to take that material and make something out of it.

Some reporters give their subjects a look at a story before publication. Did you share any of these stories with Swallow or Kelley?

The John Swallow story is the first time I've ever let somebody see a story in advance. I did it for two reasons. One, because of the subject matter—it was complicated—and, even though I had very rudimentary descriptions of math in there, I wanted to make sure they were accurate. Second, because the reporting of the story was done over such a long period of time, I wanted to make sure I hadn't mischaracterized something because parts of it were not fresh in my mind.

Your reconstructions are vivid and credible. What are your secrets for reporting and writing reconstructed scenes?

Whenever I'm doing this type of story, I know it's going to take a lot of reporting. I tell people that I'm going to be asking a lot of questions. They're going to think some of these questions are really stupid because I'm going to be asking stuff like what they were wearing at a certain time and what music was playing in the background when this happened, and stuff that they think has nothing to do with the story. The reason I'm asking these questions is that I want it to be sort of like a movie, like a dream. I want it to be as vivid to the reader as it is to them, as having experienced these things. I think almost every time people get that. I think in one way it's sort of exciting to them because they think, "It's like I'm going to be in a movie of my life." So I think people get that pretty quickly.

Is there a checklist of questions you ask?

I'm always thinking about the sensory things—sight, sound, smell, taste, and touch. So I'm asking a lot of questions, most of the answers to which don't end up being important, so I don't put them in the paper. In the John Swallow story, for example, when he has one of his breakthroughs, the question I asked was, "What do you remember about that? What do you remember about the surroundings?" He had a breakthrough at this little French fast-food joint—it was like McDonald's basically—and he remembered the steam coming up off the coffee. He remembered this woman pushing a baby stroller. So I thought that was a pretty good sensory thing that sort of put you there. It captivates the reader in a way. It keeps them going in the story. So I look for those sorts of things a lot—little sensory things. I love smells in stories because I don't think we put them in stories very often. I love being able to describe the way the grass smelled if somebody's walking across a field. So I'm always asking those sort of things and thinking about that. I think as you're doing the reporting, the more you ask somebody about that stuff, the more likely they are to remember it that way or to tell it to you in that fashion.

You said that these are the best stories of your life.

I think so.

Why?

They're a culmination of what I've learned. I've learned not to use so many quotes. I've learned that the biggest part of a story is that narrative drive. I've learned to leave out a lot of stuff. I've learned to capture things in scenes. Now, I haven't mastered any of those things. I mean there's a long way to go on any of that. But these are pretty good examples of what I've learned as a journalist. I mean, if you asked, "What have you learned about how to be a reporter?" I could hand you one of these stories and say, "This pretty much sums it up."

Writers' Workshop

Talking Points

1) Tommy Tomlinson says he relied on metaphors to convey the arcane mathematics of John Swallow's world in "A Beautiful Find." Discuss the value—and possible dangers—of journalists using a device from the poet's toolbox.

2) One of the hallmarks of Tomlinson's writing is his sparing use of quotes. This characteristic reflects his belief that "quotes really have to have some deep insight into the person I'm talking about or to the subject of the story, or it has to move the story forward in a really compelling way even better and faster than I could." Contrast the use of quotes in "A Beautiful Find" and "Michael Kelley's Obstacle Course" and consider how they reflect that philosophy.

Assignment Desk

1) Tomlinson uses metaphors to help readers understand the challenging world of mathematics. In what other areas that journalists cover would metaphor provide a helpful bridge in understanding? Identify difficult concepts in your beat or specialty area and look for a metaphor to use.

2) ASNE award winners over the years have described the value of reading their stories aloud as part of the revision process. At *The Charlotte Observer*, Mike Gordon, who edited Tomlinson's profiles, and other editors take it one step further: They read stories aloud with the reporter sitting beside them. Experiment with the technique in your newsroom.

3) To organize his prize-winning profiles, Tomlinson took advantage of structural elements present in the material. In "A Beautiful Find," he mimicked an examination's question format to arrange the themes he wanted to explore. In the stories about Michael Kelley, the outline of a 7-minute, 20-second obstacle course provided the narrative architecture; in Part II, the elapsed time of a stopwatch adds suspense as well as structure. Such "extra literary" devices—using tarot cards to sequence a story about friendships, for instance—help writers find fresh ways to organize their stories. Using Tomlinson's work as an example, look in the world of your stories for a new blueprint.

The Star-Ledger

Amy Ellis Nutt
Finalist, Profile Writing

Amy Ellis Nutt is a feature writer for *The Star-Ledger* in Newark, N.J. She became a journalist in 1988 after a brief career teaching philosophy at the University of Massachusetts and Tufts University. Starting out as a fact-checker at *Sports Illustrated*, she worked her way up to writer-reporter and won two national writing awards from the Women's Sports Foundation and the Golf Writers Association of America.

Last year, Nutt won the ASNE Distinguished Writing Award for Non-Deadline Writing for her five-part series, "The Seekers," which explored some of the biggest unanswered questions in science. "The Seekers" also won a National Headliner Award and a first-place prize from the Newswomen's Club of New York.

In 2000 she won a first-place writing award from the National Mental Health Association for an article about electroconvulsive therapy and in 2001 the Newswomen's Club of New York recognized her for column writing.

Nutt is a graduate of Smith College and received a master's degree in philosophy from the Massachusetts Institute of Technology and a master's degree in journalism from Columbia University. She lives in Bridgewater, N.J., and credits her parents, Dave and Grace, for any innate writing talent.

The story of "The Natural Who Self-Destructed" follows the precipitous fall of a talented golfer with a gift for sabotaging his own life. Rich with the voices of those who tried to save Jeff Thomas from himself, Nutt's story is brought to life with details and anecdotes that animate a doomed life.

[This story has been excerpted because of space considerations. The full text can be read on the CD-ROM included in this edition of Best Newspaper Writing.]

The natural who self-destructed

AUGUST 31, 2003

HOBE SOUND, Fla.—There was a stillness, an end-of-the-road kind of sadness about him.

Rita Mercer sensed it the last time she saw him, sitting slumped in a beat-up armchair as he waited for his clothes to dry in the motel laundry room.

"He said he was down about his family," she says. "He showed me the picture in his wallet of him, his woman and a little child."

Mercer knew about the drugs, too. Saw the people coming and going from the man's room all the time. Sometimes even saw the drugs—rock cocaine, pills, marijuana.

Drugs and alcohol weren't unusual at the Heritage Inn, a down-at-the-heel kind of place wedged between trailer parks and self-storage warehouses.

What did seem out of place was this man. "He isn't from here," Mercer would tell people. "He's different." She just couldn't say how.

Around the motel, 44-year-old Jeff Thomas was seen as a loner, an alcoholic drug addict who managed to pull himself together every day to caddie at the golf course on the other side of Route 1.

What wasn't known by Mercer, or anyone else, was that the man who drove each morning from his $16-a-day efficiency to the exclusive McArthur Golf Club was *the* Jeff Thomas—winner of more than 50 golf titles and the greatest amateur golfer ever to come out of New Jersey.

On July 30, Thomas' decomposing body was found sprawled across his bed, face up, in the last place on Earth he called home.

How he got there is the story of how a natural-born winner, despite his gifts—or maybe because of them—was a natural-born loser as well.

SO GOOD

There was magic in his hands, that's what everyone said. He didn't have a classic, controlled swing. It was more like a big sweeping hook, and when the ball land-ed—more often than not in the middle of the fairway—it seemed to roll forever.

"He just blew me away with his shot-making," says Kevin Kennedy, a teammate of Thomas' at Ramapo College in 1978 and '79. "He had such feeling in his hands. He was so good, he could have flushed a ball with a 2-iron off the hood of a car."

Off the course, however, Thomas was a loose can-non. In high school he was fired from a caddie job at Plainfield Country Club after he stole a member's Ping putter, and as early as junior high he was selling his own prescription medicine at school.

"Jeff was mischievous," says older brother Alan Thomas. "He'd always take a risk and get in trouble. We'd be throwing rocks in the parking lot and he was the first one to get caught."

A gentle, even outgoing person most of the time, Thomas had a buried anger that sometimes rocketed to the surface.

"He made more enemies than you could shake a stick at," says Eddie Famula, a former head pro who knew him in the 1980s and '90s.

Golf may have been his only friend.

When he joined the Ramapo team, Thomas already had won the first of what would become a record eight New Jersey State Amateur titles, as well as both the jun-ior and men's club championships at Plainfield West, a public nine-holer directly across the street from the de-cidedly more upscale Plainfield Country Club.

Thomas won those early tournaments with a starter set of Spalding clubs with leather grips so worn they were glazed and slick. "He didn't even wear a golf glove. It was crazy," says Kennedy. "He could just flat out hit a golf ball."

Thomas was 13 when he began playing regularly with his father, Charlie. The elder Thomas had played on two state championship golf teams in 1947 and 1948 when he attended North Plainfield High School, and his competitive instincts were passed down to his sons Alan, Jeff and Chris.

"I wasn't bad," says Alan Thomas, a 46-year-old re-search chemist in Gilbert, Ariz. "But Jeff learned it so fast he ended up kicking my butt. I got so disgusted with it, he was so good. So I went and played basketball."

Thomas had tunnel vision when it came to golf. He played on the South Plainfield High School team, and two years after graduation was still playing every day at Plainfield West.

That was when Ramapo College golf coach Vince Nardiello heard about the former high school phenom and recruited him. A four-time All American at Ramapo, Thomas led the school in 1982 to its first Division III title in golf.

On the golf course, he was a brilliant manipulator of the ball—"He could hit it in his sleep," says Nardiello. But Thomas also enjoyed playing the role of the renegade—snubbing his nose at any authority figure he could find. By the time he got to college, Thomas was a heavy pot smoker and drinker. While other players arrived at away matches with luggage and clubs, Thomas arrived with luggage and clubs and a case of Heineken.

"We had to take a vote whether to keep him on the team because of his off-course antics," says Kennedy, who now owns a golf cart company in Myrtle Beach, S.C.

At Ramapo, Thomas showed up drunk for a match his freshman year; he stole cigarettes and cigars from a store on a team trip, and cold-cocked Kennedy after he suggested Thomas stop ripping telephones out of a hotel wall.

"He had a world of talent. He had [PGA] Tour potential," says Nardiello. "But it was difficult to have him on the team....In 23 years of coaching he was the only guy I ever kicked off the team. He also accomplished more than any other player I ever had."

When Thomas ran out of eligibility at Ramapo, he needed only 16 credits to get a degree, but it didn't matter if he couldn't play golf.

"I begged him to come back and finish," says Nardiello. "He was a smart guy. He got A's and B's without buying a book....But he was the most self-destructive person I ever met."

Time and again, however, it was his talent, his gift for striking a ball with a bladed club, that earned Thomas yet another chance.

"He was a Dr. Jekyll and Mr. Hyde," says Tom Kaufmann, a bartender at the Polish National Home in South Plainfield who frequently played with Thomas at Plainfield West. "He was basically a nice guy, but when he drank he rubbed a lot of people the wrong way. Because of his talent they looked the other way. They thought, 'Hey, here's a guy who's going to be big; he's going to be on TV someday.'"

So people would hire Thomas knowing about his unreliability. Rarely did he repay them for the opportunity. He lost a part-time job as a bartender for hitting a customer over the head with a bottle, and lasted a week as a limousine driver before being fired.

When asked why they liked him, invariably his friends answer with a story, not about the man, but about the golf:

The 80-footer Thomas drained at the 1979 NCAA Division III championship; the time he beat another amateur, a friend, at Seminole Golf Club in North Palm Beach, Fla., by one stroke—while on crutches with a sprained ankle.

"The first time we hung out on a golf course together, we were in the dark [at Plainfield West]," says Kaufmann, "and Jeff says to me, 'Hey, let's hit one-handed bunker shots!' And I say, 'Yeah, right.' You couldn't see a thing. And doesn't he take the first swing with one hand in the pitch black and sink it. He was amazing."

In 1983 and '85, Thomas won two more state amateur titles, then finished third in the state event in 1986 while still nursing a broken heel.

By the time he won his seventh state amateur in 1991, Thomas had piled up more than 30 titles. That same year he lost the Metropolitan Golf Association's prestigious amateur tournament, the Ike, in a playoff, despite tying New York's Old Westbury course record of 68—not once, but twice.

[The full text of this story can be read on the CD-ROM included in this edition of Best Newspaper Writing.]

Lessons Learned

BY AMY ELLIS NUTT

Of the three profiles included in my entry, "The Natural Who Self-Destructed" was the longest and most difficult to write. How do you do a story about a person's life and death when all you know is his name? That was the dilemma I faced when *Star-Ledger* managing editor Rick Everett asked me last August if I wanted to follow up on a one-paragraph announcement in the paper reporting that the body of former New Jersey amateur golf champion Jeff Thomas had been found in a cheap motel in south Florida.

I told him I'd love to. But I said I didn't want to write a story from old clips; I asked if I could fly down to Florida to do the reporting, to see for myself where Thomas lived and died and talk to those who were the last to see him alive.

Forty-eight hours after crisscrossing the treasure coast in and around Hobe Sound, I felt I knew more about Jeff Thomas than just about anyone else—more, it turned out, than most of the friends who'd known him for the past two decades; more even than his brothers, who'd lost contact with Thomas in recent years.

In doing so, I learned again how important it is to see and feel and hear and touch a story—up close—especially when the person at the center of that story can no longer speak for himself. If I had not gone down to Florida to trace Thomas's last days, I wouldn't have found the caddy or the golf club employee who knew him best during the last few months of his life and who testified to his humor, competitiveness, and reliability. I wouldn't have been led by them to the owner of the fresh produce market who often played golf with Thomas and understood how the sport was both a lifeline and a trap for his friend, and how a bad back had led to Thomas's addiction to painkillers.

By visiting the motel where Thomas had lived for 10 months, I was able to persuade the owner to let me see the room where he had died three weeks earlier: the gouges in the walls from Thomas manically driving golf balls off the carpet; a copy of the Bible and beat writer Jack Kerouac's classic, *On the Road,* in the bedroom, and a single beer bottle still sitting in the refrigerator.

Most important of all, by going to Florida I was able to talk to other people who lived at the motel and who saw more of Thomas in the last days of his life than anyone else.

A professor of mine at the Columbia University journalism school once said that a reporter should never leave an interview or the scene of a story without knowing what the lead of his or her story will be. I've always extended that admonition to include knowing a story's kicker as well.

As I lingered at the Heritage Inn in Hobe Sound in late August talking to the chambermaid and anyone else I could find, a woman shyly approached me and asked if I knew Jeff Thomas. I told her I didn't, but that I wanted to talk to those who did. Two hours later, Rita Mercer, a witness to Jeff Thomas's last acts of kindness—and desperation—had provided me with both my lead and my kicker. I knew that the story of a man who had only been a name to me days earlier was now a complex, deeply textured portrait.

I was ready to go home and write.

Newsday

Chuck Culpepper
Finalist, Profile Writing

Chuck Culpepper writes sports features for *Newsday* with an eye toward
stories that relate something about life
in general. Realizing a long-held daydream from his
small-town childhood in Suffolk, Va., he lives skyward
in a 39th-floor apartment in Manhattan.

He joined *Newsday* in October 2002 after two and a
half peripatetic years collecting hotel soaps as sports
columnist at *The Oregonian,* which followed nine peripatetic years collecting hotel soaps as sports columnist
at the *Lexington Herald-Leader* in Kentucky. He won
two Associated Press Sports Editors awards for feature
writing while in Lexington.

Before that, he worked for two newspapers that have
ceased publication, the *National Sports Daily* and the
Los Angeles *Herald Examiner*. He has spent at least two
days in each of the 50 states.

In "Frosty, the Football Coach," he mines the rich
trove of anecdotes and unusual tactics of Frosty Westering, the Pacific Lutheran University football coach who
retired after the 2003 season at age 75. Defying almost
every premise football followers have come to hold as
true, espousing love as a motivator superior to fear, Westering has been called "a great man" by those who know
him and by those who have read about him.

*[This story has been excerpted because of space con-
siderations. The full text can be read on the CD-ROM
included in this edition of Best Newspaper Writing.]*

Frosty, the football coach

OCTOBER 5, 2003

TACOMA, Wash.—Get ready to unlearn almost everything you've presumed true about football. Such as the head coach.

You know a head coach has to be an imperious chairman of the joint chiefs of staff or the whole operation will careen into anarchy. Actually, that's a crock.

A contagious bale of energy known as Frosty Westering, 75, no pushover, former Marine Corps drill instructor, insists that his Pacific Lutheran University players call him "Frosty" and corrects them when they use "Coach." He adores when they spot him on the campus and yell at him—"Frosty, you dropped something!"—then hide behind a tree while he scans the ground. He'll say, "You guys got me on that one!"

They urged him to do a belly flop into the hotel pool on their Sept. 13 trip to California. He complied. They exulted. Former player John Gradwohl recalls a sopping game day in Oregon in the late 1980s when Frosty delighted the crowd with a running flop into the mud, emerging with dark splotches on his then-perpetual yellow windbreaker.

Three Saturdays ago, the Lutes faced fourth-and-12, and quarterback Dusty Macauley went to Frosty and said, "Let's go for it," and Frosty said, "You're kidding," and a small chorus said, "No, let's do it," and Frosty beamed and said, "Let's do it, then!"

The Lutes converted, not that it's all that relevant to Frosty. You know how coaches must state concrete goals or perish? That's also false. Players have never heard Frosty so much as mention playoffs or conference titles or any kind of material championship hardware. No, he's spent 39 coaching years and that exalted total of 300 victories and four national titles and four runner-up finishes and the early stages of this, his final season, begging them, just begging them, to relish the journey.

Sure, but all your life you've known that no football player steeped in essential machismo ever gets caught singing. Well, the world has misled you so stridently. The Lutes sing almost as often as they breathe. Without provocation, they fill their pregame locker rooms with such standards as "Leaving on a Jet Plane," "Stand By Me" and "Rawhide." While warming up for the 1999 NCAA Division III championship game in Salem, Va., they sang "The 12 Days of Christmas." After all, it was Dec. 18.

Pacific Lutheran spotted Rowan (N.J.) 60 pounds per lineman yet still won, 42-13.

After Frosty's 300th win Sept. 20, they sang James Taylor's "Steamroller," with offensive lineman Dave LaSalata leading. Three defenders recently gave a reporter a ride in a pickup truck, and in a startling moment, these hard hitters sang, "Leaving on a Jet Plane." "So kiss me and smile for me/Tell me that you'll wait for me...," defensive back Geoffrey Schock crooned from the driver's seat.

They sing this also to airline crews, who invariably come to adore them for their respect for others' jobs, their steadfast attention to safety instructions, their learned capacity to click all their seat belts simultaneously. "The captain, and myself, the first officer, found ourselves overwhelmed by the excitement created by coach Frosty Westering, his entire staff, and the whole football team," an Alaska Air Lines pilot wrote, unsolicited, to Pacific Lutheran president Loren Anderson on Sept. 15.

This was, of course, after the team disembarked, then formed a "Go" tunnel outside the jetway, then welcomed the pilots and flight attendants to run through for high-fives.

"Singing creates energy," Frosty explained. "When you're singing, there's a lifting of yourself. Singing is a bonding, too, when your buddies are singing and you're singing, too."

"Usually, the people singing are the not-cool people," said Kyle Sells, a fairly amazed freshman from Boise, Idaho. "But in this group, if you're not singing, then you are not cool."

It's about "losing your embarrassment," Schock said.

But surely, players require putdowns—tear 'em down, build 'em up. Poppycock, says Frosty, who orders them to give each other "put-ups."

But it's essential to mourn losses, wallow in them, remember the feeling so you'll avoid feeling it again. Balderdash, says Frosty.

Anderson, the school president, said sometimes he feels "depressed" after a game—he breaks out laughing at the mention—but that "if those feelings cross Frosty's mind, he has never shown it."

Donna Westering has never seen Frosty mope over any of his mere 94 defeats, and she's been married to him for 52 years and five children and 13 grandchildren. Alumnus tight end Doug Burton, from the early 1990s, said, "You're able to absolutely release it all on the field because there's no fear of failure."

Schock said, "I wouldn't be a better person for winning a national championship."

Defensive back Mark Gunderson said, "If you're not enough without it, you'll never be enough with it."

No. 1 or no one? Frosty won't abide it. Losing means you've just completed the privilege of playing. Losing means time for the Afterglow, Frosty's brainchild in which 300 to 500 fans, parents, siblings, girlfriends, coaches and players gather just after the scoreboard clock has struck :00. Players thank fans for coming. Fans thank players for inspiring them to combat strife. Frosty serves as maestro, but anyone can address the crowd. Anyone with a recent or pending birthday receives the throng's rendition of "Happy Birthday."

Have the Lutes just won? Have the Lutes just lost? You can't tell during the Afterglow.

[*The full text of this story can be read on the CD-ROM included in this edition of Best Newspaper Writing.*]

Lessons Learned

BY CHUCK CULPEPPER

I suppose I must listen more attentively to my inklings, which I've seldom trusted and often found at least somewhat loopy, a qualm sometimes bolstered by colleagues and superiors.

In 1999, I read a brief *Sports Illustrated* feature about Frosty Westering, the septuagenarian head football coach at a pretty gumdrop of a university in Tacoma, Wash.— Pacific Lutheran. Of all the unusual details that struck me, one proved especially durable: His players, entrenched in his emphasis on singing as a consciousness-raising act, spent warm-ups for the NCAA Division III championship game of December 1999 crooning "The Twelve Days of Christmas." I had watched football ever since age 7, and that defied just about every notion I'd acquired.

I found Mr. Westering too potentially intriguing to fit into a 620-word column, my role from 2000 to 2002 at *The Oregonian*, despite my proximity to his glow at the time. Still, even as I headed for *Newsday* in October 2002, I'd think occasionally about the idea before dismissing it as too small for New York—or for just about anywhere.

In September 2003, I learned of Westering's decision to make the 2003 season his last. Now-or-never carried the day. But I was nobody's salesman as I began selling the story over the telephone. I feared coming off as a flake and made sure to sound casual, unmarried to the concept. The school, after all, sits about as far from New York as you can get. Almost nobody in New York would've heard of it. It has won four national championships, but in small divisions before smallish crowds.

Luckily my editor was one Sandy Keenan, far from the only time I'd state that sentiment. But even though she's unafraid of the unconventional, I hurried through a few facts on the way to some other topic. Westering has his players cheer flight attendants and pilots on road trips. He stops practice to have players gaze at Mount

Rainier. They sang "The Twelve Days of Christmas" before the championship (which they won handily).

"The Twelve Days of Christmas" seemed to clinch it for Sandy.

I've been to Olympic opening ceremonies in three countries, to 11 Super Bowls, to four Wimbledons, to a World Cup celebration on the streets of Paris, to a tractor pull in the southern part of a great state called Kentucky. Nothing has exceeded the three days at Pacific Lutheran. While often we sportswriters ravenously make a story out of one or two uncanny facts, here came a torrent.

He cancels several practices every August so his players can help all the freshmen move into dormitories. He insists his players call him "Frosty" and loves for them to holler his name on campus, then hide behind trees or buildings. Win or lose, he leads the players and a lingering patch of fans in a ritual "Afterglow" wherein they revel in their Saturday. Anyone can speak to the gathering.

The players have uncommonly excellent social skills; when he places a reporter at a dining table with several of them—another uncoachlike act—they're neither scared nor dismissive nor shy. The players readily say they love each other and that it makes them play harder. Ten have included as a groomsman at their weddings one John Nelson, who has spent his life in a wheelchair, and whom Frosty eventually hired as an assistant coach after he passed him on campus one day and invited him to an Afterglow.

Covering college football frequently begs for cynicism and probably qualifies one to cover anything from politics to pornography. But I find that on my best days in general since September 2003, I'll usually have thought of Frosty at least once. *Newsday* had no gripping reason to fund and run this feature, and I barely mustered the gumption to pitch it, but since the experience and the response, I'm less inclined to worry about how flaky I might sound and more inclined to heed my nagging inklings. The best stories often lurk in the "wrong" places.

COPLEY
news service

S. Lynne Walker
Diversity Writing

S. Lynne Walker decided to become a journalist when she was 16. Although the Watergate news coverage at the time drew many of her peers into newspapers, it wasn't Woodward and Bernstein who attracted her to the craft. Her hero was Art Buchwald, a columnist famous for his humor and political satire pieces.

She yearned to be a humor writer. The funny thing is she never became one. "I now know, as a seasoned journalist, that the hardest thing you can possibly do is make someone laugh when you're writing. I was never able to do that," Walker says.

But Buchwald served as an inspiration for her to pursue journalism. At 18, the Atlanta native started working full time on the night shift at *The Honolulu Advertiser* while a full-time day student at the University of Hawaii. That experience fueled a passion for reporting and writing that remains as strong nearly 30 years later as it was the day she started out as a "copy kid."

"I just think that journalism was probably what I was born to do and I love it. I just love it with all my heart," she says.

Captivated by the stories she recalls reading in *The Atlanta Journal*, which she would sneak off and read on her front steps at the age of 10, she became determined to write compelling stories. Walker says, "I try as often as I can to write out of the box, to write in a style slightly different than the style I was taught when I went to journalism school."

She has pursued that goal at the *Advertiser*, the *Tampa Times, The Sacramento Union, The San Diego Union-Tribune,* and now as the Copley News Service bureau chief in Mexico City.

Walker, 47, pushes the boundaries of her writing by devouring all the information she can gather. In her daily work, she seeks all the tiny pieces that add to a good story and give people a real flavor of what went on. On her big projects, she drills as deeply as she can to unearth the great details that will keep the reader's attention.

Her passion for storytelling, context, and detail shows in the four-part series about Beardstown, Ill., that she wrote for *The State Journal-Register* in Springfield, Ill. The series, "Beardstown: Reflections of a Changing America," shows the challenges that emerge when a small, isolated, homogenous community finds itself transformed because of the influx of Hispanics seeking work.

Walker sees her stories as a window not only on Beardstown but also on many towns across the United States that are experiencing racial and cultural changes.

—Aly Colón

[*Parts 3 and 4 of Walker's series have not been included here because of space considerations. The full text of those stories can be read on the CD-ROM included in this edition of Best Newspaper Writing.*

The award for Distinguished Writing on Diversity is funded by the Freedom Forum, which has partnered with ASNE on many diversity efforts.]

Beardstown: Reflections of a changing America

For more than 200 years, the peoples of the world have been welcomed in America, a country built upon the backs of immigrants. In cities and in small towns, new waves of immigrants look to improve their lives and those of their families in the same land of hope, opportunity and prosperity sought by their forefathers.

Here in central Illinois, the Illinois River community of Beardstown is no longer an enclave of mostly white residents. It has become a reflection of America's continually changing face, an international community with a significant population of Hispanics—and a growing number of Africans—who have come to work for Excel Corp., the pork processing plant. A demographic change that is taking place across the country can be seen in microcosm in Beardstown.

Off and on for the past seven months, reporter S. Lynne Walker of the Mexico City bureau of Copley News Service lived in Beardstown. Walker's fluency in Spanish allowed her to understand a side of the immigrants' story not widely heard in central Illinois. The work of Walker and photographer Kristen Schmid Schurter offers an intimate look at the clash and commingling of distinctly different cultures.

Beginning today, we are pleased to present the first part of their four-day report examining one community's 15-year adventure in social change.

Barry Locher
Editor, *The State Journal-Register*
Springfield, Ill.

Tension in the air

NOVEMBER 9, 2003

BEARDSTOWN, Ill.—On winter afternoons, in the sliver of twilight dividing day from night, Mayor Bob Walters drove along his town's quiet streets troubled by the changes he feared were coming.

Beardstown was an all-white community of 5,200 people built by German immigrants. No one remembered an African American ever setting down roots in this Illinois River town. When Mexican immigrants began flowing into the state, they, too, had bypassed Beardstown.

An intimacy had grown from that cultural isolation.

Bike-riding children waved to octogenarians resting in porch swings. People turned out for fish fries, baseball games and Fourth of July fireworks. Everybody knew everybody's name.

But in that winter of 1986, Walters could feel the comfortable rhythm of small-town life slipping away.

In just two years, three Beardstown employers had closed their doors, eliminating 500 jobs. Now, the town's biggest employer—the Oscar Mayer pork slaughterhouse—was shutting down, idling another 820 people. With no hope of finding work, families were beginning to leave.

Walters, who worked for 18 years as a ham boner at Oscar Mayer, had reservations about what many saw as the salvation of his dying town.

Excel Corp., the second-largest meatpacker in America, wanted to reopen the Oscar Mayer plant, and most of the town's residents were enthusiastic about the offer. They thought life would be the way it used to be, with an influx of money, thriving businesses and jobs for their children and grandchildren.

But during his travels as a representative for the United Food and Commercial Workers Union (UFCW), Walters had seen what happened when meatpackers, operating on profit margins of just 2 or 3 percent, opened plants in the rural Midwest.

Yes, they hired local folks. But they also recruited a stream of immigrants, most of them Mexican, to feed their insatiable demand for strong, young workers.

What Walters had seen on his trips across the Midwest was already starting to attract the attention of the nation's top demographers. By the late 1980s, they were recording the transformation that occurred when the meatpacking industry moved into small American towns.

People from different cultures who spoke different languages were crowding into communities where white, English-speaking Americans had lived for generations.

The new arrivals brought new music, new foods and new holidays. They also brought new social problems.

They weren't creating towns, as earlier waves of Europeans had done, but moving into tight-knit communities. Sometimes, the towns lost their identities and people from neighboring communities poked fun at them, calling them "Little Mexico."

Walters didn't know these new immigrants as people, but he knew their presence was changing a way of life in America's heartland.

He knew his own town, too. In 1858, the people of Beardstown had gathered in the town square to hear Abraham Lincoln deliver a stump speech opposing slavery. But a century later, they had hung a noose in that same park, warning blacks to stay away.

"It had been an all-white, redneck community for 160 years," Walters said. "For a community like that to have a different ethnic group come in, well, it's hard to adjust."

* * *

On a sweltering June afternoon in 1987, Excel quietly opened the company's first pork-processing plant in Beardstown. With no fanfare, the town took its place in the dramatic demographic change sweeping America.

By the year 2000, Beardstown's Hispanic population would grow 3,229 percent.

Illinois welcomed Excel because economically depressed Cass County, home to Beardstown, was one of the poorest in the state.

Gov. Jim Thompson signed special legislation waiving the requirement that Excel's parent company, privately held grain giant Cargill Inc., open its financial records before being allowed to locate in a free-enterprise zone at the outskirts of town. Excel received all the economic benefits Illinois had to offer, including state funds for job training.

But Beardstown already had a labor force trained in the meatpacking business. With downstate Illinois facing rising unemployment, Excel dropped the starting wage from $8.75 to $6.50 an hour.

At one of his first meetings with Excel officials, Walters pushed the company to hire former Oscar Mayer workers.

"I wanted Americans to hold the jobs," he said. "There were a lot of local people looking for work. I wanted to give them the opportunity first."

Excel finally agreed to hire 250 Oscar Mayer workers. Another 100 employees came from nearby towns.

Every day, more than 5,000 hogs were chopped into pieces and boxed for shipment. The plant's work force put bacon on America's breakfast table, sent pig tails to canners for pork 'n' beans and shipped snouts to Alabama for pickling.

The money that Excel's workers earned flowed back into Beardstown's economy. Hardee's and McDonald's opened hamburger franchises to compete with the town's old-fashioned coffee shops serving biscuits and gravy. In 1989, Sam Walton Jr. phoned Walters from his private plane to say he'd be landing at Beardstown's tiny airport to look at a site for the town's first Wal-Mart.

The visit was so sudden, "we didn't even have time to get out the marching band," Walters said. Still, "they said they liked what they'd seen, that they liked our town."

Walters took great pride in pointing out that in Excel's early years, no Hispanics moved to Beardstown.

Although the 1990 census recorded 31 Hispanics, Walters insisted, "There were no Hispanics here. I'd like to think I had a lot to do with that."

He wasn't motivated by racism, Walters said, but his years of experience in the meatpacking industry.

"They take Hispanics, blacks and the downtrodden to work in their plants—those who don't have the computer skills or the basics for today's work environment," he said. "They seem to prey on that type of people. They take advantage of the disadvantaged."

As he left office in 1990, Walters gave his successor some advice.

"I told him, 'If you don't stay after Excel, you are going to have a lot of Hispanics and a lot of Asians come in here and take those jobs.'

"That's exactly what happened," he said.

* * *

The first Hispanics who showed up at Excel didn't last long.

When Excel hired Brad Hunter, a former Oscar Mayer worker, in 1989, "there was very few coloreds and very few Mexicans," he recalled. "Every time we'd try to tell them to do something, they'd look at us stupid. So we'd start harassing them and they'd quit."

But two things changed the equation: Excel stepped up its production, increasing the need for workers. And worker compensation costs began to soar, with injury claims reaching $7.8 million a year by 1994, according to UFCW representative Duke Walters, who is the mayor's brother.

In the dangerous meatpacking industry, accidents were inevitable. Workers carved up a 265-pound hog every 4.5 seconds, and in the process cut themselves with knives, hurt their backs and suffered from repetitive stress injury, Walters said.

Excel's most serious accident came in 1990, when workers inhaled ammonia gas that leaked from a cooler where slaughtered hogs were kept, according to Occupational Safety & Health Administration records. Seventeen workers inhaled the toxic fumes; seven had to be hospitalized.

When Walters sat down at the bargaining table with Excel in 1994, the company made it clear that "if they continued to have those costs…we were probably looking at closure."

Employee turnover was also a problem, reportedly hitting 100 percent a year by the mid-1990s. The company's slaughterhouse was strategically located near farms in Illinois' sparsely populated countryside that produced the hogs Excel slaughtered. But there weren't enough workers living nearby, so when Excel increased production, the company had to import its labor.

Every week, Excel officials interviewed job candidates, but "they weren't able to get enough people in the job pool here," said Walters. "In order to build the factory and get the people they needed, they had to go outside the area."

So Excel began to look for workers from south of the border who acknowledged they didn't gripe about every ache and pain.

"After starving to death, after sneaking across the border, people are prepared to do anything. There is no pain," said a Hispanic man working in Beardstown. "If I came into the United States under a pile of avocados, what right do I have to complain?"

Excel confirmed in a written statement that "we have done mobile recruiting in areas of high unemployment where people were looking for work opportunities. This included northern states as well as southern and western."

The company, which refused repeated requests over the past seven months for a face-to-face interview with a representative, sent recruiters to California, Arizona and the Texas border towns of Laredo, Eagle Pass, Brownsville and El Paso, drawing job candidates with spots on Spanish-language radio.

Excel sent nurse Lisa Mincy to the Texas-Mexico border at least 10 times during the eight years she worked at the plant. Sometimes, Mincy administered drug tests and gave physicals to 35 job seekers a day during the two- to four-day trips.

"One guy rode his bike 12 miles to get to me," said Mincy, who left Excel last year. "It was hot. It was like 110 degrees that day."

Those who passed Excel's physical exam got a $400 advance and a one-way bus ticket to Beardstown.

* * *

Nobody can remember when the first Mexican families moved into Beardstown. Suddenly, they were just there.

The Rev. Eugene Weitzel recalls looking out at his congregation at St. Alexius Catholic Church in 1995 and seeing a handful of Mexicans in the pews. Soon, they were knocking at his door, asking for a Spanish-speaking priest.

Buffy Tillitt-Pratt, a longtime real estate agent and a member of the famous Beardstown Ladies Investment Club, can still recall the first time a Mexican family stopped by to ask if she might have a place for rent.

"It is against the law to discriminate. Some of the people in Beardstown probably did not realize that at first," said Tillitt-Pratt, who rented them a three-bedroom house she owned.

Principal Pam DeSollar remembers a Mexican mother and father walking into her kindergarten office and using hand signals to enroll their 6-year-old son.

"How were we going to talk to this family? How were we going to fill out the forms?" DeSollar said she wondered at the time. "We couldn't communicate."

DeSollar's concern was echoed throughout the town. For the first time in their lives, Beardstown residents weren't able to talk with their neighbors.

They didn't understand anything the Mexicans said or did. And the Mexican families didn't understand the stuffy, small-town rules that now dictated their lives.

Police officers showed up at Mexican homes because American neighbors complained the mariachi music was too loud. City officials arrived to caution Mexicans that their lawn had grown taller than Beardstown's 8-inch limit. Police were constantly ticketing Hispanics for driving without insurance and driver's licenses.

"We didn't know the laws," said Antonio Carrillo, 36, a father of three who works at Excel. "That was part of the problem."

The police department was unprepared for the arrival of Spanish-speaking residents. None of the officers was bilingual. During routine traffic stops, police officer Jacob Swan pulled out his own license to show the new residents which ID he wanted to see.

The town's schools were also caught off guard. In 1993, the district had just one Spanish-speaking student. By 1996, it had several dozen.

Immigration agents showed up at the Excel plant in 1995 and pulled 60 workers off the production line for questioning.

"Everybody who wasn't Caucasian, they called into the office," said Sergio Ruiz, 36, who is now a chief steward for the UFCW, Local 431. "They asked you questions and they said, 'Leave. Stay. Leave. Stay.'"

Despite the scare, Excel's Hispanic work force continued to grow.

Ruiz brought 26 Hispanics to work with him at Excel in July 1993. At the time, there were only about 15 Hispanics working at the plant, he said. Excel also paid its employees to help with the recruiting, handing out $150 for each new worker.

When the number of Hispanics reached nearly 500, businesses began to cater to the new residents' tastes.

Su Casa, a Mexican-owned grocery store, opened near Beardstown's historic town square and offered tortillas, chilies and nopal cactus. A bar, El Flamingo, was opened by an American woman and her Mexican husband.

But as the Hispanics' presence became more obvious, ambivalence by some longtime Beardstown residents turned to resentment.

Martha Martinez, 29, was denied her right to register to vote at the same time she applied for a driver's license, which she was entitled to under Illinois' "motor-voter" law. She asked why and was told, "it was because I was a naturalized citizen, not a citizen citizen."

Martinez's family was also the target of hate crimes.

"They threw flaming rags at the house," said her husband, 35-year-old Alejandro. "They punctured our tires. They said we came to take their jobs."

* * *

On Aug. 10, 1996, Beardstown was rocked by its first murder in seven years.

Jorge Arambula, a 28-year-old Mexican who worked at Excel, was accused of fatally shooting Beardstown resident Travis Brewer, 22, at El Flamingo. Brewer was a friend of another Beardstown man, whose ex-wife was living with Arambula.

The next night, a 6-foot-high makeshift cross was doused with diesel fuel and set ablaze in front of the bar.

Arambula was detained five days later at his home in Monterrey, Mexico. But Mexican law enforcement authorities refused to extradite him to Illinois. He has never been tried for the murder in Mexico, and the case remains open at the Beardstown Police Department.

The decision infuriated Beardstown residents. On Aug. 16, 1996, El Flamingo was gutted by fire, and anonymous callers warned the owner of Su Casa his business would be next. He stripped his shelves and closed the store.

Police soon arrested a 28-year-old resident of nearby Rushville, but Illinois state police patrolled the town for weeks.

When rumors circulated that the Ku Klux Klan was headed to Beardstown, the Mexican community braced for the arrival with its own whispered threat.

"For every one of us they kill," one Mexican resident remembers people saying, "we're going to kill five of them."

Conquering the great divide

NOVEMBER 10, 2003

BEARDSTOWN, Ill.—Shaken residents of Beardstown flocked to church services on Aug. 18, 1996, as bells pealed for unity and ministers exhorted their congregations to overcome "the darkness of hate."

But when people heard those words, they knew the sheltered lives they once enjoyed had slipped from their grasp.

Eight days earlier, a Mexican immigrant had [been accused of murdering] a Beardstown man. The incident had been followed by a cross-burning and arson. In the aftermath of the violence, lifelong residents were torn between fear and uncertainty.

Beardstown's residents had been shaped by where they lived, where they went to school, the things they had in common. Now, like the residents of many small towns across the United States, they were seeing their community reshaped by immigrants who'd made their way north from Mexico.

By 1996, the meatpacking industry had opened plants in almost 150 Midwestern towns. Other industries were also beginning to draw Hispanics to communities throughout small-town America. In Dalton, Ga., Hispanics manufactured carpet. In Kennett Square, Pa., they harvested year-round mushroom crops. In Rogers, Ark., they cut and boxed poultry.

With each passing month, more Hispanics were recruited to Beardstown for jobs at Excel Corp.'s pork slaughterhouse. The new arrivals brought lifestyles and attitudes that made Americans feel uneasy.

They saw Mexican flags popping up all over town and heard Spanish spoken in the aisles of the Wal-Mart store. Hispanic children rode their bikes past the town square where a plaque cited Abraham Lincoln's famous anti-segregation speech, "A house divided cannot stand."

Hispanics also worried about the town's future. They had moved here after dangerous trips across the border or from jobs in big cities where they'd lived in poor, crime-ridden neighborhoods. Many felt that in Beardstown, they'd found not just a job, but a place in the United States they could call home.

They weren't herded into ghettos, as they had been in other meatpacking towns. Some bought houses on the town's tree-lined streets and were looking forward to raising their children. They appreciated the low crime rate and the city services that were provided without the "gratuities" they were used to paying in Mexico.

The good things about Beardstown reminded Marisela Chavez of her hometown in the Pacific Coast state of Michoacan.

Her Beardstown neighbors sent greeting cards to Chavez's two daughters on their birthdays, at Easter and Christmas. Chavez smiled as she remembered the moment her daughters opened the Christmas cards and found $20 bills tucked inside.

"I think the people in Beardstown are like we are in our pueblo. They all know each other. They know where everybody works, who their children are," said Chavez, 38, who moved to Beardstown in 1995 and works with the school system's bilingual program.

Like other Hispanics, Chavez believed a mix of Anglos and Hispanics made Beardstown a stronger community.

When the town's 11 churches called a meeting after the arson, 60 people showed up to discuss their concerns about the growing tension.

By the end of the meeting, Anglos and Hispanics had formed an alliance called Beardstown United. Plans were made to enter a float in the town's Fall Fun Festival, and a block party was planned for October.

Beardstown United noted that the racial divide touched every facet of the residents' lives.

Although the town had been built by immigrants in the early 1880s and had been home to people of foreign ancestry ever since, "this new wave was different," said Loraine Brasel, who was a member of Beardstown United.

"They came right from Mexico with no established support group here. They didn't speak English. So they formed their own cohesive group," she said. "It was like having a little country dropped right in the middle of Beardstown."

There were concerns about whether the schools were teaching Hispanic children to assimilate into American life. People were also beginning to complain about the new Spanish-language Masses being offered at St. Alexius Catholic Church.

In 1996, Beardstown wasn't a community, but two separate groups of people: Anglos and Hispanics.

* * *

At St. Alexius Catholic Church, the Rev. Eugene Weitzel heard the hushed complaints.

People were uncomfortable with his staunch defense of Beardstown's Hispanic residents and his decision to offer separate Spanish-language Masses.

It had been almost a year since four Hispanics knocked at his door and asked him to offer a Mass in Spanish. Weitzel, a 76-year-old Springfield native who didn't speak Spanish, readily accepted their proposal.

At first, most of his Spanish-speaking parishioners were men who'd left their families in Mexico when they came to Beardstown for work. But as Beardstown's Hispanic population grew with the arrival of women and children, so did attendance at Spanish-language Masses.

From the beginning, there was "tension between the two groups," Weitzel said. "This is a redneck town. They are slow to accept outsiders. Whenever we have people who are different, we seem to have a fear of them."

Weitzel said opposition was so strong that four or five families eventually left the parish.

"There are people here in my own parish who would be happy as a lark if they'd just leave town," Weitzel said. "One of the men came up to me and said, 'If they can't speak the language, then get the hell out.' Well, come on. His folks came over from Germany and they didn't speak the language."

Weitzel's outspoken remarks became a lightning rod for criticism about Hispanic residents.

"Father Weitzel has been the worst thing for Mexicans, because he tried to push the Mexicans on Americans instead of letting people try to live together," said Eugene Gyure, a 64-year-old retiree who attends St. Alexius.

Many in Beardstown insisted they didn't feel animosity toward Hispanic churchgoers.

"People at the church don't like the separatism. They

want to be one parish," said Jackie Tanner, 47, who moved to Beardstown in 1998. "They don't like two services. They don't like two youth groups. Resentment. That's what you have when you separate a lot."

Edmundo Bernal, a 35-year-old Excel worker who had attended bilingual Masses in Chicago, was dismayed by the separation. "We share the same religion. The only difference is that we have a different language," he said.

* * *

The racial divide was also clear in the schools. In a town where friendships were formed in kindergarten, it was hard for youngsters who didn't speak English to squeeze into the closed circle.

Victor Sanchez remembers feeling alone and alienated in 1998 as he walked down halls filled with Anglo students.

"I was, like, shocked because I hadn't seen so many white people in one place," he said. "I felt strange. It's hard to get along with people when you don't talk the same language."

Victor and his family came to Beardstown from the central Mexico state of Hidalgo. The 13-year-old Victor was placed in seventh-grade English as a second language, or ESL, classes, where most of Beardstown's 153 Hispanic children—about 12 percent of the district's student body—were enrolled.

Victor picked up English quickly. In three months, he learned enough to help his mother, who worked at Excel, adjust to life in Beardstown.

"If you don't learn English fast, you get stuck," he said.

But as his language skills improved, he began to understand the comments Anglo students were making about their Hispanic classmates.

"Beaners. Wetbacks. Go back to Mexico," Victor remembered some kids saying.

"They think they are better than us," he said. "They think when the Latinos are coming here, they are going to steal their work. But the companies prefer Latinos, you know? Because we can work more. Because we need more."

Georgeanne Osmer, who teaches family and consumer science at Beardstown High School and helps coach the girls' softball team, watched her students segregate themselves.

"If I have four tables in my food class—four kitchens—I can guarantee that all the Hispanics will be at one table," she said. "There's not animosity, but there's not a cohesiveness, a togetherness."

Tomas Alvarez was thrust into this divided world when he arrived in July 1998 at the age of 12. His father had been called from Guadalajara to lead a growing Spanish-speaking congregation at the Church of the Nazarene.

Tomas didn't speak English, so he was sent to ESL classes with Victor.

But after his first year, Tomas said, "It was obvious I wasn't learning much. I learned more from my friends than from the ESL teacher."

Tomas' teachers recommended that he be moved to English-speaking classes, and in eighth grade he became an A student. Tomas, who plays football and has helped the school district update its Web site, will be going to college after he graduates in May.

He's certain that if he'd stayed in ESL classes, he would have faced the same future as several of his classmates. "I know some real smart people who stayed in ESL," said Tomas. "They're out at Excel now."

* * *

For Hispanic parents who worked Excel's grueling jobs in extreme heat and cold, amid blood and fetid smells, Beardstown's schools offered their children a way out of a life of manual labor.

Like the immigrants who came to America before them, Hispanic mothers and fathers wanted their children to become professionals. For them, having children who ended up cutting meat at Excel represented their own failure.

But the school system wasn't prepared for students like Elvia Montoya, the first Hispanic student to graduate from Beardstown High's ESL program.

When Montoya arrived in Beardstown, she didn't speak English, so an interpreter accompanied her to most of her classes.

Her goal was to get her master's degree and become a Spanish teacher. But after she graduated in 1998, her

English skills were so poor that she couldn't even get into the local community college.

"Sometimes, I blame myself for not learning more, or I don't know if it was their fault because the program was just beginning," said Montoya, 24, who works as an interpreter at a Hispanic community outreach center in Beardstown. "I didn't come out of high school with good English; I came out with enough English to survive."

Kathy Haut, one of Montoya's ESL teachers and now coordinator of the bilingual program, said the arrival of Hispanic students "put a huge burden on the school system."

One 15-year-old Mexican boy who had been selling flowers on the streets of Tijuana arrived with a second-grade education. Another teenager came from the Mexican countryside, where he had been working his family's fields with oxen and a plow. When teachers asked him to use a computer to do his schoolwork, Haut said, he couldn't figure out how to switch it on.

"How are you going to have quality teachers for all those children? You're not," Haut said. "You're just doing the best you can. Parents don't understand that we can't just go out and pick up bilingual teachers. They can do it Chicago. They can do it in San Francisco. But who wants to come here?"

She's frustrated because she hasn't been able to solve the problems of bilingual education.

"As glad as I am that these people are here, they have to understand how hard it is to go from a school system that's 150 years old and all Anglo to suddenly having a bilingual program," Haut said. "If they think this school is going to be a Mexican school, no, it's not. It's going to be an Anglo institution."

Hispanic parents said Haut's staff pressured them to keep their children separate from Anglo students. They were warned that moving their children from ESL to regular classes would be tantamount to robbing them of their culture.

Haut blamed Hispanic parents for not getting involved in their children's education and suggested they might not understand educators' reasons for keeping their children in ESL classes.

For Hispanic parents, "it's a status symbol to be able

to speak English," she said. "It's the language of power. It's like distancing themselves from their past."

Dora Sanchez ran into the ESL problem when a bilingual teacher said her daughter, Arely Madrid, should go into regular fifth-grade classes.

Sanchez persisted even after a different staffer from the bilingual program visited her at home and said Arely would be more immersed in her culture and her Spanish would be better if she stayed in ESL.

On the first day of school, however, Sanchez was shocked to discover that Arely was back in ESL. Weeks passed before the dispute was settled and Arely was moved to English-speaking classes.

Although Arely started later than the other students, her grades were exemplary. This year, she'll be on the honor roll.

"Give me a whole room of Arelys," said her sixth-grade teacher, Susan DeWitt. "She's an outstanding student."

Sanchez was convinced she had made the right decision.

"Of course it is important that they learn their culture and their Spanish. What parent doesn't want their child to be prepared? That is why we are here," Sanchez said. "But if the bilingual program doesn't have the same quality as the English classes, we don't want them to go."

* * *

Anglo and Hispanic children in Beardstown's two kindergartens offered hope the town would be united in the future.

From the moment the first Hispanic child was enrolled in 1993, principal Pam DeSollar threw herself into the task of educating Beardstown's youngest residents.

At that age, the children were color-blind about their fellow classmates and eager to soak up a new language.

"We had to change the way we worked. We had to fight right to the state level to get the resources we think we're entitled to," said DeSollar, principal of Grand and Washington kindergartens. "We've been challenged. But am I sorry about that? No."

DeSollar, 60, who grew up in California's San Fernando Valley, moved to Beardstown after she married her husband, who is from an established local family. When she arrived in 1965, she found a backwater town that seemed disconnected from the rest of the world. The local grocery store didn't stock the ingredients she needed to fix her favorite meals, so she ordered her re-fried beans and canned chilies by the case.

DeSollar saw the arrival of Hispanic families in small-town America as a natural progression of the wave of immigration that had started in California and other border states. "If Excel stays here, we will contin-ue to see this growth," DeSollar said. "What I hope is that we don't become two communities. Our country is bilingual. And it's only going to become more bilingual in the future."

By the late 1990s, everybody in town seemed to un-derstand the Hispanics were here to stay. The challenge facing Beardstown was to find a way for Anglos and Hispanics to grow together instead of growing apart.

[Parts 3 and 4 of Walker's series can be read on the CD-ROM included in this edition of Best Newspaper Writing.]

A conversation with
S. Lynne Walker

ALY COLÓN: What was the catalyst for writing "Beardstown: Reflections of a Changing America"?

S. LYNNE WALKER: Barry Locher, the editor at *The State Journal-Register* in Springfield, had talked to me two years ago about Beardstown at a company meeting. He said Hispanic immigrants were coming in and changes were taking place there. He said, "I know this is a really good story, and I'd love for you to do it." Because of my responsibilities—I'm one person covering an entire country with a hundred million people—it took me a while to get to it. But I never lost sight of it and I never gave up on it. And he never gave up.

Why you?

One of the reasons he wanted me was because I am bilingual. He felt that they had not been able to reach the Spanish-speaking part of the community in an effective way, that they were missing half of the story. Our original thought was that we would, at some point during the work on the series, go to the villages where most of the Mexicans living in Beardstown had come from. But as we began to get into it, I talked to Barry and the managing editor, and I said, "This doesn't feel right to me, to go to Mexico on this one, because I think the story is in Beardstown. This is really the story of this town and the people who've always lived there and the people who are just now arriving. I don't think going to their villages is going to add to the story. And it may detract." Beardstown's story was many towns' story in America. Beardstown is Anytown, U.S.A. So I thought that's what we wanted to tell. It was a story about a small town in the Midwest, which reflected many small towns in America.

Did living in Mexico and being bilingual provide an opportunity to do this kind of story?

Yes. In Springfield, they had not been able to reach the Hispanic community. I didn't think that was going to be a problem for me. I simply went out and started talking to people. Because I live in Mexico, it's easy to break the ice. I started talking about something [Mexican president] Vicente Fox said or things that people were really familiar with—some food I had had when I was in their state. It became very comfortable for them to talk to me. My language skills are strong, so they didn't feel awkward in conversation with me. That is important, too, because if people feel like you don't really understand them, or they don't understand you, it makes them nervous. They don't know if you really understand what they are saying or if it's going to be misinterpreted. We didn't have that barrier to overcome.

Another thing I did was talk to community leaders on the Hispanic side. They gave me advice. One good piece of advice was to go to the Spanish-speaking Mass. Let people see me there. That's a non-threatening situation. I talked to people before and after church. I met some people who invited me into their homes. Once I got going, there was no end to the number of people I could talk to.

How important do you think the language skill was in your reporting?

It was crucial. Absolutely crucial. I think you relate to people in a different way if you speak their language. Imagine if someone came to you and wanted to speak another language that you barely knew and they wanted to interview you. Think about how uncomfortable you would feel about whether you were getting your message across or what they were really doing. It would be difficult.

What I found was that when you don't speak a lot of Spanish, you get these sort of flat, superficial answers because that's the easiest thing to say. For example, "How was your life in Mexico?" "Very hard." That doesn't tell me anything. I need to know what you had for breakfast, for lunch, for dinner. I need to know what you're doing to get your kids to school.

Why do you need to know that?

I was interviewing somebody in Mexico once, and I started talking to him about shoes. I got the most incredible answers because I asked him, "How much do your clothes cost? How do you pay for clothes?" He was so poor; he's a father of many children. He said the shoes cost 40 pesos. That's $4. He said they last six months. "I can buy two pairs a year. Our children have to have sturdy shoes because they go to school. They're not allowed to go to school unless they have sturdy shoes....For my wife, there's no money left over for shoes. So she doesn't have any." He said none of the women there have shoes because there's no money left over for them. It's a small thing, shoes. But it was just an incredibly powerful thing. It says so much to you about people's lives. And you don't get that if you don't speak their language.

What advice would you give to journalists who want to tell a truer picture of communities such as Beardstown, where new groups are emerging rapidly?

Well, I think it'd be good if they could learn Spanish. But until you do that—it takes a long time—you go to the community leaders in the Hispanic community who are bilingual. Sometimes they will help you.

Did you start out speaking Spanish?

I did not start out speaking Spanish. In my first major project that I did in 1988, people helped me interpret. They gave so incredibly generously of their time. So you can go out with people who are in a social work function or community activism, people who are in touch all the time and who your interview subjects have confidence in because they introduce you. That would be the second option. Now, I wanted to say one more thing. A lot of the Hispanic community leaders in Beardstown are bilingual. I always spoke to them in Spanish, unless they preferred to change the interview themselves to English. One of them said to me in Spanish, "I have been interviewed many, many times by many reporters." He named some big papers in the Midwest. And he said, "This is the very first time I have spoken to a reporter in Spanish." I believe because of that, he told me some very personal things that he might not have if we were speaking in English.

How did you learn your Spanish?

Well, I should say first of all, I'm a native of Atlanta. So I certainly did not learn it there. When I was growing up, we didn't learn Spanish in school. I did not start to learn Spanish until I was an adult and well into my journalism career.

What prompted you to learn it?

When I was at the paper in San Diego, I was covering agriculture, among other things. I had asked for that beat assignment. I was also covering aerospace. I always told people I covered anything that started with "A." It became apparent to me when I was covering agriculture that I really was not getting all of the story. I would go out and interview growers, California growers, and they would say, "Some of my people make $15 an hour in piecework." In those days—$15 an hour's pretty good now— but it was great money then. I just didn't believe many people out there were making $15 an hour. However, I couldn't ask anybody. So I was hamstrung. I really was not getting what I needed to know.

So what did you do?

I proposed a very ambitious series in 1988. I was going to follow migrant workers through an entire season in San Diego and then go home with them. Had I known what was involved, I would never have done it. But I was young and enthusiastic. Among the proposals for that project was that I would learn Spanish while I was doing it. The managing editor of the paper offered to help pay for my Spanish lessons, so I took her up on that.

So I was going to Spanish-language classes three times a week. I was doing my regular aerospace beat during the day. And then on the nights that I wasn't in Spanish class, I would go out to the migrant labor camps and talk to people and interview them and work on my series. The classes I had were very good; they were specialized.

San Diego's a lab, if you want to learn Spanish. When I was driving home at night, I used to listen to the Major League Baseball games on the radio in Spanish. I'm not a baseball fan at all. But there's a lot of emotion and excitement in it. And you can begin to understand what people are saying, especially when they yell, "Home run." I did that and then I went to these classes. So that's how I started to learn Spanish. I later paid for a tutor on my own to help me continue. After that I lived in a very impoverished part of Mexico for six months with a family. I didn't go to a language school. I went to a place where no one spoke English.

How did you find the people and the place?

I met them through the series. After the series was over, they made the mistake of saying the door was always open. Unfortunately, I showed up. That was really fun because I spent a lot of time with the children in that village. They'd come running home from school to tell me what they'd learned that day. I sat down with them because everything they said was helping me learn. So that's an unusual way of learning Spanish, but it really worked. The other thing it helped me learn was that Mexico was at the bottom of the economic ladder. So I didn't start at the top, at the places where people wear suits and ties and polished shoes. I started at the bottom. That has helped me all the way through my coverage of Mexico in understanding at least half the population of that country.

Talk about the challenges that come with doing this kind of coverage in the context of other communities in which they might have not only Hispanics but other groups. What did you learn about what needs to be done as a journalist to get the story that is actually taking place, as opposed to the flat explanation of the world that we might hear otherwise?

The first thing I told Barry was that I would be living in Beardstown. Springfield is only 45 miles away, so it's not like you can't get back and forth. But I said, "I will be living there because I need to be in the community to understand what's really going on. I need to be able to go to anybody's house at any moment, could be 6 in the morning, could be 11 at night." That became important because these were shift workers, as it turned out. People did have unusual schedules. I needed to be there so I could feel that community, sense what was going on, and have all the time in the world to talk to people. I think as a reporter you have to spend a lot of time in these communities. You need to check in with people every day or every couple of days. Because just in the normal course of conversation, it's amazing what will come out. People don't even think about mentioning it to you because it's just part of life there. It can't be an occasional pass if you're really interested in covering it.

Today many journalists feel pressured to produce a lot, and on deadline, and frequently. How do you make that work?

I'll just use my own example. When I did the project in '88, I did both. I promised my editors I'd never let my beat coverage drop. And I did dailies. But I just kept working on this long-term project. So if you're in a newsroom, I understand the pressures of that. I understand the difficulty. And as you're doing your long-term project, you will see daily stories that will come out of that. So there is a payoff for the paper, too.

Did you have a plan for writing in the narrative order that you did, or did that emerge from the reporting?

No. That was very difficult. Probably the hardest thing. It took a lot of thinking and going back and forth. What I first set out to do was to find out what the situation was, find out what people were saying, and find out what the elements were. We could have done it thematically every day. I worked with this terrific editor in San Diego, Susan White, and I do want to talk more about relationships between reporters and editors.

We talked about it several different ways. At first, we thought maybe one section would be called "Poverty and Prosperity," one section "Education," one section "Law Enforcement." Then we thought of picking key characters and telling the story through them. But I began to fret over that because I thought if we did that, it would leave out so many other people I'd talked to whose voices would not be heard. But you have to be careful. You can't throw everybody in your story because it just becomes a mishmash.

I thought I really was not going to be doing justice to this town if we just focused on five or six people. In the end, we decided together, almost at the same time, that the main character was the town itself. The people come in and out of that. We decided the most organized, stream-lined, and logical, readable thing would be just to tell it from the beginning to the end.

What about the length?

One thing Barry had said was he wanted to try to hold it to three days. He didn't limit me on inch length, within rea-son. But he felt he couldn't hold readers for four days. This is another concern in our business because you can just go on and on. At the last meeting we had I said, "I just cannot make this work in three days, and I want to tell you how I see this breaking out." I spent about 45 minutes go-ing over an outline of part one and all of the elements, part two with all of the elements, part three, so that they could see how this was going to lay out. Barry agreed to go for a fourth day. I don't think we're sorry we did that because the response from the community was tremendous.

What prompted you to start the series from the point of view of Beardstown's mayor?

That was the greatest gift of all to me. On about the sec-ond or third day I was there, I called the mayor and asked if we could meet in his office. It was on a Saturday in his office at city hall. I was talking to him, kind of getting into the interview, and he says, "I suspect what you really want to talk about is the Hispanic situation." So we start-ed talking. And he told me that one of the key elements in this story was the Excel meat-packing plant, which is the real reason that all these people came. That was what would draw people. It was the catalyst for the change. He said he used to work at Excel as a ham boner. I said, "Ter-rific. Then you know about the conditions in the plant, you know what the work situation is, and everything." He said, "I was mayor when Excel came in. I helped the city negotiate its coming here."

He had left Beardstown for a period and was now back as mayor. I thought, "This is the thread; these are the key issues—when Excel came in, what happened, how it was then, how the community was then, what work conditions were like." So I said, "Tell me about the meat-packing industry and its conditions. Everything." He was incredibly patient with me, incredibly giving of his time, and you just can't ask for any more than that. We mustn't forget that people don't have to give us any of their time.

He's a native Beardstown resident and someone who, I came to learn, had been through the transformation that the town had been through. Oh, and he was the one who negotiated the Wal-Mart arrival, which was a big economic development for them. He just summed it up. So that's why I decided to go with him.

How did you decide what you wanted to highlight first, and how did that affect the narrative that followed?

That's always the most critical thing for me in any story. If you want to see a story like the rolling of a movie, sometimes I'm thinking, "What is the opening scene?" The opening scene is the moment when that town is at the edge of deciding yes or no on the Excel plant. It brings good things. It brings things that may be difficult for them. The mayor knew it. He'd been to other Midwest towns in his work with the UFCW as a labor rep. He had seen how other Midwestern towns had totally changed. He knew what was going to happen if they came in. I thought, "This is the moment, the moment when you make the decision, that's going to change your town forever."

What did you want these stories to convey to the reader?

When I went in, I didn't know what I wanted to convey. But in the end, I wanted readers to hear the voices of the longtime residents because you can understand their concerns and frustrations. I wanted them to hear the voices of the new residents because if you hear their voices, you can also understand them. I wanted readers to know the role of this massive corporation in America and this change and understand that that's a key role in the change of many towns like this. I wanted them to see what a town goes through over a period of time. The mayor said they had no safety net then. There was no state or federal help—they just had to find their own way on this. I wanted people to see how a town finds its own way. I wanted them to see how a town reaches a crisis point when you can end up on the national news because something so bad has happened. And how a town decides which way to go at that critical moment. I wanted readers to feel all of those things.

In the end, I wanted readers to be slightly conflicted. In other words, I don't think you can come down on one side or the other on this. I hoped at the end you could see both sides. But I also wanted readers to understand that this is what is going to be happening in America now. This is the massive change. And we wanted people to see that, yes, they do assimilate. There is some controversy over that.

One of the things I was struck by is the thread of the story from things being good to a world upended. Why did you approach it that way?

I think it's probably human nature when you have lived in a sort of isolated way. Even though it's not very far from Springfield, they had lived in this isolated, insulated way for so long, and then—and it is human nature—you feel comfortable, I think, with your own kind, right? So to then have people come in. You cannot speak to them or with them. So you don't really know what they're about, you don't really know what's going on, you don't really know if they're good or bad people. You don't know anything. It does upend your world. And this is also a part of the difficulty of change that these towns in America are going through. It's real. It's there. I don't think there's any sense in denying it or underplaying it. So the issue becomes, if you're not really comfortable with this, but it happens and it's beyond your control, how do you deal with it?

So in a sense you were trying to reflect their perspective, how they were seeing the world, and then showing how that basically evolved.

Yes, and I took it from their perspective first because they were there first, and then I introduced the people as they began to come into the picture.

How much reporting and writing time did it take to do the whole series?

I worked on it for seven months. I lived in Beardstown for five weeks. Within the seven months, I made four trips there. The writing, I would say, took at least three weeks. When it really got down to deadline, I sat in my chair in Mexico City for 15 hours a day. I hardly got up. I hurt my hip and my back because you're really not supposed to sit in your chair for 15 hours at a time. You're not designed for that. Then it got to the point where I thought I still had questions. I wanted to be very meticulous on this. I felt we had established such a personal contact that it was going to be hard to do some things over the phone. Because I had so many questions, I decided to go back one more time. I finished the series in Beardstown, in the place where it began.

How did you organize your notes?

I have no earthly idea. All I did was write volume one, volume two, and then, in the end, I began to see I didn't even know who was in the notebooks. Finally I scribbled the names of the people in each one. That's how I did it.

What propelled you to go in a particular direction? Was it what you remembered and then you checked your notebook against it?

Yeah, because I do think if you've got a big project like that, you really can waste an enormous amount of time just trying to find stuff in your notebook. It becomes a tactic in the end to avoid writing, and it becomes so distracting. So what I try to do is just write, "Insert quote about so-and-so here," or, "Check fact on this here." Then I just try to sit down and start writing.

What role did the editor play?

That's where Susan White was so instrumental. She said, "This is going too slow. You've got to pick up the pace. You've got to take some stuff out." So we kept working with it and whittling it down till we thought it was pretty much where we wanted to be. She was as crucial as the language skills.

This is an editor I've worked with since 1996 when I did my 14-part narrative on crossing the border. We have our own rhythm and style now. I always work with her before, during, and after the reporting. Before I leave, I say, "Given that this is the overall idea of the story, what are some things we should be looking for?" I note all of these things down. Then I would call in and say, "You're never going to believe who I talked to today. Just listen to this." And I'd read her a quote. Well, she remembers stuff and writes it down on a pad sometimes. So if I forgot it in the end, she said, "What about this? You didn't even put that in there. I remember that so vividly." So that's the way we work back and forth.

Then we read the entire thing out loud on the long-distance telephone with her in San Diego and me in Mexico City. The entire thing. To see how it sounded and to rework and cut and everything. That's an enormous commitment of time on the part of an editor, but it's just absolutely crucial.

I don't think that with something like this you can come in at the end and just drop the whole thing on an editor and expect it to be right. If you've been working all the way through, then you're on the same page. The editing is much faster and more streamlined. And if you're missing something, you're both in agreement on that and it's very precise and you go back for that.

How did you decide when to use a racial or ethnic identification in the story?

Well, I think that's one of the stickiest issues. First of all, the term "Anglo," the very use of that word, is difficult because a lot of people in Beardstown don't like it.

Why don't they like that term?

One woman said to me, "You can call me 'cracker,' you can call me 'honky.' But don't call me 'Anglo.'" She said "I am an American. I'm a white American." So I thought, "Am I going to go all the way through this story and call everybody white?" That didn't seem exactly right to me. You know "Hispanic" is a more sweeping word for a lot of people from a lot of different countries. Mexican is more specific; in some cases, people were Mexican. That's where they're from and I knew it. But the community as a whole now is Hispanic. I've met someone from Colombia. There are people from Puerto Rico, from the Dominican Republic. There are people from all over the place. About 95 percent are Mexicans, and so that's the reason in some cases I use "Mexican," because in the beginning, the arrivals were Mexicans. Then others came.

What role, if any, did race or ethnicity play in the reporting process?

I have very strong feelings about racism and the treatment of people and races and what everybody has to offer in different cultures, what they bring to the table, and what you can learn from them. That's what I've been doing in Mexico for 11 years. It is my home now. I feel very strongly about this, but that doesn't mean I don't comprehend what people who are white feel. I understand. I'm not saying it's right, but I can comprehend it and I'm willing to listen, and I want to get their voices because they reflect many people in America. The problem is most people won't tell you, and I worked really hard to get people to talk with me about that. Because if I had not done that, people would have said, "This is a syrupy, one-sided sob story about Mexicans." And I don't mean my peers; I mean the people in the community. They have feelings about this, and I had to have that in the story. But my rule was if you're going to say something really bad about another race, you have to give me your name, because we're not going to let people take shots at other people behind anonymity.

Did your race either help or hurt you in any way with either group, or did that seem to be a non-factor in moving through the communities?

Well, again, let's be candid. We always feel more comfortable with people like ourselves, and so I think within the white community I didn't appear to be a threat and I probably seemed like someone you could let into your home and sit down and talk. Now, on the Hispanic side, under many circumstances my race might have been a problem simply because of the threat it posed, being an American and I could turn them in. All those fears that you have if you're undocumented. I got over that right away because of my knowledge of Mexico and my Spanish and my sort of conversational approach to them. Many people did not ask me not to use their names, even though they were undocumented. I made that decision myself because I know what newspapers really mean. I know the power we have, and I know what can happen to them. Most people did not ask for anonymity.

Is there anything you want to bring up about how you cover people of diverse backgrounds that you think journalists need to keep in mind?

I have a pretty simple formula and that is just to look people in the eyes and tell them I'm really interested in their story and ask if they'd just take a few minutes and talk with me. Just really be willing and open to going wherever the conversation takes us and to listen to whatever they have to say, because it may take you in a direction you had never dreamed. If you're patient and you listen, you'll find out the most incredible things. So I guess that's what I would say. Just have time and be willing to listen a lot. I think that most human beings really want to be listened to. They really want to have someone be interested in them and someone they can tell something to, and I think if you keep that in mind, it will help you with anybody.

Writers' Workshop

Talking Points

1) Sometimes S. Lynne Walker identifies individuals by race or ethnicity. Look at the series to see where she does that. When does she do it? How does it affect how a reader understands the individual? Does it help the reader?

2) Walker says she wanted to communicate more effectively with a community that didn't speak English. What steps did she take? How did that affect her reporting and writing?

3) Walker uses a narrative approach to her series. How would you explain the relationship of the individual stories to the whole? How would you describe what each story in the series accomplished? What was the thread that wove them together?

Assignment Desk

1) Walker crafted her Beardstown series to show how a community in transition sees the transformation it is experiencing. Identify the people, the institutions, and the events that help illustrate that change. Look at your own community and determine what elements would enable you to describe the evolution that involves different groups in your community.

2) What's your race/ethnicity? How would it affect your understanding of different races/ethnicities? What could you do to address the challenges involved in dealing with any differences or similarities?

3) In her interview, Walker talks about how she wrote daily stories as well as worked on projects. How could you devise a strategy for doing the same thing?

Los Angeles Times

Jill Leovy

Finalist, Diversity Writing

Jill Leovy is a staff writer at the *Los Angeles Times*. She grew up in Seattle and has a bachelor's degree in history from the University of Washington in Seattle.

Before joining the *Times* in 1993, she worked for *The News Tribune* in Tacoma, Wash., and *The Seattle Times*. In her 11 years in Los Angeles, she has covered community news, business, city hall, and education.

Leovy started on the police beat in 2001 after covering the terrorist attacks from Ground Zero in New York. She continues to cover issues related to homicide and street violence, working out of the Los Angeles Police Department's 77th Street precinct in South Central L.A.

Her story, "No End to Murder's Grief," is, like the rest of Leovy's "Mortal Wounds" series, gripping in a way that propels the reader to the next sentence in spite of the tragic story that will unfold there.

[*This story has been excerpted because of space considerations. The full text of this story, as well as the entire "Mortal Wounds" series, can be read on the CD-ROM as part of Brian Vander Brug's winning Community Service Photojournalism package.*]

No end to murder's grief

AUGUST 9, 2003

A year ago Thursday, on a warm summer evening in Compton, Kevin Blanchard was murdered.

There was nothing especially noteworthy about the killing. Kevin, 19, fit a typical profile of homicide victims in Los Angeles County. The young black man's death came and went, and his name was added to the list of nearly 15,000 slain in the last decade.

Events of this week, though, tell another story—that of an explosion that ripped through a community after the bullet hit, and has reverberated since.

As the day marking Kevin's murder drew near, members of his family braced themselves for what they called "the anniversary," a modern ritual, like sidewalk memorials and candlelight vigils, that has grown around urban homicide. August has become the peak time for such anniversaries in Los Angeles County.

With Kevin's approaching, his mother, Patricia, listlessly made plans and changed them, discussed prayer vigils and poetry readings. Nothing seemed adequate.

Her plans still in flux, she rose the morning of the anniversary of Kevin's death and felt a familiar shock.

It was as if no time had passed. "My body felt the same weakness, everything. Just like it was," she said, "just like on that day a year ago."

Kevin DeShawn Blanchard was shot in the head as he drove down a residential street on the west side of Compton.

He careened into a garage. Neighbors heard him try to restart his car. Then there was silence.

The killing was like many in Compton: It seemed to make no sense. The shooter was probably involved with gangs, detectives said. Maybe the killer thought Kevin was someone else.

AWKWARD AS A CHILD

Kevin was good with his hands and didn't talk much. He had an embarrassed manner and would hold a hand over his mouth when he laughed to cover a crooked tooth.

As a child, he had been chubby. He collected baseball cards and comic books as soon as he could read. In his teenage years, he seemed to grow tall and lanky overnight.

By 19, he was a handsome youth, with prominent arching black brows, always groomed, his shirts matching his shoes, his hair styled. His friends teased him, calling him "Pretty Boy."

Kevin's confidence was slow to catch up. He was ever hanging back, letting others hold the stage. When he went to clubs with his girlfriend, Angel Beazer, he would lounge along the wall, refusing to dance.

He had been attending community college and was thinking of becoming a police officer.

His mother had just got him a white 1999 Chevrolet Monte Carlo, and he was proud of his new rims.

The night Kevin died, he was driving the new car to pick up Angel.

He was late. Angel couldn't understand why Kevin did not respond to her phone messages. By midnight, she was frantic. At least five of her high school classmates had been murdered.

"Kevin, I am not mad. I am not going to holler at you. Now I'm just worried. Please call," she pleaded into his voicemail.

SINGLE MOTHER OF 5 CHILDREN

Kevin's mother is a single parent of five from Missouri, with broad features and straight, graying hair.

Her own parents did not finish high school. But Patricia Blanchard returned to school at age 48 to earn her nursing degree. She works at Martin Luther King Jr./Drew Medical Center, treating many young victims of gunshots.

She prodded her children to follow her example. "No one can take your knowledge away," she would tell them.

At age 61, she could proudly claim that four of her children had gone to college. One had earned a master's degree.

On this night last year, she got a phone call while watching TV.

From the caller's voice, Blanchard knew something was wrong.

Worry is constant for black mothers raising sons in Compton. Every morning, Blanchard prayed for their safety. "You are a young black man," she would tell Kevin. "You have to be careful."

The caller said Kevin had been shot. The paramedics were taking him to King/Drew. Blanchard dropped the phone without hanging up, and ran out, forgetting her purse.

At the hospital, she couldn't get answers.

She tried to sit, but paced the halls instead. Nearby, she could see the double doors to the trauma bay. Whenever a doctor passed in or out, she strained to get a glimpse.

At one point, a gurney came rolling down the hall. Blanchard stepped aside to let it by and saw it carried a naked baby.

The infant had been shot. A short while later, she heard a woman screaming. Blanchard had worked at King/Drew long enough to know what that meant: a mother being told of her child's death.

Shortly after, a doctor she knew came into the waiting room.

FOUR PATIENTS IN 30 MINUTES

A surgeon from Ethiopia, Dr. Gudata Hinika is compact and bespectacled, with an elegant accent and a warm personality. Blanchard used to call him "Dr. Sunshine."

Ethiopia's murder rate is a fraction of Compton's, and Hinika did his training in a suburban U.S. hospital where gunshot wounds are all but unknown.

But at King/Drew, his first patient eight years ago was a 19-year-old woman shot in the chest. He couldn't save her. "I was just destroyed," Hinika recalled.

After a few years at King/Drew, the shock went away, but he remained uncomprehending. "I could not imagine a civilized country where anyone would do damage to this extent," he said.

On the night of Aug. 7, 2002, four gunshot victims had come into the trauma bay within 30 minutes. Among them were the 2-month-old baby and a young man with no identification.

The young man had a bullet wound to the head and

no vital signs. Hinika noticed only that he was tall and handsome.

He had no time to spare. Another patient arrived with a bullet in the chest, and he spent two hours in surgery.

Hinika emerged, and learned the infant had died. He went to tell the infant's mother, and stood by as she screamed.

The nurses told Hinika that he needed to make his second death notification of the night. They pointed to where another woman waited.

He walked in the room, saw Blanchard, and halted in confusion.

"I couldn't speak for a moment," he remembered.

Blanchard, he said, is one of the nurses he most respects, among the kindest on the staff.

"What are you doing down here, Ms. Blanchard?" he asked, but the realization was already dawning.

The young man must have been her son.

[*This story has been excerpted because of space considerations. The full text of this story, as well as Leovy's entire series, can be read on the CD-ROM included in this edition of Best Newspaper Writing.*]

Lessons Learned

BY JILL LEOVY

Listen to pain, and let it teach you. That's the essential lesson I took from a year spent interviewing more than 100 people directly affected by urban homicide.

I had been reporting for years when I started this project. But these interviews made me feel that I had to learn the job anew. They were draining, unpredictable, and had a disconcerting tendency to lurch into bewildering and unexpected terrain.

Several times, for example, sources threatened suicide in these interviews. Or they talked of plans to kill their loved ones' murderers in retaliation. Others told me that they had already killed or that they were protecting some murderer's identity. Occasionally they were hostile.

I was unprepared for the emotional strain, the ethical dilemmas, and the complex task of marshaling chaotic field experiences into material that fit the needs of my newspaper and my editors. Interviews could last five minutes, or six hours. My sources talked in circles; no amount of questioning could keep them on topic. A good number of them broke appointments or stood me up, then would ambush me out of the blue, distraught and insistent on talking. Depending on the day, they could be angry, hysterical, drunk, or unresponsive.

Only when I stopped trying to orchestrate my reporting did I get the best material. I stopped asking questions; I let people talk. Usually, it turned out that my sources wanted to talk about what was most agonizing to them—and hardest for others to listen to. To my surprise, listening to their agony, though difficult, proved to be instructive—and not just on the subject of grief. Grief proved to be a gateway into broader topics, from the mechanics of the urban gang culture to the institutional problems with police and emergency services. I learned to be quiet, to listen, and to see the power of trauma to enlighten.

I still cover urban homicide, and I continue to be humbled by its demands. My goal is not just to do project stories such as this one, but to stick with the topic long term. This has required adjustments. Homicide has taught me to pace myself, to be more understanding about the limitations of newspapers, and to be more forgiving of my editors. For myself, now, I simply try to do the best I can on stories and let go of the results.

The Washington Post

Amy Argetsinger

Finalist, Diversity Writing

Amy Argetsinger, 35, is a staff writer covering higher education for the metro section of *The Washington Post*. Born Sept. 8, 1968, in a military hospital in Seoul, South Korea, she was raised in Alexandria, Va.

She graduated from the University of Virginia in 1990 with a bachelor's degree in political and social thought and started her career at *The Rock Island Argus* and *The Dispatch* in Moline, both in western Illinois.

She joined the *Post* in 1995 and covered Maryland state politics and education policy, local schools, and local government before moving to her current beat. She lives in Washington, D.C.

The story of Kakenya Ntaiya is a riveting, universal story of fitting in, of fidelity to family, of growing up and moving away from home. It carries the paradoxical tones of naïveté and wisdom that define the story's central character.

Kenyan defied tribe's traditions but now carries its hopes

DECEMBER 28, 2003

Kakenya Ntaiya awakens to the silence of a dormitory morning.

She always awoke early back home in the western highlands of Kenya, where dawn brought the cows tramping near her window and the chickens scratching their way into the parlor and a baby sister squirming in her bed as the sun warmed the smooth mud walls around them. They were reminders of so many chores to do.

Here in this airtight dorm room the size of her mother's entire house, no chores announce themselves. Breakfast will come from cows that someone else milked and chickens she's never seen. Yet even after three years and three months at an American college, she rises early, with an awareness of all she has to accomplish.

But first Ntaiya sits on her bed and thanks the God who delivered her here, as she says she always does. The God who will help her fulfill her duties. And she prays for the family that misses her so and for the village elders who sent her away on the understanding that she would greet each morning thinking of them.

A girl will never forget her home, they said. It was the way they consoled themselves, really. No daughter of Enoosaen had ever gone to college—or practically anywhere alone, beyond those fields of corn and sugar cane and more cattle than people. Yet she had fixated on the United States, territory uncharted on the maps in their minds. A girl could get lost out there. She could be robbed, or prostituted, or worse. But the eldest of James and Anna Ntaiya's eight children had worn them down with clever arguments and won them over with big promises. The boys who had gone had stayed gone, as boys are wont to do. A girl, however, would remember. A girl would return.

For now, it's April of 2003, and the spring semester is hurtling toward exams. She lopes down the stairs, out the door, across the lawn to her 9:25 class—Economics of the Developing World. Several international students fill the seats around her, so this time it can be a South American called upon to offer a story from "back home," while Masai tribeswoman Ntaiya, exotic pride of Randolph-Macon Woman's College, slouches in the back taking notes. "Sustainability," she writes. "Meeting the needs of the present generation without compromising the needs of future generations."

Just one more year to graduation, to the diploma her neighbors back home once mocked as a fantasy.

They could never have imagined, of course, how safe she would be in the embrace of a small campus, all red brick and magnolia and cheery hellos, nor how well she would blend in by now. How she would swan through the dining hall today with a brazen, face-splitting smile, teasing one tablemate about a boyfriend, another about a peculiarly American taste for uncooked vegetables. How she could plop down in a professor's office—uninvited!—to banter about her star performance on the Model United Nations trip. Or how at her 12:15 International Law class, the child who grew up without electricity or running water would play technology guru, gently heckling a classmate who couldn't get a PowerPoint presentation to work.

"Hit 'End Task'!" Ntaiya hisses as the computer burbles unpromisingly. "You have to take the disk out."

Nor could the people of her village, who plotted their days by the sun, have imagined the pressures the United States would heave on top of those she had carried to its shores—the accumulation of ceaseless demands. The presentation on Croatian culture, not yet started but due in two days. The paper for British history. The econ quiz. Final exams. Then the summer, and what exactly? Nowhere to go, no money to fly home. And now the administrator she hoped to cajole about that campus job is telling her, kindly but firmly, that she'd better not count on it.

As her friends chatter around her in the computer lab, she stews silently before escaping into the cool spring night. But as soon as the tears rise up, a wave of shame beats them back. She endured so much to make it here, paid a price no American college woman could comprehend. If these little things at college overwhelmed her, how will she ever handle the real work ahead? So many debts to pay back home—a family to support, a school to build, a water system to improve. So many minds to change, so many children to inspire.

That was the deal, wasn't it? *A girl will never forget her home*, her community decreed. It wasn't just a prophecy, or mere solace. It was its plan for her, and she alone would have to make it true.

A LONELY PATH

By the time Ntaiya entered her village school's equivalent of eighth grade, only one other girl was in her class.

In the fabled Masai tribe into which she was born, the girls who started school tended to drop out by the middle grades, many to get married. School district officials can remember only a handful of Masai girls from her region who graduated before Ntaiya, and no others who pursued a college degree.

She attended a grammar school where most of the teachers did not hold a university diploma. With paper hard to come by, she and her classmates wrote in chalk on the concrete floor. She never possessed a textbook until high school. She never read an entire book until she was 20 years old.

There were no SAT prep courses in Enoosaen to pave Ntaiya's path to a four-year scholarship at an American college, worth roughly 80 times her mother's annual income. There were, after all, no SATs.

That a child who helped feed her family by pulling weeds for less than a dollar a day in a village 20 miles from a paved road could even have a vision of higher education—would know someone who would know a college president on the far side of the globe and could write a letter saying, *let me tell you about this girl*—reflects the evolution of the least developed corners of the world.

The first young representatives of tribal Africa emerged from rural villages in search of university educations in the 1960s and '70s, some heading to the capital cities, others overseas. The cattle-herding Masai came late to this trek: Their stoic and semi-nomadic ways beguiled a century of Western visitors—from *Out of Africa* author Isak Dinesen to today's Hollywood filmmakers—but confounded colonial attempts to impose institutions on them. It was not until the 1980s that

Ntaiya's community began growing crops to supplement the cattle that once constituted its entire livelihood and slowly gained a modest economic stability that opened the doors to schooling.

For the young rural Africans who pursue the promise of higher education, it may be a lonely journey, but it is rarely a solo effort. Many arrive on campus only because their villages raised money to finance their travel or tuition—with a hope, spoken or implicit, that these students would one day return the favor.

"You feel, definitely, a debt," said Sylvain H. Boko, an associate professor of economics at Wake Forest University who has studied the impact of globalization on African communities—and who himself was one of the first children from his village in Benin to go to college. Such emigrants "are very conscious that we left behind a lot of people who do not have the chance to achieve what we have. That haunts you."

Many leave intent on returning someday, a desire stoked by equal parts duty and nostalgia. But college has a way of altering their dreams. The major in agriculture or medicine is dumped for policy studies or literature. The village sweetheart is replaced by one from a distant city or another culture. Newfound comforts, such as e-mail or sushi, evolve into essentials. After four or six or 10 years of schooling, many find that their newly complicated lives no longer fit into the places they left behind. They still feel the debt. But they try to fulfill it by sending money and visiting regularly, while making new homes in the cities where they can enjoy the lives for which their expensive degrees prepared them.

In Enoosaen, a cluster of grass-thatched huts and rocky fields eight hours west of Nairobi and invisible on most maps, these are the potential careers: farmer, teacher or merchant selling flea spray and cotton cloth from sheet-metal shacks.

And this is the social life: The men, most married by their early twenties, talking crops and cattle under the awnings of the village center. The women, most wed by their late teens, beading bracelets around a kitchen fire. None of the four or five young men who departed Enoosaen for college has returned to live full time.

For Ntaiya, whose journey triggered a cathartic debate

in Enoosaen, the stakes are higher. She vows to return, though so have all the others. Yet the expectations for her will be greater, speculated Njeri Mbugua, a sociologist at Illinois Wesleyan University—because she is the first woman.

"She embodies in her not just her individual success, but the success of her community," said Mbugua, a native of Kenya. "They said, 'We send you out with our blessings.' Now, her community is expecting her."

IMMERSED IN A NEW CULTURE

There were days growing up, with her mother sick and father absent, that Ntaiya remembers going without food. Here, her tastes have grown agonizingly precise.

"Veggie burger," she tells the waiter at Applebee's in Lynchburg, each vowel rolling out roundly. "No lettuce, no pickle..." She pauses, tilts her head coquettishly and considers the menu again. Her friends Katherine and Adwoa watch with interest.

"No lettuce, and mayonnaise," she proclaims finally, the last word tripping out in three regal syllables.

The waiter labors to keep up, flustered by the accent or the attitude. "Veggie burger, no lettuce, no mayonnaise?" he asks.

Ntaiya glances back. "Mayonnaise should be there."

America came at her freshman year in a rush of new stimuli—television, fashion, snow, vacuum cleaners, plumbing, Wal-Mart, silverware—and a barrage of attention. Everyone wanted to talk to her, to take her to her first movie or on her first boat ride. She was the star of Randolph-Macon's fundraising banquet, hamming it up in her red Masai wrap and beaded headdress in a skit with *Good Morning America* host Charles Gibson, husband of an alumna. The applause came like thunder.

After three years, the novelty of this country has long since worn off, as has the novelty of her presence here. She is 24 now, a junior. But life has not calmed down.

She's reading—and reading, and reading, sunk in those funky old orange armchairs that survived the colonial redo of the Main Hall lobby. A couple of books a week: economics texts, Shakespearean plays. English was her third language, after her tribe's Maa and her region's Swahili, and it's still a chore, absorbing all that print to regurgitate into papers and class discussions. Sometimes it takes a second read before it all sinks in.

Or she's traveling. To the Model United Nations or mock African Union conferences in New York or Washington that have became the great outlet for her grand new intellectual passion of international relations, mixing it up with the aggressively brainy students from other colleges, finding fodder for weeks of rehash and gossip.

Or she's working. A couple of days a week at the campus nursery school, where the faculty children cling to her like kittens, and a few nights a week at the computer study hall, where she hushes her giggling classmates from behind an old wooden desk—jobs less taxing than time-consuming but essential to fulfill her scholarship's work-study requirement and to earn pocket money in the absence of a check from home.

Or she's running—three miles or more down the trail by a quiet stream, a sport she had never tried (the hours in her mother's fields leaving no time or need for exercise) until she came here and craved a way to empty her lungs and clear her brain.

Or she's talking on the phone with the best new discovery of this past year—David, a fellow Kenyan. They've met in person exactly twice since he introduced himself in a London airport more than a year ago, but he calls every night from Toronto. He has a gentle, unassuming manner completely unlike that of any other Kenyan man she knows, and he speaks in a sweet, husky voice that calms her every time she gets stressed out.

Or she's just plain having fun, which should be her occasional right, after all, as an American college student.

"Play Faith Hill!" she pleads as they pile into Katherine's silver hatchback after dinner, and Katherine dutifully cranks it up, the first song Ntaiya ever loved in this country, a joyous tune with a lithe beat and such outrageously happy lyrics—the only ones simple and clear enough for her to pick out on the radio that baffling freshman year. She croons along with it now in a soft, dreamy voice, all the way back to the dorm.

"It's the way you love me. It's a feeling like this...This kiss, this kiss!"

LONGING FOR HOME

It's only when the whirl subsides—when classes are over for the night or for the semester, when the last papers are turned in, when the chattering of friends no longer fills her room or the clamor of the hallways is silenced for a long weekend or holiday—that it all comes back to her.

What lies ahead.

And what she's left behind.

It's a warm, sticky night in summer. Ntaiya is in a bleak mood.

She can't stop thinking about home, not when she's alone in her room, siblings smiling at her from the photos taped to the walls. The boys, Benard and Daniel, young men now, frozen as skinny youngsters in this shot. Seenoi, the one Ntaiya raised when her mother was off nursing their sick father, the one who called her "Mama," wearing a skirt so big it covers her 3-year-old legs. She would be 6 by now.

And her mother, so youthful in this picture she could be Ntaiya's sister. You'd never know from this photo what hard times they've shared, working in other people's fields for 50 shillings a day, barely 70 cents, before Ntaiya nudged her mother to start their own farm and they slowly began to draw a steady income. Ntaiya worries that her mother has no one to talk to these days.

And now, after a long day at two jobs, some very bad news: Her sister Naserian is getting married. Twenty-year-old Naserian, the third child. For so many years, their mother sacrificed so much to educate her girls, to push them on to a better life than her own, and now Naserian, barely a year out of high school, is throwing it all away.

"If I were there," Ntaiya says grimly, "I could stop this marriage."

But she is not there. She doesn't even know when the wedding is to happen—or if it's happened already. She received the news the way she receives all news from home—in a letter, this one from her brother Daniel, that took three weeks to arrive. She longs for more information. Yet there are no phone lines in Enoosaen. She tries to dial the number of a village neighbor's cell phone, which she did once before several months ago for a brief, static-filled call to her mother. She can never get an answer.

Ntaiya is not there by her own choosing. Four years ago, she sat in her family's living room with two letters of admission, one from Randolph-Macon, the other from a teachers' academy in Kiambu, seven hours from home. If she had gone to Kiambu, she wouldn't have received a university education. But she would have earned her teaching credentials, and she would have finished a couple of years ago. She would be working and making money by now. And she would be home.

Instead, she picked Randolph-Macon. She had wept for days; still, it was always the choice of her heart—the U.S. college, and all the big things it could bring her way.

And so she had made the deal. If she had to leave so many responsibilities behind, then she could not go just for herself.

Times like these, she thinks ahead. About all the things she has to do when she gets back to Enoosaen. The things her community needs. The things she promised.

Like a boarding school for girls.

And a maternity clinic.

And a way to improve the drinking water, which comes up on the backs of donkeys from the river at the bottom of the cow pastures, sometimes carrying disease. And better roads, and maybe electricity. And some positive leadership from an educated woman who can demonstrate on a daily basis that schooling is important, that feminism is good.

These are ambitious things, she knows. "It's gonna work," she says on another, sunnier day. "It's gonna take some time."

But in the summer of 2003, there are things Kakenya Ntaiya is not thinking so much about yet:

Like how the path back to Enoosaen is getting longer by the day, what with her growing interest in graduate school that could end up extending her stay in the United States by two years, maybe three.

Or how the kinds of jobs she may be suited for when she receives a master's degree in international studies are not likely to return her to Enoosaen.

Or how David, with whom she is growing more serious, has years of study ahead of him in yet another country.

Asked about these things, Ntaiya sighs but refuses to entertain doubt. You have to understand, she says, how much it took for the barefoot village girl to make it to the halls of academe.

"If I can go to college," she says surely, "I feel like I can do it."

Yet college has always been full of those people who burned brighter than anyone else in their home town's memory—destined, it seemed, to change the world. Mostly, they just level off into normal lives, for who can continue shooting upward at such speed?

Lessons Learned

BY AMY ARGETSINGER

The first thing I learned from my adventures with Ka-kenya Ntaiya is that working a beat is the way to find the good stories. This may sound obvious, but it came as a bit of a surprise for me. So many of us beat reporters envy the general assignment reporters: They're the ones, it seems, who get all the adventures, who get thrown into the big stories, or who have the freedom to pursue the delicious oddball assignments with a writerly flair.

And yet, I'm fairly sure, they would never have had a chance to find Kakenya. I was a few months into a new beat, covering local higher education, when a public relations official at Randolph-Macon Woman's College called to pitch me a story. A few phrases stuck out—"Masai tribe," "one of the few Masai women to go to college," "female circumcision"—and I decided to drive down to Lynchburg. To be honest, though, I wasn't expecting much. Still, I figured that this young woman might serve as a lead for a larger story about international students and that the trip would be a good excuse to get to know another campus and more officials on my beat.

And then I met Kakenya.

In hindsight, I learned only the barest details about her on that first meeting. I didn't know yet about the pressure she felt to return as a leader for the community. But even those bare details—how she had never used a fork or a toilet before she arrived in America, how she had bargained with her parents to allow her to continue high school—convinced me that not only was she a story, she was a big story.

The story was delayed for a couple of years, as the crisis of Sept. 11 and other competing priorities got in the way. A big hurdle, though, was trying to figure out what format Kakenya's story would take. It was just so sprawling: Her childhood was one remarkable facet, and her acclimation to Randolph-Macon and American life was another. And there were the lingering questions of how and when she would fulfill her promise to return to Kenya.

It was a breakthrough for me—and the second major lesson of this process—when I realized that Kakenya could be a narrative series. It was a genre in which I had never worked and which the *Post* rarely uses. But it gave me the framework for thinking through the elements of the story, and I began seeking out examples of great serial writing from other newspapers.

The third lesson for me was how to build trust with a subject. I had previously written a few intimate profiles of ordinary people, though none of this length or depth, and I knew the potential for pitfalls: Subjects forget that you're a reporter, not a friend, and are shocked at what lands in your notebook once they've let their guard down. You want your subjects to let down their guard, but you don't want them to feel burned or embarassed by the final product. I would spend hours with Kakenya just hanging out, not even taking notes, and we did begin to think of each other as friends. But as we got closer to publication, I tried to prepare her for the experience of having her life spread out in *The Washington Post*. I shared with her some examples of other major stories the *Post* had done about ordinary people, including Anne Hull's 2002 portraits of immigrants in the American South.

Kakenya seemed okay with the prospect, but I still worried. I knew that even if she had no quarrel with any facts or quotes in the story, there would still be the shock of seeing her life spread bare upon the front page of the paper. So in the days before the stories ran, I sat her down and explained everything that would be in the stories—the quotes, the scenes, the observations—and what purpose each of them was meant to serve. She was, understandably, mortified: "Oh, my God, I can't believe you're putting all that in the paper!"

Yet by the time the early editions of the story hit the *Post*'s website, Kakenya was delighted. She had been able to work out her shock and anxiety about the story before it appeared, and, instead of getting hung up about embarrassing little details, she was able to see the story in the same way strangers would.

She later sent me a note saying that appearing in the paper was one of the great honors of her life, something she would always remember. And, yes, we can now call each other friends.

Mark Mahoney
Editorial Writing

THE POST★STAR

Mark Mahoney is a master of the editorial two-step. First, he gets people to read what he's written. Then he gets them to do something.

Like any good dancer, Mahoney has a way of breaking down his moves. He begins by figuring out what it is that really bugs him about something, whether it's the death of a child, a bone-headed expenditure by local politicians, or the conduct of a local parish priest.

Sometimes this starting point—this bugging point—can be quite personal for Mahoney.

Take his approach to an editorial about a popular priest accused of molesting an adolescent boy. By coincidence, the priest had baptized Mahoney's twin daughters, Chelsea and Christa, now 8. Mahoney began his editorial like this: "You held my babies in your hands."

Mahoney says a lot of readers were taken aback, even

offended. Some accused him of putting "your own personal thing on it." Mahoney says he responded by explaining: "I wanted to make people feel my anger and resentment."

Sometimes what he wants readers to *do* is simply to *feel*.

Mahoney, 40, who is also the father of 11-year-old Caitlin, is the primary editorial writer for *The Post-Star,* a 35,000-circulation daily in Glens Falls, N.Y.

He was born in Wappingers Falls, N.Y., and received a bachelor of science degree in communications management from Ithaca College in Ithaca, N.Y., in 1985.

He got started in the news business as a radio reporter at WEOK-WPDH in Poughkeepsie, N.Y. ("I wanted to be Don Imus"), and spent a year as a legislative correspondent at the state capital of Albany.

He joined *The Post-Star* 16 years ago as a reporter and has been writing editorials for the past 10.

He continues to sit in the newsroom, though, and spends much of his day editing copy for the paper's news section. He says that keeps him linked to the news and still leaves him enough time to produce three or four editorials a week on local topics. (The paper uses editorials produced by a wire service, on national and international topics, on the other days.)

Mahoney enjoys the feeling of connectedness that working for a small paper in a small community can provide. He lives there, he often knows the people he's writing about, and he's able to overhear people discussing his editorials at the hockey rink on weekends.

Because he's so entrenched in the community ("I've got to pay taxes, I've got to drive on the roads. I've got to educate my kids...."), there's a pretty good chance that what strikes him as worthy of comment will also resonate with his readers.

But he doesn't take that for granted. That's where the writing—and the selling—go hand in hand: "I can try to make people cry and I can try to tick them off and I can try to make them laugh...to get them reading."

—Bill Mitchell

Debate good thing for America

APRIL 13, 2003

There's an old Monty Python skit in which a guy walks into an office and declares, "I'd like to have an argument," to which the man at the desk replies, "No, you wouldn't."

That's the odd thing about the attitude of local war demonstrators—both those for and against American action in Iraq: They want to express their opinions, but they don't want anyone to give them an argument.

It's great to hear pro- and anti-war supporters exchanging viewpoints. It's refreshing to see veterans and others arguing vehemently in favor of the liberation of Iraq against those who feel peace wasn't given enough of a chance to succeed. It's great to hear people go back and forth over whether one can oppose the war without opposing the people in uniform.

But what's bothersome is when you hear one group of Americans say that another group of Americans has no right to express an opinion if that opinion doesn't fall in line with theirs.

It's difficult, sometimes, for people with strong opinions to separate the act of free speech from the subject matter of the speech.

One group of citizens that's particularly offended by the anti-war protesters is war veterans. Based on the subject matter, they've got every reason to be offended. Like the young men and women fighting in the Persian Gulf now, they endured hardships and put their lives on the line. Many of their brethren were either killed or maimed fighting for this country. To them, to speak ill of the fight is to speak ill of the fighters. Discord among citizens, they say, sends the wrong message to our enemies and to the people putting their lives on the line.

They feel that a country needs to present a united front, particularly in times of war. And that those who don't want to unite should either shut up or find some other country.

But maintaining unity in a society that celebrates personal freedom is no easy task.

Even James Madison, one of the most vigilant and articulate defenders of personal freedom in American history, struggled to find a balance between maintaining order and maintaining personal liberty. In the end, he said liberty must be preserved.

"Liberty is to faction what air is to fire, an aliment without which it instantly expires," he wrote in *Federalist No. 10* in 1787. "But it could not be less folly to abolish liberty, which is essential to political life, because it nourishes faction, than it would be to wish the annihilation of air, which is essential to animal life, because it imparts to fire its destructive agency."

If television pictures of Iraqi citizens dancing in the streets and flinging their shoes at images of their deposed dictator remind us of anything, it's that we should celebrate the freedom that being Americans allows— celebrate the air that's essential for life in a free society.

As difficult as it is to swallow for some, discord is a sign of this nation's strength, not weakness.

Lacking Madison's historic stature, but equaling him in eloquence and wisdom, is a young soldier from South Glens Falls stationed in Kuwait. Army combat engineer Sarah Secor, like Madison, recognized the importance of preserving liberty in a free society. In a letter to the editor of this newspaper, she expressed her support for her mission and encouraged fellow citizens to stand behind the troops. But she also cheered the war protesters for their willingness to stand up for their views.

"We live in the land of the free. Thank God for that!" she wrote.

In our zeal to express our views on the war, let's remember that there's no better example of the freedoms we enjoy than a good old-fashioned argument.

Inaction hurts local taxpayers

MAY 8, 2003

What is so hard about this?

What is so hard about forcing an amusement park to collect a reasonable and legal amount of sales tax on the actual price of admission, just like other parks are required to do?

Why is it so difficult for Warren County's two state legislators, Sen. Elizabeth Little and Assemblywoman Teresa Sayward, to get some action on this issue—which could mean $1 million or more in extra tax revenue for the taxpayers they represent?

Why is it so hard for Ms. Little and Ms. Sayward to even find out the status of "negotiations" between their own state Taxation and Finance Department and the owners of the Great Escape amusement park?

What right do the political appointees in the state Tax Department have to exclude elected state legislators from discussions with a company about paying its taxes? And anyway, what is there to "negotiate"? A tax is a tax, and the law's the law. Enforce it. Don't negotiate it.

Why aren't our legislators demanding—rather than requesting—to be informed?

Why are county leaders—facing significant cuts in state aid and raising property taxes to offset the growing cost of state mandates—sitting quietly by while $1 million to $2 million from out-of-town visitors goes uncollected? Are they afraid that Great Escape will pull up stakes in the middle of the night like some traveling carnival and leave town? Ask yourself if a company making millions of dollars a year here would abandon this huge investment just so it doesn't have to collect another $2 in sales tax.

And why wouldn't the state Legislature, ever on the lookout for ways to take people's money, push Great Escape to collect its fair share of tax?

Why, nearly one year after this issue was first raised, haven't we seen a resolution?

It shouldn't be this hard.

The whole issue centers on Great Escape's silly definition of "general admission." Park officials claim that only $2.80 of the $33.99 admission price is for actual admission to the park. The remaining $31, they say, is for the price of the rides themselves, which is not subject to sales tax.

The logical conclusion to Great Escape's definition of "general admission" is that you could get into the park at that price, as long as you don't ride the rides. But you can't. All parkgoers pay the combination price for admission and rides, regardless of whether they ride the rides or not.

For each ticket sold to the park, the county and state now split 20 cents, for a total of $180,000 a year.

Allowing for discount admissions, if Great Escape collected sales tax on the average admission paid by its 900,000 annual visitors, Warren County could see an additional $500,000 to $1 million in sales tax. At the same time, the tax would only add about $2.40 to the park's highest admission price.

Instead of crossing their fingers and hoping it all turns out OK, our elected officials should be actively fighting for that money. When they were campaigning for votes, they promised to act in the best interests of us—the taxpayers.

It's time they made good on that promise.

A chance to learn
from baby's death

There are a lot more ways to silence a baby's screams than just falling asleep with your hand over its mouth.

You can ignore the desperate pleas of an abuser's own sister when she claims that her niece is being sexually abused and neglected.

When a police officer calls to report a suspected offense, you can refuse to look up the person's criminal record or make a couple of phone calls to find out if there have been any earlier allegations.

Or you can procrastinate the prosecution of a serious infant assault case for years, until the suspect disappears into the crowd and the case sifts to the bottom of the priority pile.

Fred Beagle suffocated his 7-week-old daughter Jade by placing his hand over her mouth until she died. He, alone, is directly responsible for the infant's death, and will serve 5 to 15 years in prison for his actions.

But there were plenty of people over the years who were in a position to prevent the tragedy, had they simply taken a bit more time to follow up on abuse allegations against Mr. Beagle and taken more seriously the threat to children in his care.

Massachusetts prosecutors had the best opportunity to intervene five years ago.

Mr. Beagle was arrested on felony charges in 1998 in connection with the suspected abuse of his son, then less than a year old. During Mr. Beagle's recent murder trial in Warren County, the district attorney's office spelled out more than a dozen incidents documenting the abuse, which included six bone fractures and 27 bruises. In 2001, a Massachusetts psychologist issued a report on Mr. Beagle and his then-girlfriend, stating that "any child in their care is in lethal danger and at the highest level of risk."

Yet even now, the case, incredibly, has yet to be prosecuted. If Fred Beagle is in prison, he can't father a child, and he can't abuse the children he already has.

Fast forward to 2002. Four weeks before Jade was killed by her father in November, Fred Beagle's sister was so fearful for the baby's safety that she called police. Police found no physical evidence the child had been abused, but an officer reported the case to the state Child Abuse Hotline.

The Office of Child and Family Services has five criteria for triggering a child protective services investigation; although the criteria appeared to have been met, the office said they were not and therefore no report was made.

What would it have taken for someone to express just a minimal interest in the case, such as phoning the sister to find out why she took such a drastic step as calling police on her brother? Or maybe they could have checked up on Mr. Beagle's criminal history.

They would likely have discovered the pending felony charge from Massachusetts and learned that two children had been ripped from his custody because of fears for their safety.

Hindsight is always 20-20, and no one likes to be second-guessed for spot judgment calls they might regret. But there are lessons to be learned by the miscalculations in this saga—lessons that might prevent another Fred Beagle from slipping through the cracks, and spare another infant from sharing Jade Beagle's fate.

Every credible allegation of abuse should be treated as if the child was in real danger, at the very least with a few appropriately placed phone calls. No allegations should be dismissed until they can be completely discounted.

If the process is the problem, fix it. If miscommunication is to blame, hold a meeting and work out a better system. If money is lacking, lobby for more. If not enough incentive exists to investigate all legitimate complaints, take a look at a photo of Jade Beagle.

It was in the paper. Right next to her obituary.

Another new toy
for Queensbury

JUNE 13, 2003

This is a joke, right?

Queensbury takes a lot of ribbing for its Taj Mahal fire stations, its fleet of expensive late-model vehicles, its indoor car-wash bay and the $50,000 rock garden at the corner of Bay and Quaker.

So obviously, when one of its fire departments comes to the Town Board seeking to buy a $47,000 Army truck to fight brush fires, they're just poking a little fun at themselves. You know, a little self-effacing humor to soften their spendthrift reputation.

If only Queensbury taxpayers were so lucky.

The South Queensbury Fire Company actually wants to replace its aging brush truck with a Humvee—one of those big Army truck things favored by macho drivers who've outgrown their SUVs. The 8- to 10-year-old truck would cost $29,000 and be outfitted with $18,000 in firefighting equipment—for a total initial outlay of $47,000. That cost doesn't include the extremely high cost of Humvee replacement parts or the relatively low number of qualified Humvee repairmen nearby.

They say they need this specialized piece of firefighting equipment to fight brush fires, as well as to pull stuck firetrucks out of the mud and respond to plane crashes at the Warren County airport.

There are just a few holes in the arguments. First, most brush and forest fires in Queensbury are accessible by trucks or all-terrain vehicles, and fires in very remote areas of Queensbury are rare. Aside from the occasional forest fires on West Mountain, the last real tough remote-area blaze in Queensbury was on French Mountain in 1995. Firefighters in other Adirondack towns have far greater need to access remote areas than Queensbury. Realistically, how often is one Queensbury fire company going to use one of these things?

The other arguments are equally flimsy. How many firetrucks have had to be pulled out of the mud lately? How many plane crashes have occurred at the big flat

Warren County airport that couldn't be handled by existing firefighting equipment? In addition, Humvees are more than 7 feet wide, making them difficult to use on mountain trails, and they have very little capacity to transport equipment and manpower into a remote fire site.

A $47,000 Humvee might be a nice new toy for Queensbury's volunteers, but it's questionable how much use it will get outside of parades. And you know Queensbury. If one fire company gets one, they're all going to want one.

If this go-anywhere piece of equipment is truly necessary to fight fires in remote areas of the region, then the state Department of Environmental Conservation—which has jurisdiction over virtually all forest fires in the state—should take the lead in purchasing one. Local fire companies could be asked to contribute something to the cost. And the truck should be kept at a location where it could reach most remote fires the quickest.

Before the town of Queensbury adds another punchline to its list of expensive jokes, it should take a realistic look at how often this piece of equipment will be used and exhaust other less expensive alternatives first.

Lake George movie
deal is goofy

JULY 11, 2003

M-I-C-K-E-Y M-O-U-S-E.

Mickey Mouse is a good way to sum up the silly situation going on in Lake George regarding a Disney-owned radio station's plan—then un-plan—to show free Disney movies in Shepard Park.

When Mayor Robert Blais first announced Albany radio station WDDY's offer to hold family movie nights in the park, including providing free popcorn for the kiddies, everyone thought it was a supercalifragilistic idea.

The village would get one of those wholesome, tattoo-free family events it's always after, and the fledgling radio station would get access to a small world of potential new listeners.

But just as suddenly as the idea appeared, the beauty turned to a beast.

Mayor Blais read the fine print on the contract and found out the radio station was seeking compensation for its "free" movie night—from $5,000 to $8,000, depending on which deal the village wanted to take. It turns out the radio station expected the village not only to provide the theater and the audience, but also the movie projector and the screen. We wonder if the popcorn was ever really free.

Suddenly, what started out as a win-win proposition for the radio station and the village has turned into a win situation for the radio station, but an expensive, disappointing lesson for Lake George.

With the movie night idea out there and getting raves, the village risks looking penny-wise and pound-foolish for not spending the cash for the event. If the village can't find the money in its budget, officials will have to go around to businesses, hats in hand, looking for sponsors.

It shouldn't have to be that way. And it all falls on the radio station.

First of all, money shouldn't be an issue for WDDY. The AM station is owned by Disney, a corporation that last year brought in $25.3 billion in revenue—thanks largely to the types of families that spend summer vacations in Lake George. This is the same Disney that charges $18 for a new video, then tacks on 11 minutes of commercials at the beginning to entice your children to nag you to spend more money on Disney products. A company that's made billions off of families shouldn't be extorting a small tourist village in the Adirondacks for $5,000 for a movie screen and a projector to show its movies.

Secondly, this event is as much a commercial for the radio station as it is for Disney.

WDDY is touted on its Web site as a member of Radio Disney. The top three performers on its play list are the D-Tent Boys, Hillary Duff (Lizzie McGuire) and Kelly Clarkson, all of whom perform G-rated bubblegum music for the 12-and-under crowd. The same audience that will watch Disney movies in Shepard Park is the same one that will listen to this radio station. Does it really make financial sense to demand compensation from the village when the station is getting all that exposure for the price of splashing some light on a wall?

There's no reason for any money to exchange hands here. Showing Disney movies in Shepard Park helps Lake George. And it helps the radio station.

Hakuna Matata.

A conversation with
Mark Mahoney

BILL MITCHELL: You describe your secret as picking topics that interest you and then persuading readers they should care, too. Could you elaborate?

MARK MAHONEY: I always view myself and this paper, really, as members of the public. As a reader, I look at the same things that I think would strike the public as important or as problematic or as disturbing. So the first thing is you find something that gets under your skin, and then you start looking at what the problems are. Why is it bothering you? What's wrong with this picture?

Do you want me to go into specifics?

Sure.

The editorial I'm thinking of was the one about the baby who was killed. The baby died when the guy fell asleep or the baby was crying and the guy put his hand over her mouth to keep her quiet and she suffocated, and so, okay, that's terrible. But then you look at the circumstances that led up to this: the Massachusetts people not fully prosecuting the earlier child abuse case; the social services people letting this thing slide. This guy was allowed to have children and be out of prison when he should have been in prison. They could have caught this earlier, before he killed his baby. There were all kinds of breakdowns in the system. And as I was reading the stories about this, it started to get me ticked off and it started to get our other editors mad. Yes, he killed a child, but, boy, there were a lot of people at fault here, and there's a systematic problem that's bothering us. So the first thing you do is really focus on what's riling you up and then look at the factors that went into it and point them out to people.

When you're writing editorials, you have to interpret the news for people, tell them why something's bad. They might read the story and they might not get fired up. But then you say, "Hey, look what they did wrong here, look what they missed here, and look what happened here."

What comes next?

The writing part. How are you going to approach this thing? Do you want to lecture them? Do you want to rile them up? Do you want to put them into action? My approach was to slap them in the face. So I wanted to say right at the beginning just what I said earlier—that there's a lot of things that led up to this. Then it's just a matter of tying it all together and making your case and then—always at the end—I think you have to advocate something. If you don't take a position, if you just list the facts, then big deal. They get that from the story. You have to point out what's wrong and then interpret what it is and then talk to people about what can be done to solve this situation, to resolve it.

What got me started was I flipped through the obituaries and I saw the baby's obit in the paper, and I saw the photo and that almost made me cry right then. So I knew that if I showed people that image, they would get it. Nobody likes to see a picture of a dead baby in the paper. So I wanted to remind them, "Hey, this is what's at stake here. You open your obituary page, and there's a picture of a dead baby because of all these failures in the system."

Did you think about publishing the baby's photo with the editorial?

We don't usually do that. I almost liked describing it better.

Let's back up a bit and talk a little more about your setup at _The Post-Star_. How many editorials do you write each week?

I usually write three or four a week. There's really not enough going on in this town to write every single day.

Is there an editorial page every day?

There's an editorial page every day, and we run a national editorial on three or four of the days. We try to spread them out so that we write local ones on Wednesday and Friday, and then we always have a local one on Sunday, too. For a paper our size, there's only one editorial writer. I always tell the managing editor, "You start making me write one every day, I'm going to have to start writing about the weather, and then I'm going to quit." Because it seems like some days that's all there is to write about.

What about candidate endorsements?

If you want to be engaged in the public discourse, the election is a big part of that. I think you should be writing about this election and encouraging people to vote and telling them why it's important and how this matters. Help coalesce the news for people, put some ideas in their heads, and get them thinking for themselves and maybe spur them to action. Even if they don't vote for the candidate you endorse, they might vote.

Do you have an editorial board?

Well, for the candidate endorsements, we get everybody together and we just bat it around.

When you say everybody, whom do you mean?

The managing editor, our city editor, our assistant city editor, our news editor, the copy desk guy, and our Sunday editor will sit in for the endorsements. The publisher will sit in when we do the presidential endorsement. When you have just two or three people making the decision, it's a little easier. I like to have balanced editorials. If you don't put the other side in, you lose a lot of credibility; we can lose half the people we're writing to, so you have to give credence to the other arguments. That doesn't mean you've got to walk down the middle. You decide whose argument is better and then go with that.

Let's talk about how you get your ideas. What ticks you off or attracts your attention? Are you getting most of these three ideas a week from stories that are already in the paper? From community meetings?

Part of it is we sit down and we talk about what we want to focus on for the year. For example, we decided we're going to be the voice for the taxpayer. We started looking for stories and ideas that might fit. We hammer on the budget processes all the time to the point at which they really are kind of afraid of what we might write. In doing that, we've served to rile up the citizens and get them involved.

Does this overall focus for the year help shape news coverage as well as the editorial page?

It does. We're not trying to push an agenda, but if we say, "Hey, we want to find out everything we can about taxes," we'll push the reporter to do more budget stories. Do a salary story now. Do this, do that. I think it almost kind of feeds on itself. Our opinion is we want to protect taxpayers. We want to let them know what's going on so that they can act on their own behalf. We're finding now that when we set an editorial agenda, it translates into the reporting agenda. Again, not taking a side but reporting it, and then commenting on whatever comes out of that. We never tell our reporters how to write a story, but we'll pick the facts that they get. Go get the facts and then we'll interpret them and see where we go from there.

What about separation of opinion and news in the newspaper?

We're very careful to walk that line. We make sure that the reporters know their job is just to report straight. If it doesn't jibe with whatever they think we think, then it doesn't. But they are to go out there and just get straight information. The way we interpret it is our business on the opinion side. And that seems to work, and the reporters can really go out and honestly say with a straight face, "I've got nothing to do with the opinion." And I think it's worked.

How big is the reporting staff?

We've got about 12 reporters.

Does the managing editor edit your editorials?

Yeah. We talk about them beforehand, we bat ideas around. He'll say, "I think this," and I don't ever have a problem offering my opinion. Most of the time I agree with the paper's position, but if I don't, I still write it. We have discussions and he'll add stuff and say, "Maybe you want to tone this down," or, "I want you to include more of this, maybe move this a little bit higher." He pretty much lets me do the writing. We have a good working relationship. I'll go write it and then I'll throw it by him and then sometimes he'll turn the whole thing on its ear. Or he will say, "How about we focus on this?" or, "This gets a little wordy," or, "This gets a little thick," or, "I don't think this is quite what you really want to say." So, yeah, there's a lot of give and take. I like that. I appreciate that a lot.

You edit news copy as well as write editorials, correct?

I edit a lot of daily copy. If you get too distant, you start to lose touch with what's really going on. When you're talking to the reporters, you get that in-between-the-lines stuff, the real stuff that's going on, what almost doesn't make it into the story. Especially with us, where you have a small, young staff; maybe they know stuff but then sometimes it doesn't show up in their stories. I have a really good working relationship with the reporters, and I'll have them look over some editorials just for facts. I tell them, "You can't change the opinion, but if you see that I got a number wrong or if you say, 'I really wouldn't emphasize this because this really isn't quite the way it is,' I want that insight."

What's the setup in the newsroom?

Our core group of editors sits in the middle—we have little quads with low walls, and the reporters are all around us. The managing editor has his own office. The door's always open. I really try to stay in touch with the people who are out there writing the stories so that we can get an idea of some trends. They see a lot of stuff, and they're out there more than we are. We're in here writing and editing and doing what we've got to do. They're our eyes and ears. So I think it's really good that I edit daily copy and look through stories and talk to these guys about them and ask them questions. It's nice really—I don't know if it's strange for other papers, but we have a really nice give-and-take relationship between the managing editor and our frontline editors and the reporters. A lot of give and take, a lot of communication, and I think that helps in the editorial writing and opinion writing.

When did you begin writing editorials?

I think it was about 1994. I started doing one or two a week—we had few local editorials. The managing editor was writing one maybe every other Sunday or something like that. We had three or four people writing them, and you had a lot of different styles and some people were better at it than others. When Ken Tingley became managing editor three or four years ago, he said, "You're the guy and you're going to write more." I try to mix up the styles enough so that they don't all read the same. I try to have three or four or five different ways of approaching editorials.

What are some of those approaches?

I look at each situation individually and see what I think it would take to make the point the best. Sometimes I try to use humor or sarcasm or irony. In the Disney one, they're talking about showing movies in a little tourist village. We got riled up because Disney's got a billion dollars, and they wanted to charge the village $8,000. The village has 1,000 people; they don't have $8,000 for the stupid thing. I thought it would be funny if I started dropping in Disney terms throughout the editorial. You know, make the point but also kind of keep it interesting: "supercalifragilistic," "the beauty turned to a beast," and at the end "Hakuna Matata." I was making my point, but I was trying to make it lighter. This is not an editorial about whether we should invade Iraq; this is about showing a movie in Lake George. You've got to keep it in perspective.

Do you recall any reader reaction?

They thought it was funny. That was one of those editorials that strikes a chord, too. It wasn't a life-and-death issue, but it was one of those things where you just go, "Jeez, you're right, that's just idiotic." I also got a lot of reaction to the Humvee editorial. This town of Queensbury has a lot of money. It's a big mall town, so they've got a lot of sales tax revenue and sometimes they spend it stupidly. When the reporter came over and said, "The fire department's going to buy a Humvee," I said, "That's a joke, right?" Because that would be your initial reaction. Like this town with all these useless, wasteful expenses, now they want a Humvee? So I did some research on Humvees and talked about how many people they can carry and why they're not really good in the woods or on trails or for fighting fires. I asked if there were any problems where they needed something other than a fire truck. How many fire trucks get stuck in the mud where a regular tow truck or something couldn't pull it out? The answer was none. Then we saw how many Humvee dealers around here could actually fix these things and they're very few, and parts are expensive. So it just seemed like a ridiculous thing, and we wanted to point it out. We got a lot of reaction to that one. People were saying, "Good for you. It's horrible."

What happened? Did Queensbury buy the Humvee?

They wound up buying the damn thing. You might say, "They bought the Humvee anyway so nobody listened to you," but what it does is stir people up. It puts things in people's minds. The town is much more cognizant of fire department spending because they know we're going to cream them for it. They've made a lot of changes so they're not just automatically agreeing to all these frivolous purchases. Part of it is because in the back of their minds, they know they're going to get trashed by us, and I think we've made a difference that way. You nibble at the edges a little bit and you take some bites. One knockout punch sometimes doesn't really make the change. If you're persistent and you remind people there is wasteful spending, more examples of wasteful spending, another damn thing they're doing, that's so you can effect changes. You start to get people worked up, so then people start to get ticked off, and I think that's when they start to get involved and they start talking about it. Our managing editor has this theory and I agree with it—it's that you keep at it, you keep poking at it, you keep pecking, you keep reminding people. You write a lot of stories, you write a lot of editorials, you remind them this is going on. Sometimes one thing will go in one ear and out the other, so sometimes you've got to keep it in front of their faces.

Do you share your editorial agenda for the year with your readers?

I know some papers do that, or they set out the 10 things they plan to do or their goals for the year. We haven't done that. I think the way that you show that you're doing it is just do it.

I like to think that we're contributing at some level to improving the community. You know, you don't want to take too much credit. I don't think that's realistic. But I think you can move the readers and you can inspire them and you can get them going and then they do a lot on their own. I found out early on you can't make the politicians change their minds. What you do is you get somebody mad at them. "Hey, why are my taxes going up? I read it in the paper." That does it. They hear that stuff.

What other themes, in addition to tax advocate?

We do a lot of positive editorials. You get the feeling you start to tear stuff down a lot, but we do a lot of building. We want to see them do stuff that's right, that promotes economic development, that brings in business. That started to catch on as an editorial theme for us: Build up the community. We have people in for editorial board meetings to give us ideas, and we have this tech park here and we're supporting that and telling the community to be prepared and have smart growth and be ready to accept this development rather than fight it. Some people say, "We don't want this stuff in our back yard; we like things the way they are." Well, it's coming and you should be ready for it and you can plan for it. We want to keep the taxes down, which everybody does, but we also want to build up the region. Build up these resources and when somebody comes in with a good idea, support it. We live here and we want the place to be better.

How have you found editorial writing different from reporting? Do you like it better?

I never thought I had more than one opinion on any-thing, and now I have a million opinions. I love the writing. I think you have a lot more freedom as an editorial writer. I do. They pretty much let me write any way I want. I can write about drunken monkeys, and I can write a Disney editorial that no one else would even think of approaching like that. Or I can try to make people cry and I can try to tick them off and I can try to make them laugh or whatever, but somehow get them reading it. When you have the freedom to write and argue and be persuasive, I think that helps the community. None of us is in this for the money or the hours or anything like that, so really the only thing you're hanging it on is making a difference. That sounds corny, but really if you're not making a difference, if you're just spitting in the wind, then, really, what's the point? It's just kind of filling in space.

Say more about how your work editing news stories influences your editorial writing and vice versa.

As I try to be better at my job, I'm demanding more and saying, "Don't just settle for the dull lead; look for something different." We've sort of got that as the philosophy in the paper. I'm not the only one who has it. I think you see that if you encourage people to take risks. One of the things I try to do with editorials is take some risks. Sometimes you make it, sometimes you don't. I think the reporters, too, they're a little afraid, especially the young ones, to have a voice. It's like they're afraid to be subjective. I tell them to just write it straight but give it some color. Sell it. I always say my job's to sell the paper's opinion. Sell the opinion. Give it your best shot. So sell this story to people. Make them read it. Make them go all the way through it. If you bore them to death, they're not going to read it and you're not going to have any impact.

What's an example of an editorial in which you took a risk?

Those I usually wind up killing. These are the ones about which the managing editor says, "You wrote this at 1 o'clock in the morning, didn't you?" I always edit from the top. Sometimes I'll read editorials in which the first 4 inches are just bull. It'll be great when I thought of it. I use that kind of writing as a device to help me get into the rhythm of what I'm writing. Sometimes you can't find your focus until you start writing. Eventually we'll say, "Oh, my God, what a bunch of crap," and we'll just hack it. So I think a lot of my failures don't make it into the paper, hopefully.

There are some that have been controversial in the newsroom, like one I wrote about this priest who was accused of being a pedophile, and they were having a big housewarming party for him. As it happens, he had baptized my twins. So I led with, "You held my babies in your hands," and a lot of people were taken aback or offended and said, "You put your own personal thing on it." I said, "I wanted to make people feel my anger and resentment." So one of the ways I did it was I gave them my own personal story. My editorial wasn't my opinion, but it gave them a personal story. I think a lot of people liked it and a lot of people were jolted by it, but some people looked at it and said, "I think you went too far on that one."

On Sept. 11, 2001, my mother sent me an e-mail and said, "Keep safe and pray." That was the hook for the whole editorial. I didn't say it was my mother, but I said it was one of the editors' moms. You draw on a lot of your experiences to write this stuff. I think if you're not, if you're not connected to the community, if you're not connected to life, if you're not connected to yourself or people's emotions, then you can't do it. Sometimes if you make it personal, if you get angry, if you just think something's funny, you want to reach into people and grab them and get their attention, you know? So how do you reach people? How do you tell a story at a party? How do you become an interesting person anywhere? You tell jokes, you get ticked off, you do whatever. I think you really want to tap into people, what makes people tick, and I think if you try to be too straightforward or too stoic or too formulaic, then you're not going to do that. They've got other stuff going on. So I do tap into emotions and the stuff that makes me mad, I write about it. I'm trying to inspire readers to do something, inspire them to be mad or have a conversation or just think. I don't mind risking personal stuff. I think that's a good risk to take.

That's an interesting way to frame a strategy for effective editorial writing—do what you would do to be a more interesting person.

It's just like that. I've got kids. I've got to pay taxes, I've got to drive on the roads. I've got to educate my kids, so I've got to be personally involved in education. Whatever people are talking about, you should be talking about. If you sit in an ivory tower—now I sound like I'm lecturing a little bit—but you really can't do that. I don't think you can be effective that way, and if you're not effective, then, like I said before, why bother? So you want to be an interesting conversationalist. You want people to know you. You want to touch people, whether it's making them cry one day or making them crack up another day, or getting them worked up that day. Whatever it is, you want to find something that's going to make them act and be a part of the community and care about what you're writing about. I'm one guy and I'm trying to reach a whole bunch of different people in a bunch of different ways, because people aren't the same every day.

What kind of results are you getting from your editorials?

Last year we actually had tangible results. We've had people say, "You guys were the ones pushing this and it got people to change their minds, it got them to do stuff, embarrassed people into doing things." I think the biggest success is getting more people talking about things and getting more people involved, and then having them change.

And the other thing you can do is encourage people to come forward who were afraid to come forward before.

When local officials said they wanted to install one of those roundabout traffic circle things, we did an editorial suggesting they try an experimental one on a temporary basis. I wrote about all these communities that had done temporary ones. This councilman came by and he said, "You know, I've been researching the same idea. I just didn't have the nerve to come forward and say it, but now I can." So you get that kind of thing.

You do see success. I think we are seeing little differences in the way people are doing their budgeting. We are seeing Queensbury being a lot more careful with its money. We hammered on an assemblywoman because she didn't seem to be doing anything. She didn't have any plan. She just said, "I want to do the best I can," and we said, "Give us some specifics. You've got the job. Do it now." And next thing you know, she came in with all these specifics. So we got her off the dime a little bit. I think they look over their shoulders when they see that. When you keep their feet to the fire, they do start to say, "How is this going to play? God, he's going to write something bad about me." And I think that's all right. And we'll write good stuff about them when they do good stuff, so that helps, too.

What's your hunch of how it might be different writing editorials in a small town versus a big city?

Having never written for a big-city paper, I don't know. But here when you're writing about stuff, these guys have got to go to church and they've got to go grocery shopping and they're out and about at the soccer games. I think people are more apt to change than if you're in Los Angeles and you've got 6 million people or whatever, and no one knows who the councilman is and would never run into him. When the councilman's got to show up at a Little League game, five people are going to corner him and say, "Hey, the paper says you're doing this. Why are you doing this?" I think you can effect change that way. I'm not going to tell Colin Powell whom to invade because he doesn't really care; but I can tell people in our town how they should be treating their local soldiers and that free speech is for everybody, maybe get people to bend a little bit and say, "Maybe I shouldn't be such a jerk to those idiots who don't agree with me." I just think at some level, as long as you can make it personal and you can stir people into action to show up and the politicians will listen to them, I think that's a good thing. I don't write national editorials because we just don't think anybody would be listening anyway.

What part of your job are you trying to get better at?

I'm always trying to improve my writing. I'm always trying to be more concise, make stronger arguments. Again, it's just kind of tapping into your life experiences and talking to people and trying to keep it fresh. I think the hardest thing is keeping it fresh. But I do always try to make sure that they are well researched. I try to make more phone calls now to talk to people and just chat, whereas a few years ago, I might have just relied on a story. I try to look for different perspectives. But I don't want to just sit on my laurels, and I don't want to write what everybody else is going to write. I want people to be surprised when they pick up the paper and read it. I want them to read it, and if they're going to be bored with the subject matter or the style, then I'm not helping anybody.

Why did you get into journalism in the first place?

I just like telling stories. I like talking to people, and I like letting people know what's going on. I've always been a newspaper reader, from the time I was little. I've always been interested in this stuff. And the local news really fascinates me because I know that it affects everybody. So I don't get bored writing about taxes and the trash plant and sewer bills. It's not mundane to me because it affects everybody's lives. It affects mine. I'm interested in it because it matters to me. So I like being in there and I like being able to make a difference. I'm not one of these big rah-rah American guys, but I like the principles on which the country was founded, and I like the citizen involvement, and I think newspapers are a prime factor in shaping the way things are.

Writers' Workshop

Talking Points

1) The ASNE judges said they gave Mark Mahoney the editorial writing award for his "pointed and persuasive ways." Mahoney describes his secret as picking topics that interest him and then persuading readers that they should care, too. Look at his editorial about sales taxes on amusement parks. Did he succeed in persuading you to care about the topic, too? Why or why not?

2) Mahoney cares about the results he gets with his editorials. What was the result of his editorial about the Humvee? How would you characterize the range of results Mahoney seeks?

3) What part of his job is Mahoney trying to get better at? What's he trying to do differently? What elements of your journalism are most in need of improvement? What are you doing to get better?

4) Mahoney says an effective way for the editorial page of a small-town paper to approach national and international issues is to address the nature of the local debate about such issues. Read "Debate Good Thing for America" and discuss how you might approach other national and international issues in your community.

Assignment Desk

1) Mahoney discusses a variety of styles that he's able to select from his writer's toolbox. What are his most effective styles? What are yours?

2) Mahoney says the key to effective editorial writing is to do what you'd do to become a more interesting person. Pick up the editorial page of your local paper. Imagine the page as a friend who has come to you for counsel on becoming a more interesting person. What advice can you offer?

3) Try writing something for the local paper's letters or op-ed page. Pick a topic you care about. Many letters and columns express anger and outrage. Try writing one that will leave readers with a grin on their faces.

Los Angeles Times

Andrew H. Malcolm
Finalist, Editorial Writing

Andrew H. Malcolm's varied career has included stints at two of the country's most prestigious newspapers and another life as an insider in state and national politics.

He has been on the editorial board of the *Los Angeles Times* since 2001 and spent 26 years at *The New York Times* as a foreign correspondent, bureau chief, national affairs correspondent, editor, and columnist. His assignments took him across the country, and to Canada, Vietnam, Thailand, Korea, and Japan.

He left New York in 1993 to direct communications for Montana's then-governor, Marc Racicot. From there, he became press secretary to Texas first lady Laura Bush and deputy communications manager for the Bush presidential campaign. He was a member of the new president's transition team before rejoining the journalism ranks in 2001.

Though fairly new to editorial writing, Malcolm has already won a National Headliner Award and the ASNE Distinguished Writing Award for Editorial Writing. He also won a George Polk Award for national reporting in 1973. He has written 10 books.

Malcolm is a 1966 graduate of Northwestern University and earned a master's of science in journalism degree in 1967. He and his wife, Connie, have four children.

He speaks French and spent a summer interning in Paris, which may have prepared him to write "Déjà Vu All Over Again." It is a double-barreled blast of sarcasm aimed at the faux arbiters of linguistic correctness.

Déjà vu all over again

OK, mes amis, this is guerre.

The French government has issued a formal linguistic edict banning "e-mail" from the French language. Serieusement. The Culture Ministry has officially prohibited the word in all government ministries, documents, publications, even Web sites. Pas de e-mail. Interdit. From now on, instead of e-mails, all French men and women will send and receive un courriel. Mon Dieu, it is an abbreviation for courrier electronique and probably seems rather clever up there in the Ministry of Culture. Is that where they transferred Inspector Clouseau?

Does anyone think in an era of instant global communications that any language—let alone une belle langue comme francais—can remain pure in isolation? Evidemment, oui.

To remain the same and forever pure these days a language must die. Not a whole lot of new words are creeping into the Latin dictionary anymore. Languages are not stuffy old castles with tall walls, guard towers and a Ministry of Moats to remain isolated from the outside world—especially from English, the SARS of language.

Adding new words and adapting the old invigorate the palette of any language. C'est dommage but the pragmatic language that proves most versatile will dominate in the Darwinian world of communications. C'est la vie. And la mort.

English has surpassed French as the de facto international language because of the ubiquity of American economics, the U.S. military and, bien sur, American culture, especially movies and music largely, like, California-based. Also, if la verite be told, being a nuclear power just sounds a lot stronger than having a force de frappe.

Deep in their coeurs, French officials know this. Every day the French have les meetings before using le cash to order a la carte from McDonald's and rendezvous at a cinema matinee. Banning e-mail and Walkman (it became baladeur) simply won't cut the moutarde.

Of course, we could have a little tete-a-tete to plot retaliation against word-banning fromage-lovers. We could give carte blanche to a special commission to ban French from English—omelet, cafe, cuisine, nom de plume, maitre d', croissant, encore, even Paris, Texas. Give French the coup de grace. But then our lives and conversations would lack that mucho grande Champagne fizz.

Lessons Learned

BY ANDREW H. MALCOLM

"Your assignment," editor John Carroll said to me in early 2001, "is to write whatever you want as long as I would never, ever, expect to see it on the editorial page of the *Los Angeles Times*." Now, what subversive wouldn't relish that?

Especially since, frankly, I never read editorials much before writing them. I thought I knew how stuffy they had to be, how dry, pompous, and "on the other hand" they sounded. And how disconnected they usually felt from anything close to home that I cared about. Many editorials were like a weather channel, packed with info and forecasts about places you are not.

There aren't many advantages to growing up, but one of them is the end to lectures from Dad, those loving, well-intentioned, one-way talks that glaze teen eyes. So I did not want to write one-way pronouncements that plop onto driveways across the West.

From Day One in my mind I have envisioned these 460-word efforts as concise, pointed, featurey chats with an intelligent friend I just haven't met yet. I want them to be stories, to give a sense of informality and journey, a feel of serendipity with unexpected twists, and to show through humor that newspaper writers are wry humans with children, families, cranky days, chuckling days, and a sense of humor. I'm not trying to fix anything here; I'm trying to tell stories with a point. In this one, I wanted to show how hopeless banning words is for any language.

The "Déjà Vu" editorial began with an odd wire report on France's Ministry of Culture banning the word "e-mail." Bells go off when I see such things in delicious anticipation of how to toy with such toys. We could play off the anti-French sentiment that had Americans boycotting their products and pouring litres of rotting grape juice into the gutter.

But after 20 minutes' thinking, I came to feel the most annoying thing for such a vapid, revealing move by a home of the Renaissance was to talk about this official

French move in the kind of butchered French that loud, over-confident American tourists in plaid pants would use while showing off in front of the Paris American Express office. That would be both funny to Americans and grating to French. Parfait!

To work, my French expressions had to look like French but have a simultaneously clear English meaning to allow chuckles, too, by those who'd never been laughed at by condescending Parisians with a tendency to look down their noses, even if they're short. Hence, such lines as "la verite be told."

The first line wrote itself: "OK, mes amis, this is guerre." I wanted it to be flip, intriguing, bilingual, lightly confrontational, and seem annoying to French-speakers. Then I had to explain the little-noticed news item, slipping in more bilingual butcherings and a little mocking: "Is that where they transferred Inspector Clouseau?"

Ten years ago, I suspect copy editors would have added: "a reference to Peter Sellers, who played the bumbling French policeman in the *Pink Panther* movies." Some newspapers still think every passing reference must be explained. With today's smarter readers I think that comes off as showing off. If they get the joke, fine. If not, there'll be another along in a minute. May Dieu bless my editors for letting such passing references pass as lightly as they should.

I try to learn or re-learn something from each of these writing exercises. In "Déjà Vu" I was re-reminded of the importance in 21st-century journalism of leaving something to the imagination, something that piques and involves readers' minds in visual ways, as TV does more loudly and chaotically. To compete, we need to move briskly from visual keyword to visual keyword so they feel entertained, even though they've been learning, too. If you have the time, writing short with tiny relevant details is the best way. Then read it aloud to yourself to check the visual rhythms, as readers do in their minds.

When John Carroll first asked how I felt about writing editorials, I replied too quickly: "I think writing editorials is the last thing I'll ever do in journalism." Today, more than three years and 400 editorials later, I realize I was probably right—and am thankful for it.

ASBURY PARK
PRESS

Randy Bergmann
Finalist, Editorial Writing

Randy Bergmann is editorial page editor of the *Asbury Park Press*, New Jersey's second-largest daily. Before joining the *Press* in 2002, he worked as a national editor for the Associated Press in New York City.

He has served as editor of *The New Jersey Herald*, a daily serving Sussex County, N.J., and managing editor of *The Princeton* (N.J.) *Packet*. Bergmann has won numerous New Jersey Press Association writing awards, including a first place in editorial writing in 2003, as well as national Gannett awards for editorial writing.

Several of his editorials on public ethics and corruption were included in the Gannett New Jersey entry that won this year's Selden Ring Award for Investigative Reporting and the National Headliner Award for Public Service. He was part of a team recognized as a finalist for the National Journalism Award for public service reporting by the Scripps Howard Foundation. The team also received a rare honorable mention in the Worth Bingham Prize for investigative journalism.

A native of Westfield, N.J., Bergmann has undergraduate and graduate degrees in journalism. He received a master of arts degree from Ohio University and has done graduate work in journalism at New York University.

Bergmann lives in Warren, N.J., with his wife, Alice, and infant son, Charles.

"A Call to Action to Clean Up a Corrupt Political System" is an opinion on steroids. It argues forcefully for an overhaul of the state legislature—a call backed up with relevant names, telephone numbers, e-mail addresses, and a "six-point program for good government."

A call to action to clean up a corrupt political system

SEPTEMBER 28, 2003

If you work hard and pay taxes, you should be shaking with rage. Your elected state senators and Assembly members have been systematically enriching themselves with your tax dollars.

Not every state legislator is a greedy, self-serving trough swiller. But the harsh reality is that most of them are.

And even if you're lucky enough to be represented by state lawmakers who haven't been exploiting the system to get rich, your legislators have ultimately failed you. They have either stood idly by and watched while their colleagues systematically looted the state treasury. Or they have been ineffective at stopping this plundering of millions upon millions of your hard-earned tax dollars.

For the past eight days, the *Asbury Park Press* and the six other Gannett New Jersey newspapers have documented how state lawmakers have perverted the political system in the series, "Profiting from Public Service." The series should be required reading for every citizen of New Jersey.

The catalog of abuses detailed in the series, staggering in its variety and scope, is sickening. While ignoring the problems that have plagued New Jersey for the past two decades—soaring property taxes, skyrocketing car insurance rates, traffic-choked highways, unaffordable housing—our legislators have been busy feathering their own nests.

The series showed clearly how the New Jersey Legislature has become corrupt to its core, a cesspool of greedy, self-serving politicians interested in just two things: getting rich off of your tax dollars and making sure you don't know it so that you'll re-elect them Nov. 4.

Our lawmakers have voted themselves the best pension plan in the state. Then, many of them have used their influence to land multiple public jobs to inflate their pensions, guaranteeing them a prosperous retirement while thousands of senior citizens choose between paying their taxes or buying food and needed prescription medicines.

Our lawmakers have made it legal for themselves to play hooky from their other taxpayer-funded jobs so they can be in Trenton passing more laws to enrich themselves and subvert the system.

Our lawmakers have put family members on their own payrolls or helped their relatives find high-paying jobs in other areas of state government, guaranteeing a hefty family income stream and assuring a fat family retirement pension.

Our lawmakers have accepted free trips, golf outings and filet mignon dinners from lobbyists trying to get laws passed for special interests or lucrative contracts for the companies they represent. Then, our lawmakers have shaken down those same lobbyists and companies for campaign contributions to help ensure they're re-elected.

Our lawmakers have used their positions and influence to build their private businesses—and then refused to tell you, the voter, the details of their personal finances or how their business relationships may lead to conflicts of interest when they vote in Trenton.

And our lawmakers have rigged the political system to virtually guarantee their re-election and block meaningful good-government reforms.

In many other states in America, what's happening in our Legislature would be outlawed. In New Jersey, it's all legal and it's all paid for by you, the hard-working taxpayer.

But it doesn't have to be this way. You can do something about it.

It's time for every citizen to rise up and take back our government. It won't be easy. But it can be done. Here's how:

All 120 legislators—80 Assembly members and 40 senators—are up for election Nov. 4. First, you must register to vote—you only have six working days, until Oct. 6, to register. So do it now. You can even download the registration form online at www.NJElections.org.

Second, you must make sure that any politician who gets your vote Nov. 4 promises you in writing to work to pass the six-point, good-government reform plan outlined alongside this editorial. We have developed this plan from the findings of our series and the recommendations of good-government experts.

Clip the plan out. Post it on your refrigerator or bulletin board. Use it as ammunition in your fight for clean government. Until the Legislature is forced to approve these reforms, none of New Jersey's most-vexing problems will be solved.

On the op-ed page, we have provided you the names, phone numbers, e-mail addresses and mailing addresses of your elected representatives—and the candidates challenging them in the Nov. 4 election.

Call them up. Send them an e-mail. Write them a letter. Tell them you're fed up and you're not going to take it anymore. Demand that they promise you in writing to pass these good-government reforms. And don't vote for anyone who won't make that promise.

Don't let apathy keep you from action. You must rise up and take back your government. Do it for yourself so that you won't have to move out of New Jersey when you retire. Do it for your children so that they can afford to live in New Jersey after we're all long gone.

[*Bergmann's "Six-Point Program for Good Government" can be read on the CD-ROM included in this edition of Best Newspaper Writing.*]

Lessons Learned

BY RANDY BERGMANN

I was drawn to journalism at an early age, by both a love for writing and a belief that journalism was a noble calling, one that would give me a chance to make the world a better place.

I believe that today more than ever. But the editorial pages of many newspapers come up short as forces for positive change. Too many of them hold back.

Why? Maybe it's the cherished principle of objectivity run amok. Maybe the obsession with providing balance has somehow leached into the opinion pages. Maybe it's fear of being branded partisan. Maybe it's the product of editorial boards that regard consensus as an inherent virtue. Consensus can be. It also can give rise to neutered writing.

Whatever the reason, many editorial pages seem to have been defanged. They lack fire, urgency, and clarion calls for action. And they all too rarely ask anything of the reader, even when it's clearly in the reader's best interest to act.

The editorial on public ethics and corruption selected for this volume is representative of an approach that characterized all of those entered in the ASNE contest. It also reflects our overall editorial philosophy at the *Asbury Park Press*, one rooted in the following principles:

- If there is a problem in need of a solution, be specific about who should take the lead in solving it. Name names.
- If the topic warrants outrage, let it out. Vent.
- Offer a plan of action. Be specific about what must be done.
- In spelling out a course of action, don't direct it only at elected officials. Involve the public.

Too often, editorials speak in measured tones that change imperceptibly from one issue to the next. The volume and balance controls should be adjusted to fit the circumstance. Our editorials on ethics and corruption bristled with heartfelt anger. In addition to dressing down public figures, we took our case directly to our readers, urging them to get up off the couch and fight back. We tried to make it as easy as possible for them to do so, including lawmakers' phone numbers, e-mail addresses, and fax numbers in editorials, and providing clip-out coupons demanding action from their representatives.

The aggressive, activist tone of the editorials and our insistence that public officials and readers take the initiative in working for change produced results—a flurry of ethics-related legislation at the state and local level, much of which has already been signed into law. More change is in the offing. Our readers pressured politicians to act, and the politicians responded.

Newspapers often talk of the need for public officials to be held accountable. But they rarely urge readers to insist on it. Citizens in this country have become jaded and complacent. Many feel powerless. Over time it becomes a self-fulfilling prophecy. As long as people believe they are impotent—a perception entrenched politicians have no desire to change—they will be. We must keep reminding our readers that they can make a difference. And we must keep reminding ourselves of our obligation to cheer them on.

Brian Vander Brug
Community Photojournalism

As the homicide rate in South Los Angeles soared, Brian Vander Brug committed himself to documenting the faces of those whose loved ones were victims of the violence. For more than a year he listened as people recounted one tragedy after another, witnessing the pain and worries of the bereaved.

The result was "Mortal Wounds," a project with *Los Angeles Times* reporter Jill Leovy that Vander Brug says was "emotionally draining." In addition to being honored by ASNE, the series received a first-place award from the National Press Photographers Association's Best of Photojournalism competition for domestic news story, and Vander Brug received a 2003 Scripps Howard Foundation National Journalism Award.

Two compelling images from "Mortal Wounds" linger in Vander Brug's mental photo album. One is a portrait of Monica Mallet peering through a bullet hole in the sheer curtains of her parents' living room. The bullet came through the window, pierced the curtains, and killed her brother in 1998. "I wanted people to look at her," Vander Brug says. The photo also received a first-place award in this year's Pictures of the Year International portrait competition.

The other image that stays with Vander Brug comes from King/Drew Medical Center. A trauma unit technician, in the process of cutting away a gunshot victim's clothes, discovered a loaded gun. "He dropped the clip, cleared the chamber, and a bullet popped out, and everybody just froze," Vander Brug says.

Born in Los Angeles in 1960, Vander Brug has been with the *Los Angeles Times* since 1990 and a staff photographer there since 1997. He previously worked at the *Hemet* (Calif.) *News*. He's a 1989 graduate of California State University in Long Beach. He and his wife, Jill Connelly, live in West Hills, Calif., with their 2-year-old daughter, Sierra.

—Kenny Irby

[*All of Brian Vander Brug's photos and Jill Leovy's six-part series that accompany them are included on the CD-ROM in this edition of Best Newspaper Writing.*]

Mortal Wounds

They have become dots on a demographer's map: black men and teenagers gunned down on the streets of Compton and Watts and Inglewood and Hyde Park. There are three on one block, six on another. More than 400 murders, on average, are added each year.

The homicide rate in South Los Angeles is double that of Bogota, Colombia. But few pay attention. Not the neighborhood that falls silent. Not the city institutions that turn numb.

Photographer Brian Vander Brug wants readers to look inside the dots. He wants them to follow the bullets as they pass through the dead and strike the living. In photo after photo, Vander Brug captures the faces of murder—those shot, those left behind—in a way that shatters complacency.

Vander Brug and staff writer Jill Leovy wade through the volatile and unpredictable worlds of emergency workers, police officers, hospital staff, and grieving families to watch the stories unfold. Then, through Vander Brug's striking images and Leovy's gripping storytelling, South Los Angeles—and its dots—become real.

The picture that emerges, brought into profound focus by Vander Brug's photographs, is one of lives forever bent by violence.

—Adapted from the Los Angeles Times ASNE contest entry

A conversation with
Brian Vander Brug

KENNY IRBY: You've spent many years covering urban issues. How was covering "Mortal Wounds" different?

BRIAN VANDER BRUG: As journalists, we report on murders all the time, but then move on to the next story. On "Mortal Wounds" we got deeper into the issue of homicide. We went back to people who had lost loved ones to see how they were getting along and found most were still in unbelievable pain. We asked mothers, fathers, sisters, and brothers to recount in detail the events surrounding the deaths in their lives. It was very emotional.

What led to your involvement?

The reporter, Jill Leovy, is a good friend. We were talking at a social gathering, and she told me about some amazing interviews she was doing to research a story on urban violence. We talked at length about where we thought the story would go, and I started tagging along on her interviews. Photo coverage began with the funeral for Kevin Blanchard, a murder victim whose family we followed for a year.

How did you and your writing colleague work as partners during the reporting process?

For a long while it seemed we were joined at the hip. I tried to go on all of the interviews, even when I thought photo opportunities were weak or unlikely. As the story was being edited, we got together to plan captions for the photos and added information that was edited out of the story into the captions.

What were some of the challenges between you two?

Coordinating time for interviews. Some days we would both be working daily stories and Jill would schedule an

Kevin Smith, 7, and his father, Kevin, stop on their way home from the boy's football practice to pay their respects at a vigil for a homicide victim. The elder Smith's nephew was gunned down around the corner in a separate shooting with similar circumstances.

interview after we'd already worked a full day. I had a newborn at home and a working wife and things got a little hectic at times. But Jill was great to work with and was a great advocate for pictures. She always thought about the visual side of the story.

How did you prepare for this assignment? Given your normal approach, how was this different?

We told our subjects everything about what we wanted to do up front. We told them we would be asking questions that would be very difficult and emotional, and that they could quit answering them whenever they wanted. They could decline being photographed and tell us to go away. I went on interviews, even when subjects said they didn't want to be photographed. After meeting them, many decided they would let me in with my cameras.

How did you develop the essential relationships for this project?

We worked our way up and down the food chain. We talked with the top people at hospitals, police agencies, and coroners' offices as well as anyone we would have to deal with along the way, including secretaries and security guards. Phone calls were followed up by personal meet-

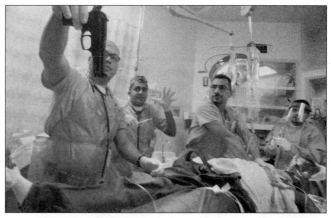

The bullet had damaged his brain. Doctors weren't getting vital signs. There were people working at John Smith's head, at his feet, on each side. They put a tube in his throat to help him breathe. They performed a "cutdown"—an incision in the ankle to infuse fluids in a patient with very low blood pressure. They shocked his chest, trying to get a heartbeat. Only once was the trauma team's rhythm broken. A technician ripping off Smith's pants found a wad of bills—and a large handgun. For a moment, everyone froze. But the gun was quickly forgotten. Smith did not survive.

ings. We always tried to schedule face-to-face meetings with sources and subjects. It really helps to actually meet a person and talk about your goals. Meeting them helps develop a more personal relationship.

What challenged you the most in covering this story?

Murder happens at all hours of the day and night. We had to be ready to go to work whenever the phone rang or pager went off. Extra hours, many unpaid, were required to do this story. We both felt if the overtime cards were filled out week after week, the editors might put the brakes on our endeavors.

Also, on one of the first nights in the trauma bay, despite having permission from the hospital CEO, the chief of surgery, and the attending physician, a charge nurse who had not been told about our activities saw my cameras and gave us both the boot. The head of the trauma bay just shrugged and said it was her prerogative, and we lost a whole weekend of shooting and reporting.

What were the most memorable lessons you learned during this assignment?

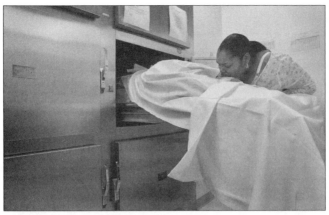

The hospital morgue is a small room with a chain and hoist and a row of stainless steel doors in the walls, like those of a commercial refrigerator. Each door opens to reveal a drawer. Ellen Atwater, 26, kisses the face of her common-law husband, John Smith, in the hospital's morgue after the 33-year-old man was shot in the head by an alleged gang member in South Los Angeles.

To really listen to subjects and to respect them. To work a story like this, you really have to care and have a lot of empathy. I think the people in our story could tell we cared about them.

Were there any major surprises for you while reporting this story?

The biggest surprise was the amount of pain in these people's lives and the extent of the effect it had on them. Many could not work or sleep. Relationships fell apart. Even years after having a loved one murdered, people's lives remain shattered. Having a loved one murdered is truly the worst thing that can happen to you. It is not like losing someone to illness or an accident. There are often concrete reasons for death, but survivors of homicide are left grasping for answers that always remain elusive. They wake up in the morning and go to bed at night asking, "Why?"

How did you cope with the emotional toll of seeing death and being with bereaved people over long periods?

It was really hard, truly the hardest thing I've ever done as

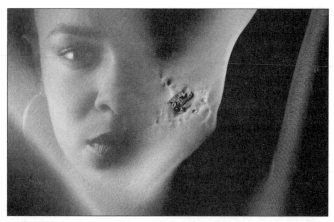

Monica Mallet peers through a sheer curtain in her parents' living room, where bullets from a drive-by shooting pierced the front window of the family's Inglewood home as well as her brother, who died as a result of the gunshot wounds he suffered in 1998. The window glass has been repaired but the hole in the curtain, as well as the Mallets' lives, have not.

a photojournalist. The pain endured by someone touched by homicide is unbelievable. After some of the interviews, many of which would last for hours, we would be left physically and emotionally exhausted. During one news conference police held to offer a reward for information on the killer of a 13-year-old boy, the family's pain was so palpable I couldn't point the camera at them anymore. I had to step outside.

Do you have any advice for others who may be thinking about covering a story like "Mortal Wounds"?

Cultivate relationships with your sources and have empathy for your subjects. They can tell if you are passionate about it and they will do anything for you.

What outcome had you hoped for when you covered this story?

We both hoped people would pay attention to this problem and would be moved to do something more to help stop the killing. We felt if this were happening in another part of the city, the outcry would be deafening and you'd see federal help, special prosecutors, and more police, etc. But the killing does go on, although the murder rate is down. In the course of reporting the story, police officials knew we were poking around and asking about detective staffing and caseloads. Before the story came out, the LAPD moved more detectives into the central part of the city to help try to solve more cases.

What are your thoughts on the need for photographers to be originators of ideas?

We should always be on the lookout for story ideas. If we aren't the originator of the idea, we should take the lead in telling the visual side of the story. Photographers should always try to think of a different way to see a story. I hate the term "think outside the box," but we should always think about doing something beyond what is expected of us.

Where do you do your best reporting?

I think my best reporting is done before I photograph a subject. I like to take a little time to talk with them and get to know them. It relaxes everyone and helps a subject forget about the camera.

What advice can you offer younger photographers when it comes to working with editors?

Always take—and even ask for—their advice. Even if things don't work out or you think it won't work out, their experience is invaluable and an editor might get you to think about another aspect or viewpoint you may have overlooked. It really helps to get edits on your picture stories throughout the process. We are lucky here at the *Los Angeles Times* in that our editors are great facilitators for photojournalism. They will give you the time it takes to do a story right if you are willing to put in the effort.

Why do you do what you do?

I get a lot of personal satisfaction from telling stories and exploring issues. I love meeting new people and seeing new things. I can't imagine not being a photographer.

The Oregonian

Rob Finch

Finalist, Photojournalism

Rob Finch began his journalism career at the University of Notre Dame, where he graduated with a bachelor's degree in history. After completing three internships, he began work in 1998 as a newspaper photographer for *The Beacon News* in Aurora, Ill.

For his work in 1999, the Missouri School of Journalism named Finch Newspaper Photographer of the Year in the annual Pictures of the Year International competition. The following year, Finch was awarded second place in that competition. In 2000, he was an exhibitor in Perpignan, France, as part of the *Visa Pour L'Image* festival, the largest annual exhibition of photojournalism in the world. He was also recognized with the "30 Under 30" award from *Photo District News*.

He joined *The Oregonian* in 2001, later accepting a nomination to the Joop Swart World Press Masterclass, a training program named for the late magazine editor and honorary chairman of *World Press Photo*. Finch was one of only two Americans chosen. In 2003, he again was named Newspaper Photographer of the Year in the annual POYi competition. Finch has been a faculty member on the annual National Press Photographers Association's Flying Short Course and Western Kentucky University's Mountain Workshop.

In "A Place Where Children Die," Finch's photographs tell a quiet, intimate story of an insidious, unseen killer that has been taking the lives of the young on the Warm Springs Reservation, a community *The Oregonian* called the "deadliest place for children in Oregon."

[*Rob Finch's photos and The Oregonian stories that accompany them are included on the CD-ROM in this edition of Best Newspaper Writing.*]

A place where children die

When *The Oregonian* figured out that kids on the Warm Springs Indian Reservation were dying at nearly four times the state average, photographer Rob Finch and reporter Julie Sullivan resolved to find a story that would go beyond the dismal statistics. They faced an unusual challenge. Warm Springs, like all Indian reservations, is a sovereign nation where suspicion of the motives of outsiders is common.

Over a period of 10 months, Finch and Sullivan attended birthday parties, tribal ceremonies, and school events. They spent days and nights and weekends on the reservation. And because they built up trust over time, they were able to photograph and observe in good times and in bad.

The raw power of Finch's images and Sullivan's passion for telling the Warm Springs stories was kindled by an intense desire to do justice to the lives of those on the reservation.

After the series' publication, the tribes promised a top-to-bottom review of how they allocate money for programs dealing with the health and welfare of children. Federal health officials have announced they will take aggressive steps to track children who might be neglected or abused, and the tribe is looking to fund programs to help save children.

—Adapted from The Oregonian ASNE contest entry

Lessons Learned

BY ROB FINCH

My reporting colleague, Julie Sullivan, and I had just finished as bad a day as we could imagine. We had been mocked, laughed at, lectured, and threatened. We had good intentions. We were just trying to do our jobs. We had been working on this story for a few months now, and we were getting nowhere.

We had the statistics. Kids died nearly four times more often on the Warm Springs Indian Reservation as the state average in Oregon and twice as often as on other Northwest Indian reservations. We knew some of the basic reasons why kids were dying: alcohol and drugs, abuse and neglect, and the number one killer—car accidents.

You would think the next step would be easy. Plug these reasons into the newspaper formula, and we would come out with The Story. Statistics plus people equals success. But in this case, it was not working. The major problem: We could not find the people.

Neither Julie nor I, nor the two other reporters working this story, Kim Christensen and Brent Walth, are Native American. We are outsiders ethnically, economically, and geographically. We are from the big newspaper over the mountain. No one wanted to talk to us beyond the standard script. Certainly no one was letting us into their lives to tell intimate stories. Not even close.

On this horrible day we had been invited to a private home medicine dance. Many of the elders would be there. They would dance all night, praying for forgiveness and cleansing. No one could leave. Yet none of what happened there could be reported or photographed. So we declined the invitation. People had asked us to fish with them. They wanted to show us their new corrals. They wanted to talk about why the elk were staying so high in the mountains this winter. They asked us to can salmon. "No, thank you. We are here to report on the problems children are having here," we would reply. We thought we were being good reporters, streamlining our process to get at the story.

What we were really doing was disrespecting the people there, simplifying their lives so they would either fit our story or be of no use. In photography I equate this to subjects becoming compositional elements in my mind, not people who I, or readers, can connect with.

So we made the 20-mile drive to the town that borders Warm Springs. We were defeated and demoralized. We had a decision to make. We either had to dump our get-the-story strategy or we had to give up, walk away, and settle for mediocrity. We both knew that the latter was not an option. We owed it to the people in Warm Springs to give it our best effort.

We decided that we would go back to what we knew—just telling stories about people. That would give us a reason to be there, a reason to ask questions, a reason to make pictures. It would also take a heck of a lot longer to do this. We would amass a collection of stories in pictures and words that would land on the cutting-room floor.

It worked. People want to tell their stories. They want to talk to the newspaper. It is important to allow them to do just that. Let them tell you about their lives, what they've done, and what they've seen. They talk. You listen. It seems so simple. But so often we complicate our job, thinking we know something that we don't, and trying to force something that we can't.

In the end, the project was a life-changing experience. It allowed me to look at prospective stories in a new way. I am a better journalist and a better person for my experiences in Warm Springs. It is all because I allowed myself to do what I knew: connect with people, earn their trust by giving my time and my ear, and let them tell me a story. I am just there to record it.

THE COMMERCIAL APPEAL

Alan Spearman

Finalist, Photojournalism

Alan Spearman is a 30-year-old photographer working at *The Commercial Appeal* in Memphis, Tenn. He was born in Atlanta, Ga., and graduated with honors from the University of Georgia.

While in college he held internships at *The Concord Monitor*, the Minneapolis *Star Tribune, The Oregonian*, and *The Miami Herald*. He also was a finalist for two consecutive years in the William Randolph Hearst photojournalism competition, and he won second place in the College Photographer of the Year competition in 1997.

Spearman joined the staff of *The Commercial Appeal* after college in 1998. Since then he has won many national and regional photojournalism awards. His photos for "Diagnosis: Dire" received an honorable mention in the 2004 National Press Photographers Association competition.

In his spare time, Spearman enjoys traveling overseas, playing guitar, and spending time with friends, family, and his girlfriend. He is making a feature-length film with another *Commercial Appeal* photographer. They plan to show it on the film festival circuit in 2006.

[*Alan Spearman's photos, and The Commercial Appeal stories that accompany them, are included on the CD-ROM in this edition of Best Newspaper Writing.*]

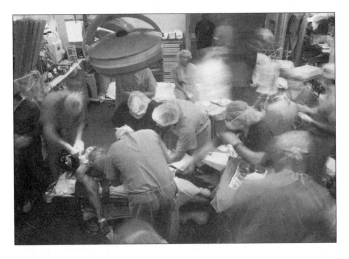

Diagnosis: Dire

The Regional Medical Center at Memphis, better known as The Med, specializes in treating trauma victims and those with high-risk pregnancies. It is an unusual hospital in that it serves poor patients from Tennessee, Arkansas, and Mississippi who, in many cases, don't have health insurance. The Med treats them anyway. As a result, the hospital is on the brink of financial disaster.

Supported largely by local, state, and federal tax dollars and other public money, The Med faced the prospect of a $15 million shortfall and the chance that it would close. Were that to happen, there would have been no place nearby to send patients who were severely burned, who had major traumatic injuries, or whose babies were born too soon.

Photographer Alan Spearman and reporter Mary Powers take readers inside The Med to tell not just a story about a budget shortfall, but a story about lives hanging in the balance.

After the package was published, Mississippi contributed $10 million to help bridge the funding gap. Several Tennessee politicians promised to find ways to keep The Med open. And congressional delegations from all three states went to work in Washington to get the hospital the money it needs.

–Adapted from The Commercial Appeal ASNE contest entry

Lessons Learned

BY ALAN SPEARMAN

The series of photographs that ultimately became "Diagnosis: Dire" stemmed from an assignment that would have just been a typical daily photo assignment. *The Commercial Appeal*'s director of photography, Dennis Copeland, caught this one just in time.

The story had a news deadline because officials from The Med were going to Nashville to discuss its budget problems with the governor and other members of state government. We had about five weeks to convince The Med that we could produce a series that might help their cause and communicate to the people of Memphis how valuable a resource this hospital is to our community. Dennis, a few metro editors, health and science reporter Mary Powers, and I met with Sandy Snell, the head of public relations for The Med, to plead our case and discuss potential legal issues. Our company lawyer dealt with lawyers from The Med on a variety of issues.

Several weeks passed, and, despite all the legal issues involved, we got the green light for the project.

The Med is a giant hospital with a lot of departments. My job was to quickly isolate the most important and unique services The Med provides and photograph them. One of the agreements we made with The Med was that a member of their public relations team had to shadow me everywhere.

I started by meeting with the heads of the major centers such as the trauma center, burn center, and the newborn intensive care center. After talking to these doctors I had a better understanding of why The Med is so important to Memphis. As it turns out, The Med was nearly out of money. If it were to close, there would be no other hospital nearby to treat indigent patients, burn victims, babies born too soon, and trauma victims.

When I began to understand how things worked at The Med, I was able to be in the right places at the right times. I had to convince the public relations department that we had to work late nights and early mornings. That meant they had to change their schedules.

Over the next two and a half weeks, I worked around the clock. We would monitor pagers from the three critical care departments. When paged, we would move from car accident and gunshot victims to emergency aneurysm surgeries to premature babies. One thing I learned is to always wear a seat belt. Many of the fatal injuries I saw were because the victims were not wearing their seat belts. I also spent hours and hours waiting for something to happen. I used this down time to make connections and friends around the hospital. I made my own rounds in the recovery rooms, spent time with victims' families, and visited the chapel. Some of these connections helped me bypass the media, which were being kept at a distance when two mortally injured firefighters were brought to the hospital for treatment.

We had to have a release signed from everybody whose picture I took. In most cases the people were so critically injured we had to get releases from family members several days after the pictures were made. I had to be very careful while shooting during surgeries. I tried to move without being noticed and not to knock anything over or get in the way. I figured if I messed up once, my access would be halted immediately. On some occasions I put a remote camera high on the walls of the operating rooms so I would be as unobtrusive as possible.

Any time I get a chance to use my skills as a photographer to help people, I am happy to do it. In this case and as a result of our news coverage, millions of dollars were given to The Med and much more is being promised by political figures in Tennessee, Arkansas, and Mississippi. The photographic success of this series was also made possible by Dennis Copeland, visuals editor Scott Sines, and editor Chris Peck. They were able to get the most powerful pictures in the paper.

Annual Bibliography

BY DAVID B. SHEDDEN

WRITING AND REPORTING BOOKS 2003

Arnold, George T. *Media Writer's Handbook*. Boston: McGraw-Hill, 2003.

Bissinger, Buzz, ed. *The Best American Sports Writing 2003*. Boston: Houghton Mifflin, 2003.

Brooks, Brian S., James Pinson, and Jean Gaddy Wilson. *Working with Words*. 5th edition. New York: Bedford/St. Martin's, 2003.

Cappon, Rene J. *The Associated Press Guide to Punctuation*. Cambridge, Mass.: Perseus Publishing, 2003.

Clark, Roy Peter, and Don Fry. *Coaching Writers: The Essential Guide for Editors and Reporters*. 2nd edition. New York: Bedford/St. Martin's Press, 2003.

Dawkins, Richard, ed. *The Best American Science and Nature Writing*. Boston: Houghton Mifflin, 2003.

Fadiman, Anne, and Robert Atwan, eds. *The Best American Essays, 2003*. Boston: Houghton Mifflin, 2003.

Fink, Conrad C. *Writing to Inform and Engage: The Essential Guide to Beginning News and Magazine Writing*. Boulder, Colo.: Westview Press, 2003.

Fleder, Rob, ed. *Sports Illustrated: Fifty Years of Great Writing*. New York: Time Books, 2003.

Frazier, Ian, ed. *The Best American Travel Writing 2003*. Boston: Houghton Mifflin, 2003.

Garlock, David, ed. *Pulitzer Prize Feature Stories*. Ames, Iowa: Iowa State Press, 2003.

Harrigan, Jane T., and Karen Brown Dunlap. *The Editorial Eye*. 2nd edition. Boston: Bedford/St. Martin's, 2003.

Itule, Bruce D., and Douglas A. Anderson. *News Writing and Reporting for Today's Media*. 6th edition. Boston: McGraw-Hill, 2003.

LaRocque, Paul. *Concise Guide to Copy Editing.* Oak Park, Ill.: Marion Street Press, 2003.

Leckey, Andrew, and Allan Sloan, eds. *The Best Business Stories of the Year.* New York: Vintage Books, 2003.

Mencher, Melvin. *News Reporting and Writing.* 9th edition. Boston: McGraw-Hill, 2003.

Murray, Donald M. *The Craft of Revision.* 5th edition. Boston: Thomson/Heinle, 2003.

Rich, Carole. *Writing and Reporting News: A Coaching Method.* 4th edition. Belmont, Calif.: Wadsworth, 2003.

Shapiro, Bruce, ed. *Shaking the Foundations: 200 Years of Investigative Journalism in America.* New York: Thunder Mouth Press/Nation Books, 2003.

Winburn, Janice. *Shop Talk and War Stories.* New York: Bedford/St. Martin's Press, 2003.

CLASSICS

Atchity, Kenneth. *A Writer's Time: A Guide to the Creative Process, From Vision Through Revision.* New York: W.W. Norton & Co., 1996.

Bell, Madison Smartt. *Narrative Design: A Writer's Guide to Structure.* New York: W.W. Norton & Co., 2000.

Berg, A. Scott. *Max Perkins: Editor of Genius.* New York: Berkley Publishing Group, 1997.

Bernstein, Theodore M. *The Careful Writer: A Modern Guide to English Usage.* New York: Free Press, 1995.

Blundell, William E. *The Art and Craft of Feature Writing: The Wall Street Journal Guide.* New York: Dutton/Plume, 1988.

Brady, John. *The Craft of Interviewing.* New York: Knopf, 1977.

Brande, Dorothea. *Becoming a Writer.* Los Angeles: J.P. Tarcher; Boston: distributed by Putnam Publishing, reprint of 1934 edition, 1981.

Cappon, Rene J. *The Associated Press Guide to News Writing*. Forest City, Calif.: IDG Books Worldwide, 2000.

Clark, Roy Peter. *Free to Write: A Journalist Teaches Young Writers*. Westport, Conn.: Heinemann, 1995.

Dillard, Annie. *The Writing Life*. New York: Harper Collins, 1999.

Elbow, Peter. *Writing With Power: Techniques for Mastering the Writing Process*. 2nd edition. New York: Oxford University Press, 1998.

Follett, Wilson. *Modern American Usage: A Guide*. Revised by Erik Wensberg. New York: Hill & Wang, 1998.

Franklin, Jon. *Writing for Story: Craft Secrets of Dramatic Nonfiction by a Two-Time Pulitzer Prize Winner*. New York: Dutton/Plume, 1994.

Garlock, David. *Pulitzer Prize Feature Stories*. Ames, Iowa: Iowa State University Press, 1998.

Goldstein, Norm, ed. *The Associated Press Stylebook and Briefing on Media Law*. Cambridge, Mass.: Perseus Publishing, 2002.

Gross, Gerald, ed. *Editors on Editing: What Writers Should Know About What Editors Do*. New York: Grove/Atlantic, 1993.

Harrington, Walt. *Intimate Journalism: The Art and Craft of Reporting Everyday Life*. Thousand Oaks, Calif.: Sage, 1997.

Hugo, Richard. *The Triggering Town: Lectures & Essays on Poetry & Writing*. New York: Norton, 1992.

Kerrane, Kevin, and Ben Yagoda. *The Art of Fact*. New York: Scribner, 1997.

Klement, Alice, and Carolyn Matalene, eds. *Telling Stories, Taking Risks: Journalism Writing at the Century's Edge*. Belmont, Calif.: Wadsworth Publishing, 1998.

McPhee, John. *The John McPhee Reader*. William L. Howard, ed. New York: Farrar, Straus & Giroux, 1990.

Metzler, Ken. *Creative Interviewing: The Writer's Guide to Gathering Information by Asking Questions*, 3rd edition. Needham Heights, Mass.: Allyn & Bacon, 1996.

Mitford, Jessica. *Poison Penmanship: The Gentle Art of Muckraking*. New York: Farrar, Straus & Giroux, 1988.

Murray, Donald. *Shoptalk: Learning to Write With Writers*. Portsmouth, N.H.: Boynton/Cook, 1990.

Perry, Susan K. *Writing in Flow: Keys to Enhanced Creativity*. Cincinnati: Writer's Digest Books, 2001.

Plimpton, George, ed. *Writers at Work: The Paris Review Interviews*. Series. New York: Viking, 1992.

Ross, Lillian. *Reporting*. New York: Simon & Schuster Trade, 1984.

Scanlan, Christopher, ed. *How I Wrote the Story*. Providence Journal Company, 1986.

Sims, Norman, ed. *Literary Journalism in the Twentieth Century*. New York: Oxford University Press, 1990.

Stafford, William, and Donald Hall, eds. *Writing the Australian Crawl: View on the Writer's Vocation*. Ann Arbor, Mich.: University of Michigan Press, 1978.

Stewart, James B. *Follow the Story: How to Write Successful Nonfiction*. New York: Simon & Schuster, 1998.

Strunk, William, Jr., and E.B. White. *The Elements of Style*. 4th edition. Needham Heights, Mass.: Allyn & Bacon, 1999.

Talese, Gay. *Fame & Obscurity*. Reprint edition. New York: Ivy Books, 1971.

White, E.B. *Essays of E.B. White*. New York: Harper Collins, 1999.

Woods, Keith, Karen Brown, Roy Peter Clark, Don Fry, and Christopher Scanlan, eds. *Best Newspaper Writing*. St. Petersburg, Fla.: The Poynter Institute. Published annually since 1979.

Zinsser, William. *On Writing Well: An Informal Guide to Writing Nonfiction*. 6th edition. New York: Harper Collins, 1998.

— *Writing to Learn*. Reading, Mass.: Addison-Wesley Educational Publishers, 1997.

— *Speaking of Journalism: 12 Writers and Editors Talk About Their Work*. New York: Harper Collins, 1994.

ARTICLES 2003

Astor, Dave. "Features of the Year." *Editor & Publisher* (November 24, 2003): 8-12.

Buttry, Steve. "Ask Early, Often, Finally: What's My Point?" *The Masthead* (Summer 2003): 12-13.

Ciurczak, Ellen. "Wondering What a Political Story Is." *Nieman Reports* (Winter 2003): 66-68.

Getler, Michael. "Covering the War Before It Started." *Nieman Reports* (Summer 2003): 77-80.

Giles, Bob. "Newspaper Editors Confront Errors." *Nieman Reports* (Summer 2003): 3.

Gorman, Kathleen. "Telling Stories Every Day." *Quill* (December 2003): 19-21.

Hallman Jr., Tom. "A Fight for Storytelling." *Quill* (December 2003): 14-18.

Hilts, Philip J. "Digging Beneath What Is Said to Be the Truth." *Nieman Reports* (Summer 2003): 32-34.

Jackson, Dennis. "Good Writing Needs Cadence." *The Masthead* (Summer 2003): 16-17.

Koren, Leslie. "Writing Stories to Reach Young Adults." *Nieman Reports* (Winter 2003): 37-39.

LaRocque, Paula. "Almost, But Not Quite." *APME News* (Winter 2003): 35.

Luechtefeld, Lori. "Interviews with the Interviewers: Dealing with Sensitive Issues." *The IRE Journal* (January/February 2003): 14-15.

McKenna, M.A.J. "The Public Health Beat: What Is It? Why Is It Important?" *Nieman Reports* (Spring 2003): 10-11.

Nelson, Jack. "Reporting on the Civil Rights Movement." *Nieman Reports* (Fall 2003): 6-8.

Partsch, Frank. "Limited Space, Tough Choices." *The Masthead* (Spring 2003): 4-5.

Rawls, Wendell. "Some of the Best Reporting is Found on the Op/Ed Page." *The Masthead* (Autumn 2003): 22-24.

Simmons, Tim. "Reporting on the Minority Education Beat." *Nieman Reports* (Fall 2003): 22-25.

Stepp, Carl Sessions. "Why Do People Read Newspapers?" *American Journalism Review* (December 2003): 64-69.

Stover, Bob. "Ignore Copy Editors at Your Own Peril." *The American Editor* (March 2003): 15.

Woods, Keith. "Tone Makes or Breaks an Editorial." *The Masthead* (Summer 2003): 6-7.

The Journalist's Toolbox

Here is a selective index that loosely follows the writing process developed by longtime columnist and author Don Murray. It references places in the book where journalists shine a light on the tools and techniques that helped make their work stand out.

Seated, left to right: Janet Weaver, dean of the faculty; Kenny Irby, visual journalism group leader; Kelly McBride, ethics faculty; Keith Woods, reporting, writing and editing group leader and *Best Newspaper Writing* editor.
Standing, left to right: Christopher Scanlan, senior writing faculty; Roy Peter Clark, Poynter vice president and senior scholar; Bill Mitchell, online editor/marketing director; Aly Colón, ethics group leader.

Poynter.

The Poynter Experience

The Poynter Institute, which opened in 1975 as the Modern Media Institute, is a school dedicated to improving the quality of journalism in the United States and wherever the press is free. Each year, the Institute hosts more than 50 professional development seminars, two programs for college students, seminars for college professors, a year-round journalism program for Tampa Bay high school students, and summer writing camps for the area's elementary and middle school children and their teachers.

The Institute coordinates and supports the National Writers Workshops each spring, joining thousands of writers in a celebration of the craft. Poynter also has established connections around the globe with training institutes and the journalists they serve.

Through its publications and website, Poynter Online, the Institute connects journalists with their peers and promotes the notion that ethics is synonymous with excellence in all areas of the craft. Poynter faculty members speak at journalism conventions, advise working journalists, consult in news organizations, and provide commentary on the everyday issues arising in the industry. Eight members of the Poynter faculty, pictured on the preceding page, played a part in producing this book.

About the CD-ROM

Included with this volume is a CD-ROM containing all the images in the winners' and finalists' entry packages for the ASNE Community Service Photojournalism category. Each package is presented with the photo captions and stories that accompanied the images. We have included full-screen images that are printable at low resolution for classroom projects and an interactive cropping tool that allows for re-editing of selected photos.

In addition, the CD includes two parts of S. Lynne Walker's series, "Beardstown: Reflections of a Changing America"; two of Dan Neil's prize-winning automotive commentaries; and full-text versions of stories by finalists Amy Ellis Nutt, Chuck Culpepper, and Randy Bergmann that were excerpted because of space limitations. These documents are provided in PDF format.

The CD project was created by Poynter's design editor Anne Conneen and multimedia editor Larry Larsen using Macromedia Flash. Kenny Irby of the Poynter faculty worked closely with editor Keith Woods and publications director Billie M. Keirstead on the presentation of the Community Service Photojournalism category.

The CD will run on both Windows and Macintosh platforms. It is designed to open at full-screen size. The Flash Player and Adobe Acrobat Reader applications are included on the CD.

We hope you find this CD useful and enjoyable.